The PR Styleguide

Formats for Public Relations Practice

BARBARA DIGGS-BROWN

Associate Professor Emerita
American University School of Communication

President and CEO
The Center for Strategic Research and Communications

THIRD EDITION

WADSWORTH
CENGAGE Learning·

Australia • Brazil • Japan • Korea • Mexico • Singapore • Spain • United Kingdom • United States

WADSWORTH
CENGAGE Learning

The PR Styleguide: Formats for Public Relations Practice, Third Edition
Barbara Diggs-Brown

Senior Publisher: Lyn Uhl

Publisher: Michael Rosenberg

Development Editor: Laurie K. Dobson

Assistant Editor: Erin Bosco

Editorial Assistant: Rebecca Donahue

Media Editor: Jessica Badiner

Marketing Program Manager: Gurpreet S. Saran

Art Director: Marissa Falco

Manufacturing Planner: Doug Bertke

Rights Acquisition Specialist: Mandy Groszko

Production Management and Composition: PreMediaGlobal

Cover Designer: Riezebos Holzbaur Design Group

For product information and technology assistance, contact us at **Cengage Learning Customer & Sales Support, 1-800-354-9706**.

For permission to use material from this text or product, submit all requests online at **www.cengage.com/permissions**. Further permissions questions can be emailed to **permissionrequest@cengage.com**.

Library of Congress Control Number: 2011942965

Student Edition:

ISBN-13: 978-1-111-34811-3

ISBN-10: 1-111-34811-1

Wadsworth
20 Channel Center Street
Boston, MA 02210
USA

Cengage Learning is a leading provider of customized learning solutions with office locations around the globe, including Singapore, the United Kingdom, Australia, Mexico, Brazil, and Japan. Locate your local office at **international.cengage.com/region**.

Cengage Learning products are represented in Canada by Nelson Education, Ltd.

For your course and learning solutions, visit **www.cengage.com.**

Purchase any of our products at your local college store or at our preferred online store **www.cengagebrain.com**.
Instructors: Please visit **login.cengage.com** and log in to access instructor-specific resources.

Printed in the United States of America
1 2 3 4 5 6 7 15 14 13 12 11

This book is dedicated with love to God and my family —Roy,
Cari-Shawn and Leon, Courtney and Todd,
and my darling Royce.

Contents

Chapter 3   Brochures   19

Chapter 4   Communication Audits   36

Chapter 5   Direct Mail Campaigns   43

Chapter 13 Public Service Advertisements and Announcements 153

Chapter 14 Speeches 167

Chapter 15 Video News Releases and Electronic Press Kits 175

Preface

*S*ubstance before form might be an old adage, but, like most adages, it doesn't always apply. As public relations practitioners, we know that our messages must have *substance* to communicate effectively. Appropriate research and effective strategic planning help us to create persuasive messages that resonate with our target audiences. But when we know what we want to say, to whom we want to say it, and identify the best opening and medium for saying it, form is everything. Helping practitioners to choose how to present a message—in the best form and style—is the purpose of this book.

The PR Styleguide: Formats for Public Relations Practice, Third Edition, is about form and style. Yes, it contains substance, but its primary goal is to demonstrate how to present your message. While it is not a writing textbook, each section has style notes for effective writing. As a guide to style and format, *The PR Styleguide* should accompany a good writing textbook in the classroom or should be used as a standalone writing tool in the office.

Intended Audience

Projects like *The PR Styleguide* are inspired by a perceived need. While teaching and working in the field, I have observed the plethora of formats and styles used for public relations media; for example, news releases, backgrounders and media kits. With this guide I hope to help practitioners understand the best formats and styles for public relations media.

For years, newspapers and wire services have published stylebooks for their writers to be consistent in grammar, spelling, and usage. With *The PR Styleguide,* now public relations professionals can adopt a consistent format for their written materials. This style guide provides professionals clear guidelines and provides readers greater understanding and acceptance for the look and feel of a news release, speech, or backgrounder. Many of my students, fellow teachers, and colleagues at public relations firms and nonprofit and social advocacy groups find themselves "reinventing the wheel" when it comes to the style and the order of a particular medium. I do not offer this guide as a panacea or cookie cutter, leaving students, teachers, and professionals little room for creativity. Instead, it is intended to serve as a guide, an organizing tool.

There are benefits to using *The PR Styleguide*. With this guide, students receive specific guidelines for media assignments, instructors can spend less time developing and grading format, and busy communication directors won't waste precious time deciding what format to choose or how to organize a communication message.

Language became a bit of a problem as I developed this *Styleguide*. You will find I use two terms which some students, teachers, and practitioners may find confusing. I refer to the communication products in this book as *media*. There are two types of media in public communication—controlled media and uncontrolled media.

As the name suggests, uncontrolled media are those products we cannot control after they leave our hands. After we send a release, media kit, or feature story to a newsgathering organization, we have no control over how it will be used by reporters and editors.

Controlled media are those products and messages that we create and over which we have the most control. Newsletters, brochures, Web pages, presentations, annual reports, and paid advertising are all controlled media.

Organization

I organized *The PR Styleguide* as simply as possible, constructing an alphabetical listing of the most frequently used media. The idea is for students, teachers, and professionals to use the book as a reference tool, so the alphabetical listing makes locating each medium easy. Each medium has its own chapter. The chapters are organized identically, providing information about each medium as outlined below.

What Are They? Defines and explains the medium as it is understood in the field. Some definitions will be more extensive than others depending on how the medium is used in the field.

Who Gets Them? Delineates some of the possible audiences or publics that would receive the medium. This section is not a complete list but is designed to get you thinking about to whom you are writing. While the audience should be a part of the research process, a review of the intended audience is critical when it is time to begin writing.

What Do They Do? Delineates the purpose of the medium and how it is best used in the practice. The most common misuse of the medium is presented as well.

How Do They Help? Lists the various benefits and advantages of using the particular medium appropriately.

What Are the Pitfalls? Explains the restrictions and limitations of the medium as a useful tool in the field.

How Should They Look? Describes the format, process, and physical attributes of the medium. This section provides a model for creating the medium, including, but not limited to, margins, fonts, headings, and contact information.

Where Should They Go? Provides the most appropriate ways to disseminate the medium and why.

Did They Work? Describes the appropriate manner for evaluating the effectiveness of the medium after it is employed.

Putting PR into Practice This new end-of-chapter set of exercises gets students doing the practice work of PR.

Example Gallery Demonstrates a complete model of the medium in its proper format as described in the format section. The larger media such as annual reports and communication audits do not have examples included.

New To This Edition

- Chapter Nine, "New Media," is new to *The PR Styleguide*. It discusses social networking sites, blogs, microblogging and more. You will notice the examples in the gallery of that chapter look similar to, but are not from, the sites you know well. Copyright and permission issues sometimes get in the way of authenticity, but when you see them, you will get the idea.

- An AP style mini-chapter acts as an introduction or *primer* for understanding Associated Press style. It is located just before Chapter 10, "Newsletters." It is the one element of the book that is not a public communication medium and does not appear in alphabetical order. Instead, it is presented just before the chapters that deal most with the media for which AP style is most appropriate (media kits notwithstanding). This primer is not intended to replace the *The Associated Press Stylebook*. It is "a one and only." Please consider it another convenient tool. The Associated Press is considered the "gold standard" of news writing. A global network, it is known for its clear, concise, and professional writing style. *The Associated Press Stylebook* is well known to journalists and most PR practitioners. It serves as the tool most used for determining proper usage, abbreviations, spelling, and definitions. It is not replaceable.

- The new Appendix C includes pre- and post-tests that will help you evaluate your writing and editing skills. These tests are similar to those you will be given when applying for an entry-level PR position. Also included in Appendix C are AP quizzes on style and usage. Use them to determine how thoroughly you have mastered writing in AP style.

- In the new Appendix D, I have provided a sample edited news release showing examples of editing marks most commonly used in the field. Use them for your assignments and become familiar with them, because you will see a lot of them when you practice.

I want *The PR Styleguide* to be valuable to students, teachers, and professionals. It should make the day-to-day teaching and learning of the practice a little easier. I think it's time our profession had its own style guide. Please contact me with ideas for making it better.

The PR Styleguide and Ethics

Some of the chapters include "Ethics Notes." Similar to "Style Notes," this section does not appear in all chapters. Instead, it appears in chapters where use of the product provokes unique ethical concerns.

When we talk about ethics, some hear *law*. It is not unusual for people to confuse ethics and law. But there really is a bright, broad stripe between the two. Many actions that are not ethical are not illegal. They are merely dilemmas, but these dilemmas often speak volumes about our character. Clearly, there are many unethical actions that are also illegal. It is important for the student and the practitioner to pay close attention to what they say about and do for the clients and organizations they represent. "Ethics Notes" serve as a brief reminder of the ethical considerations surrounding some products we create and are helpful to the student learning the practice and to busy practitioners.

The practitioner must always be careful and mindful of professional and ethical conduct. The broadest definition of behaving ethically is doing what is right and shunning what is wrong. Having a clear sense of one's personal values is essential.

An audience-centered practice requires that we consider the perspectives of our audiences when making ethical decisions. Practitioners must challenge themselves to answer a fundamental question: "What are my personal values—the principles in which I believe strongly and can never violate?" The answer to this question puts us in the position to make decisions about how we will conduct ourselves as professionals.

As a professional representing an organization, you become an associate or employee of that organization. As a result, you become a part of one of your audiences; you are associated with the codes of conduct of that organization. Texas Instruments formally established its ethics codes in the 1960s several years after it said its employees had "placed their personal imprint on the ethics of the company. They chose to conduct themselves to the highest standards of personal integrity, and they demanded the same of others."

Ethical Questions PR Practitioners Face

- Is it ethical to defend products that are unsafe or badly made or could be used illegally?
- Is it ethical to promote products in foreign markets that are banned in the United States, such as certain pesticides and herbicides?
- Is it ethical to run two contradictory campaigns, as some U.S. tobacco companies do—one to encourage young people in the United States not to smoke and another to sell cigarettes in Asia?
- Is it ethical to try to deflect criticism of public figures whose behavior is improper or illegal?
- Is it ethical to buy influence in politics by contributing to political action committees, known as PACs?
- Is it ethical for PR practitioners to work for companies or clients whose environmental or labor practices differ from their ideals?

Many of the tools described in *The PR Styleguide* are media relations tools. You can learn a lot about the ethical concerns of reporters by looking at the codes of ethics to which they ascribe. A visit to www.asne.org, the Web site of the American Society of Newspaper Editors, will provide insight into the ethical concerns and rules newspaper editors and reporters must consider. The site delineates codes for regional and national newspapers and national news services such as the Associated Press (AP). The codes specify conduct regarding interaction with public communication professionals and conduct *when reporters act as public relations professionals themselves.*

Acknowledgments

There are many who helped me in completing this project. I want to thank Michael Rosenberg, Cengage Publisher, Humanities; Laurie Dobson, Development Editor; Erin Bosco, Assistant Editor; Rebecca Donahue, Editorial Assistant; Sharmila Krishnamurthy, Project Manager, PreMediaGlobal; Christina Ciaramella, Permissions; Andrea Rosenberg, Copyeditor; Greg Teague, Proofreader; Karen Maurice, Indexer; Thanks also to my former editor, Holly Allen, who was excited about this idea from the very start.

To the reviewers of this edition and the previous edition, thank you for the time we know you *didn't* have to give your impressions. Please keep the comments coming.

Gail F. Baker, University of Florida
Vincent L. Benigni, College of Charleston
Bojinka Bishop, Ohio University
Ronald Bishop, Drexel University
Sandra Fowler, Salem State College
Joye Gordon, Kansas State University
Peter F. Jeff, Grand Valley State University
Kathryn Lee, Syracuse University
Jody Matern, North Dakota State University
Marsha Little Matthews, East Central University
Janet Rice McCoy, Morehead State University
Henry J. Ruminski, Wright State University
Karen Sindelar, Coe College
Jonathan R. Slater, SUNY College at Plattsburgh
Rochelle Tillery-Larkin, Howard University

Many graduate students were helpful in gathering information for the chapters. I thank each of you. I would also like to acknowledge the design genius of Gloria Marconi and her assistance in keeping me technologically up to date. Her guidance helped to ensure the accuracy of much of the printing and production information that seems to change with every moment.

Barbara Diggs-Brown

Introduction

Making *The PR Styleguide* Work for You

As is the case with many tools, this guide is the product of necessity. My vision for it was all about saving time and effort. Frankly, I was tired of reinventing the wheel. Practically every professor I knew was writing and rewriting guidelines for the proper format for public relations products and collateral material. Twice a year, I'd write and update format and style guidelines for student projects. I also had to lecture and diagram, updating material as technology and PR practice changed. Throughout the year, former students practicing in the field emailed and telephoned to inquire about the appropriate format to use for PR products or how product uses may have changed. To my joy, this guide is being used by professionals in for-profit and nonprofit organizations.

It would be optimum for the products in *The PR Styleguide* to be presented in the order in which they are going to be taught, but few professors teach writing, portfolio, or campaign classes identically—even if they teach within the same department. Also, the plan is for use after the classroom. Although the guide was initially conceived as a teaching tool, I intended for students to keep it as an easy reference tool after graduation. With these challenges in mind, an alphabetical organization of the guide seemed to be most practical.

Using *The PR Styleguide* can be very easy. Each chapter is dedicated to one PR medium or product only, while the numerous appendices at the end contains additional helpful information. When you are assigned to produce a particular medium, you can find the guidelines and style notes by using the table of contents or index. You may refer to the examples in the Example Gallery at the end of each chapter. For example, if you are assigned to write a news release, you can find the news release chapter in the table of contents. As you continue with your project, you can consult the examples of news releases at the end of the chapter to be sure you are adhering to the proper format. Also, the chapter provides enough information for you to determine the best type of release to use for the project, the proper style, and much more.

When you are out of the classroom and into the practice, you will be constantly on the run, implementing public relations strategy. Effective implementation means knowing how best to communicate with an audience and in what form. *The PR Styleguide* will help you with effective implementation. If you need to write a script for a public service announcement, develop requirements for a subcontractor to produce a video news release, or look for the components of a news media kit, it's all here in alphabetical order in the table of contents.

I hope you enjoy using this book. I want it to be informative and useful. Please let me know if you have ideas for making it better. Meanwhile, enjoy your classes and your work.

Barbara Diggs-Brown

Annual Reports

What Are They?

It is said that the more things change, the more they remain the same. In the early 1930s the United States government passed securities laws regarding corporate governance, financial disclosure, and the manner in which corporate accounting is managed. The corporate annual report is one of the products of securities laws. In 1995 the government eased some of its rules, allowing companies to submit summary annual reports (SAR). Corporate annual reports became less cumbersome and difficult to decipher. However, following the financial scandals and corporate malfeasance at the turn of the century, Congress passed the Sarbanes-Oxley Act (SOA or SOX) in 2002, forcing corporate boards and accounting firms to be more diligent. While accuracy has always been the watchword for annual reports, it is even more important today.

Producing annual reports is one of the most challenging projects we tackle as public communication professionals. It is a large undertaking and a highly collaborative process, requiring input from many parts of an organization.

An annual report is, as the name suggests, a yearly reporting of an organization's activities. But today's annual reports do a lot more than that. The traditional goal of annual reports was to report a company's financial performance to stockholders. By law, all public companies must submit annual reports to the Securities and Exchange Commission (SEC). Now, annual reports are less reportorial and much more promotional, due in part to two dramatic changes over the last decade.

First, annual reports are no longer the exclusive domain of corporations. Nonprofit organizations and private companies produce them to share their activities with stakeholders and other publics. Though private corporations and nonprofits are not required to report to the SEC, many of them realize the benefits of producing annual reports as evidenced by their availability. An annual report is another controlled message to the organization's most important publics and promotes its image among its target audiences.

The second major change is the way in which information is presented. When the SEC changed its rules in 1995, allowing companies to submit shorter, less technical reports to stockholders, the annual report became a more concise document, less technical and more reader-friendly. Still, it is our job as public communication professionals to keep these reports simple and clear.

Today's annual reports have many varied target audiences. They must capture the attention of the traditional financial audience—the stockholders—but may also have to appeal to employees, donors, potential investors, and the media. In fact, like most good stories, an annual report should keep the reader's interest and tell the story of the organization and the people who carry out its business and other activities.

As writers of annual reports, our goal is to create a crisp, clean, fast-reading document that is not a mere compilation of the standard data required by the SEC. This new annual report style places a great deal of emphasis on jargon-free, creative text and on graphics that capture the reader's eye. Our job is to balance this new, creative style with solid and substantive information, combining inventive design techniques with sensible yet dynamic writing. But annual reports are not just beautifully designed documents; they must be complete and thorough in the information they provide. As communication practitioners, we play a major role in the construction of our organizations' annual reports, crafting the messages and ensuring that the design enhances the function of the report.

A critical component of an organization's overall strategic communication plan, the annual report should promote an organization to its target audiences. Along with other marketing and public relations materials, it plays an important role in creating the organization's public image and should serve as much more than just a means to convey financial status. Used to their full advantage, annual reports present the financial, historical, human interest, and philanthropic work of an organization.

Who Gets Them?

As is the case when writing any strategic message, we must first determine the purpose and target audience. Of course, most organizations can list many significant publics, but the key is to identify our primary audiences, understand these audiences, and tailor our messages to them. Identifying the audience for annual reports depends greatly on the purpose of the report. In general, though, we target annual reports to at least two audiences, which can include government regulators, stockholders, potential stockholders, customers, potential customers, employees, community leaders, granting organizations, donors, legislators, and the media. And each of these audiences is reading the report for a different reason. Financial investors and philanthropists want to make sound money decisions. Foundations want to monitor the progress of the organizations they support. Community leaders and legislators are interested in organizations for a wide array of reasons that include monitoring good corporate citizenship.

What Do They Do?

The conventional purpose of annual reports is to provide required financial information to investors and the SEC. Recently, new and multifaceted purposes have emerged, and organizations are now producing annual reports that are directed at multiple target audiences. They are often written with investors, employees, donors, and the media in mind. In addition to providing the required report of their earnings, public corporations are hoping to persuade stockholders to buy more shares and to entice prospective stockholders. Private organizations and nonprofits use annual reports to publicly acknowledge their own accomplishments, encourage philanthropy, create new partnerships, and recruit volunteers. But whatever the underlying goal may be, the use of annual reports has expanded to encompass a wide variety of subject matter related to the organization's primary interests.

Like most public relations and marketing materials, annual reports should make an organization stand out among its competitors, highlighting the organization's strengths and pointing to how it is unique. Again, a successful annual report is one that looks and feels like the rest of the organization's communication tools, enabling the reader to immediately identify the annual report with the organization and its other reports, marketing brochures, recruiting literature, media kits, and newsletters. Themes, copy, and graphics should work together to create a document that the reader identifies with the organization and its previous communication tools and mission.

As public communication professionals ushering the annual report through the production process, we must keep in mind that a lack of information is as detrimental to the reader of an annual report as too much information. If potential investors, donors, or granting organizations think that an organization has produced an inadequate annual report, it is unlikely they will trust that organization with their investment, donation, or grant.

How Do They Help?

Annual reports can benefit public, private, or not-for-profit organizations because they are an information source completely controlled by the organization. The theme and focus of the annual report can be used by the organization to deliver any message it chooses. These messages can be conveyed to the organization's employees, its local and national community, and competitors—not just investors or donors.

This unique opportunity allows the organization to focus on more than just the bottom line. Because they are used to discuss all aspects of an organization, annual reports can provide answers to anticipated questions from the target audience. As writers, we can use the annual report to present a human side of the organization by highlighting accomplishments of employees, philanthropy, volunteer efforts, and community or civic engagement. When we use them as a proactive crisis management tool, annual reports inform critical audiences about the actions management takes to ameliorate any weaknesses the organization has.

What Are the Pitfalls?

One hurdle we face as communicators is getting the target audience to read the information we send to them. Annual reports have become so common over the last few decades that they are often mistaken for junk mail and tossed in the trash without even being opened. The challenge for us is to make the report stand out so that it is opened and read. An annual report has the potential to reach all target audiences and convey the entire image of an organization, but only if written and produced correctly. The limitations of an annual report are determined by how much time, energy, and money the organization is willing to invest in the document.

Clarity and brevity are important in writing an effective annual report. But most organizations have a multiple clearance process that prevents clear and concise writing in annual reports. Because of the financial and legal implications of what is reported, many different divisions of an organization try to present information that is accurate but rarely simple. One solution to complicated language, jargon, and outright obfuscation caused by multiple agendas is to organize the narrative portions around a theme. The theme can keep the information structured and simple.

An alternative to providing a lot of complicated information is the SAR, mentioned at the beginning of the chapter. The SAR is shorter and less complicated than the traditional report. However, investors sometimes find the SAR unreliable because it sacrifices critical financial data in the attempt to make the information more readable.

How Should They Look?

Style Notes

To achieve the annual report's principal objectives, we must write clear, concise, and easy-to-read information in a quick, exciting, and appropriate manner. Our challenge in producing an effective annual report is to include all the basic information while creating a document that is unique and reflects the image of the organization. There are certain legal and stylistic guidelines that every annual report must follow, but there are also ways to infuse creativity. Incorporating a theme adds a creative cohesive element that the writer can implement throughout every aspect of the report's format. A document with a consistent look throughout has a much higher chance of being read cover to cover.

Today's annual reports look more like magazines than official reports. They can utilize any number of different formats, though the most popular is the booklet. With this format, all the pages are printed on both sides and bound together with centerfold staples or glued—known as perfect binding. We should try to give the reports "scan-ability" so that readers can get a general idea of what is included in the report after scanning it for a few minutes. Graphic elements such as headlines, subheads, pull quotes, bullets, and charts give the report scan-ability.

The average annual report is about 40 pages in length. Some banks and other financial institutions produce annual reports of 100 pages or more. Most do not exceed, or need to go beyond, approximately 40 pages to effectively convey their message.

Format

Front Cover

As is the case with most publications, an annual report's front cover must catch the reader's eye and create interest immediately. Innovative graphics, color photos, and artwork that reflect the theme can really make an annual report stand out. The cover is the reader's first impression of the annual report and the organization. It sets the tone for the report and can determine whether the document will be read or merely thrown in the trash. The organization's name and reporting year must appear prominently on the front cover.

Table of Contents

A table of contents is a critical element. It allows readers to save valuable time when searching for items of interest. The use of bold large type, color, and topic summaries highlights the most important headings.

Narrative Section

We should use creative language in the narrative section to describe all aspects of an organization—from its employees and day-to-day activities to philanthropic work. In this section we can help our organization connect with its audiences on a personal level. The narrative section begins to build on the theme of the annual report. Our job is to maintain that theme throughout the narrative portion through both the writing and the visual elements such as graphs, charts, photos, and layout. The written copy and visuals should complement each other. Specific elements included within the body of the narrative are background summary of the organization; its products and services; events; major purchases, sales, and mergers; status of resources; and legal issues.

Letter from a Chief Executive

This message is written from the perspective of senior executives such as the chief executive officer, chief financial officer, chairperson, and/or president. The letter can be drafted by an assigned writer. If more than one letter is included, it is crucial that the messages vary in subject matter. Often these letters offer a brief summary of how the past year's financial performance has affected the company as a whole. Drafting these letters requires some of our best skills as writers. We must include both positive and negative information in order to help maintain a level of trust between the organization and its audiences. We must use the discussion of negative occurrences as an opportunity for the CEO or executive director to explain how the organization has learned from its mistakes and how management will use this information in the future to prevent such occurrences.

Executive messages also include projections and visions for the organization's future. While understanding past performance is important, people want to invest money and time with organizations that have goals and aspirations and that do not just focus on the past. Executive letters should reflect these ideas throughout the copy and design.

It is also a good idea for executive letters to focus on a societal issue that somehow affects the company, such as the environment or health.

And finally, we need to give the target audience a sense that the organization has an intelligent, socially responsible, and ambitious leader at the helm. This is a perfect opportunity to present a positive and influential image to the target audience while generating excitement within the organization.

Description of the Organization

The description of the organization enhances the messages that the chief executive or other executives have already presented in the executive letter(s). In this section we can include information about the organization's products, programs and/or services, activities, location, major employee accomplishments or awards, analysis of past performance, and plans for the future. This section includes photographs, tables, and graphs that amplify or demonstrate the copy about the organization's products, programs, and/or services. We might include photos of employees at work or participating in philanthropic activities or community events that the organization sponsors. We also need to include all pertinent information about the organization that will engage the reader while incorporating the theme throughout all aspects of the description.

Financial Summary, or Financial Section

This section is the foundation of the annual report. Here is where it is important for us to consult the organization's investor relations or major gifts/contributions executive or consultant. The financial section paints a picture of the organization that accurately reflects the statistics provided. Efforts by the SEC to modify its reporting rules have allowed public companies to create a far more readable document for their audiences, but the list of requirements for this section is still long:

- audited financial statements
- quarterly financial data
- five-year historical summary of financial data
- description of the business
- business segment information
- two-year market price history of company's stock
- management's discussion/analysis of company's financial conditions
- results of operations
- company directors and executives

Although private companies and nonprofit organizations are not required by law to include all of this data, they do need to provide similar information such as a mission statement, the state of the organization, the financial condition of the organization, and situational analyses, which anticipate audience questions regarding specific financial situations.

Back Cover

The back cover gives us the opportunity to leave the reader with one last bit of information. Most back covers include the organization's name, telephone number, and mailing, email, and Web site addresses, along with any logos or trademarks. Again, the theme should be prominent.

As writers who think strategically, we know that deadlines are critical to all publications. Producing a quality annual report requires an extensive planning process, beginning at least six months ahead of the intended date of distribution. Much of the money that is budgeted for the development of annual reports stems from the production and printing costs. Because most annual reports are printed on high-quality paper stock and incorporate high-resolution graphics, photos, and charts, the costs for this one project can escalate very rapidly. Printing costs can run as much as $3 to $25 per copy. It is important to have a good relationship with a competent, professional, and flexible printer who understands the enormity of the investment.

Where Should They Go?

Before we enter the writing stage, we must concern ourselves with how a publication will be distributed. There are always design concerns about distribution that can affect decisions about written copy. Most annual reports are still sent through the U.S. Postal Service. Public companies send them directly to stockholders with proxy statements. For a brief period, some companies experimented with video and audio annual reports, but this never gained much popularity.

Because the Internet continues to change the face of communication and business, many organizations are using this medium and its technology to distribute annual reports. Organizations post annual reports on the Internet in three ways. A text-only file can be read immediately; however, it does not include any visuals. A PDF file must be downloaded but can sustain visuals. An interactive report is an innovative version but is limited by the recipient's software. Currently, most annual reports are written in simple text and PDF files, while only a few are interactive.

Organizations are now supplementing their hard-copy reports with online alternatives. Because the SEC now requires electronic filing for public companies, many of them make their annual reports available electronically to their financial audiences as well.

Did They Work?

Our goal is to write effective annual reports that are both informative and easy to read. Like all public communication materials, they must be written clearly and concisely while conveying a lot of information. The annual report requires extra diligence about maintaining accuracy and disclosing all pertinent data in order to ensure credibility. A theme that is interesting as well as representative of the organization's image is also critical to the report's success. But it is difficult to determine whether or not an annual report has been successful. Many organizations include survey questionnaires in an attempt to assess public response.

Ethics Notes

As a public communication practitioner, you are not responsible for the financial decisions or accounting procedures of your organization, unless you are a senior officer. All organizations—for-profit and nonprofit— have senior officers. Senior officers are responsible for ensuring the organization has internal systems controls and accepted accounting principles and that they are compliant with established accounting procedures. Senior officers must be sure the organization keeps books, records, and accounts that are accurate and fairly reflect the transactions and dispositions of the assets of the organization. They make sure that all disclosures in reports and documents submitted to the SEC and in all public communication are full, fair, accurate, timely, and understandable.

As the public communication professional, it is your job to check and double-check with all the colleagues who present information for the annual report. Your job is to ensure that the proper clearances have been completed. In addition, you are responsible for reporting any discrepancies or misconduct you observe.

Putting PR into Practice

1. Conduct online research to identify and select an annual report from a for-profit organization and one from a nonprofit.
    a. Compare and contrast the style of each of the documents. How are they organized similarly? Differently?
    b. Is there a section in the for-profit annual report you feel would enhance the quality and clarity of the nonprofit report? Why?
    c. How would you describe the tone of each?
    d. Who would you say is the primary target audience of each?
2. With the client organization you have chosen for this course or an organization with which you are closely affiliated in mind, are there elements of the annual reports you reviewed that you think would work for your client? Explain.
3. Find and review annual reports online to increase your understanding of how letters from organizations are featured in annual reports. Now write a brief letter from the chief executive officer, president, or executive director of your client organization that could be featured in the organization's annual report.

Chapter 2

Audio News Releases

What Are They?

An audio news release (ANR) is the radio counterpart to the video news release (VNR). Most ANRs are dependent on actualities—sound bites from news-makers such as organization executives, celebrities, or experts. Public communication practitioners supply prerecorded background information to news outlets, which construct original stories from this information.

Like a written news release, an ANR is designed to generate media coverage that will ultimately reach a specific audience. Radio is one of the most effective promotional vehicles for reaching target audiences. Because of its ubiquity in the American home and automobile, radio is an ideal medium for gaining publicity and creating awareness. Many organizations choose to hire a broadcast public relations firm to produce their ANRs and to guide them through the process. For a full range of audio news release services, it is best to contract with an ANR company. Companies like Medialink Worldwide, MultiVu, and News Generation supply prerecorded background information to news outlets, which construct original stories from this information. As practitioners, we need to understand the process and the unique elements that make up the ANR.

Who Gets Them?

We cannot begin the writing process—or serve as producer for an ANR project—until we understand the target audience and how that audience best receives information. ANRs can be successful only if we know who our target audience is, the message most likely to resonate well with the audience, and where on the radio spectrum the audience is listening. If our organization has hired a broadcast public relations firm, we have to make sure it has conducted the best research to target our audience.

The audience for an ANR depends on the message and purpose of the release. The audience can be as narrow as hobbyists or as broad as members of an entire community. An ANR will capture a specific audience through sound and messages that appeal to its special interest. Radio is one of the most effective ways to reach niche audiences because radio stations are keenly aware of their demographics and they reach highly delineated audiences. The introduction of satellite radio in 2001 created more narrowly defined audience segmentation for communication professionals to consider. Digital radio has more than 100 channels and offers music and talk to niche audiences interested in entertainment such as sports, opera show tunes and NASCAR. ANRs target consumers, businesses, and specialized audiences.

What Do They Do?

The goal of ANRs is to convey messages to target audiences through radio news. ANR producers accomplish this by planning, writing, and then creating a news release that suits a specific radio station's format and audience. Because radio stations have individualized formats designed to attract and keep listeners with particular demographics, the producer can tailor the release to capture the attention of a station's distinct audience. It is important to note that television/radio partnerships have increased the competition, as many radio stations can now receive stories from their television partners.

We can use an ANR to disseminate news about an organization's milestones, special events, or other newsworthy occurrences that have an impact on an audience. The prerecorded and scripted ANR is designed to reach the audience and convey a distinct and significant message.

ANRs are effective, time sensitive, and cost efficient for both the organization and news media outlets. The production costs of an ANR include on-location recording, studio time, talent fees (if professional voices are used), and distribution charges that differ depending on location.

How Do They Help?

When effectively executed, ANRs can help an organization to reach a wide variety of audiences. To some extent, the organization is in control of the information it disseminates to the desired target audience, and the content of the release is organized and produced to portray the organization in the best possible light. ANRs can offer an attractive alternative to live radio interviews during which the organization's spokesperson can be caught off guard by a question or appear nervous or unprepared on air. ANRs convey a specific, controlled message free of any mistakes or misunderstandings and at a reasonable cost. But some news editors prefer to acquire at least one interview or sound bite on their own.

The skyrocketing cost of producing the news has left many radio news departments woefully understaffed. ANRs provide sound to be used at the discretion of newsrooms free of charge, enabling them to produce and cover more stories than their limited budgets normally afford and supplying them with numerous editorial options without restrictions.

What Are the Pitfalls?

Some news directors are wary of prepackaged broadcast news pieces including ANRs because they are concerned that the information is biased. Most news directors edit the story in order to fit a particular timeframe or to create a more obvious connection to their audiences. The disadvantage to public communication practitioners is that the news producer can manipulate and change the story. In addition, there is no immediate opportunity for further clarification or explanation from the organization or newsmaker.

One of the other serious obstacles to the use of ANRs is no longer as much of a concern. Not long ago, news directors gave ANRs very low priority because private organizations—not journalists or news establishments—produced them. But recent studies indicate that news directors have become more comfortable with this particular public relations product.

Placing an ANR often takes a great deal of persuasion on the part of a public communication media specialist. In order to convince a station to use the release, we have to be sure the featured topic is both timely and newsworthy. As with any other type of news release, the topic of an ANR must be relevant to the target audience.

Another precautionary note regarding ANRs: Don't make generalizations regarding audience demographics. One size does not always fit all. For example, when targeting the Hispanic/Latino market, we cannot assume that New York Puerto Rican radio is similar to Miami Cuban Hispanic radio.

How Should They Look?

Style Notes

A typical ANR is approximately 60 seconds long. ANRs are often individually tailored to match the format of the station receiving it. The overall tone of an ANR is less formal than that of its video and print counterparts. Unlike a traditional news release, ANRs often utilize creative methods to highlight the news—an approach that complements the relaxed and very personal tone of the radio medium. The strategy is to engage listeners' interest by appealing to their sense of individuality and their relationship with the radio personalities.

Short, succinct sentences are important because radio audiences cannot follow long, complicated sentences and complex information. As well, maintaining a simple format makes it easier for an announcer to sustain a consistent style of delivery.

The writing style and tone of an ANR are not the only unique elements of the medium. Within the composition of an ANR is an element known as the **actuality.** The actuality portion of the release includes the voice(s) of one or more newsmakers, experts, and/or spokespersons for the featured organization. Whereas the narrator/announcer employed for the introductions and various transitions within the story is often a voice professional or communication professional, the newsmaker is almost always someone qualified to talk about the topic—the expert.

Just as most printed news releases offer some background for the story and often provide context for a quote from a newsmaker, so does an ANR in a unique way. A narrator or an announcer in an ANR supplies all necessary or relevant background information as it relates to the story. This often includes logistical information, point of reference in regard to the newsmaker(s), and any other newsworthy information that relates to the story. We should avoid using a publicity spokesperson who has little or no connection to the story because it decreases the credibility of the ANR.

Process and Format

We move through six phases in developing an ANR: research, actuality taping, scriptwriting, narration recording, editing of the final product, and monitoring and evaluation.

Thorough and effective research is critical to the success of media message development and media campaigns. The ANR is not an exception. Appropriate research is the basis on which messages are developed, newsmakers are identified, and audiences are understood. The organization collects all related data and information prior to mapping out the content of an ANR and presents an analysis of their effect on the target audience. Often a research firm is brought in to conduct the necessary research. During the research phase, our contribution as practitioners is monitoring the process and providing data.

After all the news is collected and the newsmakers are identified and ready to offer a recorded quote—a **sound bite**—questions must be developed to obtain an effective sound bite. The communication practitioner prepares these questions.

There are a variety of ways in which a newsmaker can supply a sound bite. Most producers prefer to record sound in a professional recording studio, which offers soundproof booths, state-of-the-art recording equipment, and playback capabilities to ensure the sound is flawless. But it is difficult, if not impossible, to have the opportunity to record under such ideal circumstances because of time constraints, distance, or expense. Usually, then, sound-bite recordings are made on location (by going to the expert) or even over the telephone.

Any sound bite in an ANR is an actuality. Most ANRs include two to four sound-bite actualities that highlight differing perspectives. Sound bites should be limited to 7 to 12 seconds each. This maintains a format of short and succinct sound most often used in radio.

Once the actualities are obtained, scriptwriting can begin. While an outline should have been developed and approved prior to this stage, a fully refined script can now be formatted. The ultimate purpose of the script is to provide hard copy as a guide for news directors to use when developing and editing their stories. Scripts are also used by the announcer/narrator during recording sessions.

ANR scripts must include a title, or **slug,** running time, date, and contact information. The narration section of the script is written in all uppercase letters and triple spaced. The actuality portion of the script should be written in upper- and lowercase letters and single spaced. Any words or names that are difficult to pronounce should be supplemented with phonetic spelling in parentheses.

Following the approval of a finalized script, a professional narrator or announcer records the narrated portion. This section usually highlights background information on the topic, introduces the actuality and newsmaker, and provides details of how to obtain further information on the topic. It is important for the narrator to state all phone numbers and contact names two or more times to call special attention to that important information.

The producer edits the final ANR, incorporating the most effective sound bites along with the ideal narration recordings, and blends them for a seamless 60- to 90-second ANR. The final tape always includes audio tone for recording engineers to set their sound levels; a countdown to alert engineers when the ANR will begin; a disclaimer that offers free and unrestricted use of the provided sound; and an introduction that includes the name and sponsor of the ANR.

Where Should They Go?

Practitioners who are well versed in media relations pitch ANRs to the news media. As with any news release, the person pitching the story should know the appropriate contact person at the radio station and the opportune time to call. Knowing the news cycles and understanding the news director's job can make all the difference in getting the audio news release on air.

When the radio station agrees to use the ANR, it can be distributed to the news director through a number of different means. Satellite transmission, telephone calls, hard copies, and the Internet are the most popular options for transmitting an audio news release.

The use of satellites makes the distribution process both fast and successful. The ANR is uplinked to a satellite by the organization and then downlinked by the radio station. This method is possible only if the news station has the time, staff, and accessibility to receive information by satellite.

An ANR can also be sent via the telephone lines. To do this, the person pitching the piece calls a radio station to pitch the actuality. If the news director is interested, the ANR can be immediately played over the telephone and recorded by the news station.

Hard-copy releases are sent with both the tape and the script by mail, or they can be hand delivered to the studio by courier. There are many different varieties of tape formats, including reel-to-reel, digital recordings, and cassettes (rarely used for broadcast purposes).

The Internet plays a major role in distributing ANRs. Organizations or broadcast public relations firms that possess the technological hardware create a release as an MP3 file, offering a flexible alternative to standard recordings. These files allow radio stations all over the world to download and then play the ANR over both the Internet and traditional radio stations, and they are available to the general public. The radio media relations companies like News Generation post the ANRs on their own Web site and direct news stations there to pick up the client's ANR.

Did They Work?

Radio is a very difficult medium to monitor. It is impossible to count the exact number of listeners to a specific radio station at any given time. Therefore, stations rely on radio-rating companies, such as Arbitron, to survey listeners and compile statistical data to estimate audience numbers.

Although radio-monitoring reports are considered faulty, ANR producers often request that stations complete these reports to help gauge the possible success of the release. The monitoring report should display the number of times the release ran as well as the stations' audience sizes and demographics.

Additional evaluation methods used to verify the effectiveness of an ANR include follow-up phone calls, radio show transcripts, and organization membership or sales figures. Radio show transcripts demonstrate how the ANR was used. Membership or sales increases may be the result of listeners hearing the ANR.

Putting PR into Practice

Writing an ANR script is good practice for writing for the ear. Follow each of the first four phases of the six-phase process described on page 12 to accomplish the development steps of creating an ANR.

1. Consider the client you chose for the course or go to the Web site for your hometown or your college or university. Conduct enough research to identify an issue, concern, or important topic affecting one of the organization's primary audiences.

2. Select the appropriate organization spokesperson and justify your choice.

3. Develop a set of questions designed to obtain the sound bite(s) you need.

4. Write your sound bite or actually have it recorded.

5. Now write your script.

An *Example Gallery* for Audio News Releases
begins on the following page.

Example Gallery
Audio News Releases

Emerald Heights Office of the Mayor   Total Time: 1:42   **❶**
Emergency Water Restrictions   Steve Mangel, Producer

ANNOUNCER: IN RESPONSE TO SOME OF THE MOST SEVERE

DROUGHT CONDITIONS EXPERIENCED BY THE MIDWEST IN MORE

THAN A DECADE, THE MAYOR OF EMERALD HEIGHTS, JUDITH   **❷**

GOLD, HAS ISSUED AN EXECUTIVE ORDER IMPOSING LEVEL ONE

WATER RESTRICTIONS TO HELP EASE THE DEPLETION OF THE

TOWN'S WATER SUPPLY. MAYOR JUDITH GOLD:

> GOLD: "While this entire region has been severely affected by this
> ongoing drought, our town is being especially hard hit. Although area
> residents have voluntarily scaled back their water usage, it is unfortunately   **❸**
> not enough. We will continue to monitor this situation and hopefully
> reduce the restrictions as soon as the water supply is replenished."

ANNOUNCER: LEVEL ONE WATER RESTRICTIONS PROHIBIT THE

USE OF WATER FOR WASHING PAVED SURFACES, WATERING LAWNS,

GARDENS, LANDSCAPED AREAS, TREES, SHRUBS AND OTHER

-more-   **❹**

Page 1 of 2

An audio news release script from a city government designed
to persuade members of the community.

❶ HEADING: Identifies the client, the slug, the date, the length of the ANR, and the producer. Short, two- to three-word title slug to identify clip.

❷ BODY: The script is written in all uppercase letters and triple spaced for easy reading by an announcer.

❸ SOUND BITES: Quotes written in normal print and single spaced, approximately 15 seconds long. Two quotes are optimal.

❹ PAGE SLUGS: At the bottom of each page, -more- indicates the copy continues on the next page. -30- or -###- or -end- indicates the end.

15

Example Gallery
Audio News Releases

OUTDOOR PLANTS. ORNAMENTAL USES OF WATER SUCH AS

ARTIFICIAL WATERFALLS, MISTING MACHINES AND REFLECTING

POOLS, AS WELL AS NONCOMMERCIAL WASHING OR CLEANING OF

MOBILE EQUIPMENT INCLUDING AUTOMOBILES, TRUCKS,

TRAILERS AND BOATS ARE ALSO PROHIBITED.

CITY COUNCILMAN, GEORGE MAXIM, AGREES THAT THE

RESTRICTIONS WILL BE HARD ON THE RESIDENTS, BUT WILL

PAY OFF FOR EVERYONE IN THE LONG RUN.

> MAXIM: "I was glad to see the mayor move so swiftly in setting up these water restrictions. It is important during times like these for all residents of Emerald Heights to pull together to get through this water shortage successfully."

ANNOUNCER: FOR MORE INFORMATION REGARDING THE LEVEL

⑤ ONE WATER RESTRICTIONS, CONTACT STEVE MANGEL AT THE

MAYOR'S OFFICE 555-2233. THAT NUMBER IS 555-2233.

④ -###-

④ PAGE SLUGS: At the bottom of each page, -more- indicates the copy continues on the next page. -30- or -###- or -end- indicates the end.

⑤ CONTACT INFORMATION: Contact information read by the announcer at the end.

Example Gallery
Audio News Releases

Formative Enterprises
Youth Exercise Classes

Total Time: 1:18
Staci Kaufman, Producer

①

ANNOUNCER: AS PART OF THE NATIONAL FITNESS INITIATIVE,

FORMATIVE ENTERPRISES IS BRINGING YOUTH FITNESS CLASSES

TO CHILDREN OF LOW-INCOME FAMILIES ACROSS THE COUNTRY

FREE OF CHARGE. CONSIDERED TO BE THE PREMIER

MANUFACTURER OF YOUTH FITNESS PRODUCTS, FORMATIVE IS

②

DONATING OVER FOUR MILLION DOLLARS IN EQUIPMENT AND

TRAINING TO COMMUNITY CENTERS THAT SERVICE SOME OF THE

POOREST NEIGHBORHOODS IN THE COUNTRY. JAIME MOLACK, CEO

OF FORMATIVE ENTERPRISES, EXPLAINS THE PROGRAM.

> MOLACK: "While children around the world use our exercise equipment every day, there are still areas in our own country where kids are forced to exercise with old, worn-out equipment. It is about time these children found out just how much fun exercise can be."

③

-more-

④

Page 1 of 2

An audio news release script from a for-profit corporation designed to inform an audience about its public service.

① HEADING: Identifies the client, the slug, the date, the length of the ANR and the producer. Short, two- to three-word title slug to identify clip.

② BODY: The script is written in all uppercase letters and is triple spaced for easy reading by an announcer.

③ SOUND BITES: Quotes written in normal print and single spaced, approximately 15 seconds long. Two quotes are optimal.

④ PAGE SLUGS: At the bottom of each page, -more- indicates the copy continues on the next page. -30- or -###- or -end- indicates the end.

Example Gallery
Audio News Releases

ANNOUNCER: BESIDES THE SUBSTANTIAL EQUIPMENT DONATION,

FORMATIVE ENTERPRISES IS ALSO ESTABLISHING YOUTH EXERCISE

PROGRAMS SO KIDS IN THESE LOW-INCOME NEIGHBORHOODS WILL

BE ABLE TO EXERCISE WITH THEIR FRIENDS IN A STRUCTURED

ENVIRONMENT.

YOUTH DIRECTOR, JOHN PETERS, DISCUSSES THE BENEFITS OF

THE NEW PROGRAM.

> PETERS: "The equipment at our youth center is so old that many of the
> neighborhood kids have stopped coming to the center altogether. Now we
> have updated equipment and a new program that seem to really pique the
> interest of these kids."

ANNOUNCER: FOR MORE INFORMATION ON THE NEW YOUTH

❺ EXERCISE PROGRAMS AND HOW TO VOLUNTEER, CONTACT

CATHERINE MORRIS OF FORMATIVE ENTERPRISES AT 1-800-555-5597.

AGAIN THAT NUMBER IS 1-800-555-5597.

❹   -###-

Page 2 of 2

❹ PAGE SLUGS: At the bottom of each page, -more- indicates the copy continues on the next page. -30- or -###- or -end- indicates the end.

❺ CONTACT INFORMATION: Contact information read by the announcer at the end.

Brochures

What Are They?

As communication practitioners, we will write and/or monitor the production of brochures more than any other public communication product. Organizations use brochures to convey messages and information to a well-defined target audience. The most commonly recognized of all public communication products, these staples of marketing and public relations take the form of a printed leaflet or pamphlet, a booklet, or even a Web-posted brochure.

Leaflets and pamphlets are formatted on a single piece of paper folded into sections called **panels.** The most commonly used brochure, the two-fold leaflet, has six panels with type and artwork throughout. Other popular formats include four- and eight-panel leaflets that are formatted on a single piece of paper of varying size.

A booklet is two or more pieces of paper bound together. Booklets are longer in length and have more content than leaflets. All the pages are printed on both sides and are often bound together with centerfold staples called saddle stitching or, depending on length, bound together by glue called perfect binding.

There are advantages and drawbacks to Web-posted brochures. On the plus side, Web brochures don't cost anything to print, can reach an unlimited audience who can access the information within hours of it being posted, and can be updated as needed without reprinting. Web-posted brochures can also be downloaded as PDFs, allowing the target audience to generate a printed copy that it can keep. On the negative side, end users have to print out the brochures on their own printers. Although online brochures can always be viewed in color, unless the consumer has a color printer they are almost always printed out in black and white. If your message depends on color, then an online brochure may not be the best solution. With broadband use, these types of brochures have gained in popularity. In effect, the cost of printing and postage, instead of being borne by the client, is passed on to the consumer.

All three brochure types are designed to enhance the uniqueness of an organization's message. Corporations, small businesses, nonprofits, schools, museums, and politicians are among the many groups that use brochures to help convey a message in a brief and streamlined format.

Coordinating messages and content, selecting the typeface, choosing the visuals, selecting the layout, and designing the overall look all help define a brochure and determine its expense and success. As public communication practitioners, we have to strike a balance between the amount of information and the design in order to create an effective, easy-to-read, and attractive brochure. Our job is to shepherd the brochure through all of its stages to help ensure it is effective.

Who Gets Them?

As always, it is important to understand the audience we are attempting to inform or persuade so that we can tailor the message to its particular needs. By understanding the targeted audience and creating a brochure that offers benefits to the audience and meets its needs, it is more likely that the brochure will accomplish our goal.

The audience is determined by the goal of the organization and the research conducted to ascertain that audience's interests. Depending on the type of organization and purpose of the brochure, target audiences can include customers, clients, employees, stakeholders and stockholders, workshop participants, organization membership, and government agencies.

What Do They Do?

Effective brochures inform, educate, or persuade the reader about the intended message. They do so by attracting the reader's interest through an eye-catching cover design and then holding the reader's attention throughout the body using clear, concise, and organized writing in order to convey a specific message.

It is crucial to determine the intended shelf life of the brochure from the outset. The shelf life is how long a brochure will be used by the organization. If the brochure will be reused, for how long will it be used? If a brochure should be updated, how often should this be done? Also, creating a timetable for the brochure helps create a calendar for the organization, indicating when to start designing the next brochure. Organizations that plan ahead and outline their specific objectives or goals generally have success in designing their brochures. These important communication strategy questions must be answered thoroughly before brochure development can begin.

Effective brochures maintain a clear, focused message targeted to a specific audience. As public communication practitioners, we must constantly stay aware of the brochure's objectives throughout the process. This means we must also remind management of the primary message; an organization without a clear understanding of its goals will miss an opportunity to effectively convey its message.

There are some commonly used messages that run throughout the many different types of brochures. Certain brochures are used in orientations, or to describe rules, regulations, or safety concerns. Other popular message choices include describing benefits or policies. A brochure might also be used to help in recruitment, training, sales, or even promotions.

It is critical to the success of a brochure to limit its focus to one clear message. Narrowing the focus to either a product-oriented or informational brochure increases the opportunity for reaching the goal. The purpose of a product-oriented brochure is to sell and/or persuade the reader to use the featured item or service. We accomplish this through persuasive language that is expressive, compares and contrasts, and is personal—sometimes emotional—for the reader. The reader is looking for personal benefits, so it is best if we can outline these benefits in language that is meaningful to the target audience.

Informational brochures attempt to convey the importance of an issue or idea rather than a tangible object. The language we use for an informational brochure tends to be more authoritative and fact oriented than persuasive because the purpose is to persuade the audience that this information is important to them.

Effective brochures capture the reader's attention by emphasizing an organization's individuality and creativity. Each organization has interesting ideas and unique capabilities. To establish individuality, we emphasize the organization's unique aspects, highlighting those elements that make the organization stand out from the crowd so that the audience will be able to distinguish the organization from its competitors.

How Do They Help?

We use brochures to convey an organization's vision to its most important audiences, and when we work to produce brochures correctly, they will communicate that vision in a quick, concise, creative way. Unlike annual reports and newsletters, brochures present an organization's message with less copy and more aplomb.

Brochures can be designed and produced fairly quickly and with small budgets. When the idea or theme is time-specific, such as a special event or an anniversary, a brochure is a quick and easy way to deliver the message. Brochures can also be *hooks* that engage audiences and persuade them to learn more about an organization.

What Are the Pitfalls?

One of a brochure's major benefits—its size—is also its downfall. Because a brochure is customarily a brief document providing condensed material, it requires elimination of some key information. This space constraint is one of the biggest obstacles we face in designing an effective brochure. Successful brochures have impressive design and style elements in order to maximize space, highlight important points, and convey a clear message in a minimum amount of space.

Budgets are also a limiting factor. Brochures can range in design from full-color documents with photographs and elaborate graphics and art to simple, one-color designs. Budget is often the defining variable. Trying to produce an expensive brochure on a restricted budget results in a poor document and can limit the effectiveness of the message because the audience does not respond to the design.

How Should They Look?

Style Notes

Designing a brochure involves first—and most importantly—identifying a purpose and goal for the document. The goals are accomplished through the overall message and themes presented throughout the brochure. Our job is to write a message that highlights two or three key points in order to get the most out of the limited space available. Limiting the message to two or three key points also increases the likelihood that the reader will remember the message.

Brochure copy should be able to pass the "scan-ability" test (people scan copy for key information rather than read in depth). We accomplish this by writing headlines that create bold statements and quick summaries. Bullets bring clarity to facts and figures that can be used to support the primary message. Copy written with positive language that is concise, jargon-free, and in the active voice is easily read and understood.

Brochures also use testimonials from customers and clients who express appreciation for the organization's products, services, or programs. Testimonials are appealing to target audiences because audiences are looking for personal benefits. Many organizations use short surveys as a way to evaluate the audience reaction. As writers, we have to remember to obtain permission to publish testimonials.

Effective brochures always point the way to additional information and give the target audience an action to take. They should supply names, addresses, telephone numbers, Web site URLs and other contact information to help the audience act.

Process and Format

The Three Stages

The **manuscript stage** is the writing phase. During this stage, the copywriter writes the copy or edits the copy written by the client. During this stage, editors check that the writing clearly conveys the overall themes and messages.

The **design stage** is when the graphic designer takes the edited manuscript, adds photos or illustrations, and designs the overall look of the piece. This is when format, size, number of pages, type of paper, number of ink colors, and how it will be mailed are considered and decided upon, usually in consultation with the writer and the client.

The **comprehensive layout stage** is the point at which we review the copy, design, and layout. Following our review, the client or an executive of the organization gives the final approval to move to the next stage. Moving forward and producing a brochure without establishing the total satisfaction of the leaders of the organization can result in additional time and money to complete the project—and in the frustration of rewrites and redesign.

Once the comprehensive layout is accepted and approved, the job will be sent to the printer, who creates a blueline proof. The **blueline stage** is the last opportunity to make any changes. This stage got its name from the blue color that results when a proof is burned from the film negatives onto special photosensitive paper. Bluelines are sometimes still used for one-, two-, or three-color printing jobs. Now printers use an electronic proofing system called an HP Blueline, which shows the actual colors of the job and is not really blue.

Full-color jobs require a color proof to make sure the colors are accurate. Color proofs used to be called **chromalins** and were an accurate representation of what the finished job would look like. At that time, the four negatives (one for each color) were adjusted—before the plates were made. As almost all printing is now produced from electronic files (see digital printing discussion in "Reproduction," below), the traditional chromalin has become, more often than not, a high-resolution PDF.

If the job is already on the press, the proof is called a **press proof.** If color is a critical consideration, making adjustments at this point may be necessary. No matter what the printing process, however, waiting until the last minute to make changes is always costly. This is not the appropriate time to find out that the organization's leadership is unhappy with the overall design, writing, or message. Making changes at this point is extremely expensive and frustrating because they require new input from the designer and the writers, and the printer may have to start all over. Maintaining open communication with the organization's leadership and understanding the process of producing a brochure can help to avoid these types of costly mistakes.

Panels

There are many styles and sizes of brochures, classified according to the number of folds used in the design. The one-fold format is a four-panel brochure; two folds (bi-fold) create a six-panel brochure; and three folds (tri-fold) result in an eight-panel brochure. The most common sizes are 8½″ × 5½″ (8½″ × 11″ folded in half) and 8½″ × 11″ (letter size), which can be folded in thirds to 8½″ × 3″ (bi-folds). For a tri-fold, an 8½″ × 14″ sheet folds to eight panels. An 8½″ × 11″ bound booklet

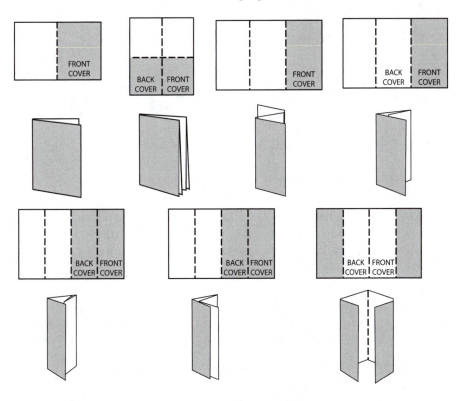

is also a choice. This is actually an $11'' \times 17''$ sheet folded in half. The most popular size used is the traditional $4'' \times 9''$ six-panel brochure, which fits a #10 business envelope.

Shown in the diagrams above are several common folding methods. It is important to work closely with your designer and printer to determine the folding method that works best for your project. There are many names for the folding patterns—three-panel, gate, barrel, accordion, French, half-and-half, and right-angle, to name a few. Pay little attention to the names. Always discuss the number of panels and demonstrate what you want. It is the safest way to ensure the quality of your brochure.

The elements outlined for this style below can and should be applied to the other styles and sizes listed above.

Panel One The first/cover panel is known as the "hook" or the "eye-catcher." Writers must use creativity and style effectively on the cover panel. This copy and its accompanying visual elements may make the difference between a brochure being read and its being thrown in the trash. The organization's name, the theme of the brochure, and possibly a slogan, teaser, or tagline are all elements of the front panel. The front panel rarely includes statistics or in-depth information. Too much information on the front panel will not engage readers but might intimidate or bore them.

Panel Two The second panel builds interest by giving background and a limited amount of information. It includes **cross headlines** (stretching across more than one panel) and bold titles that engage readers' eyes and attention. Panel Two is usually a self-contained panel and rarely continues onto Panel Three or Panel Four.

Panels Three and Four These two panels contain the main elements of the brochure. This is the place to convey the key message. Unlike Panel Two, these are not necessarily self-contained panels. They can be treated as one large page, with information extending unbroken from one page onto the other. Topics and other features can also begin on Panel Three and continue onto Panel Four. Photographs and artwork are also most commonly included on these panels.

Panel Five This panel is considered the brochure's "wild card." It can be used as a teaser to promote other details. It can also be used as an application (e.g., membership, enrollment, or admission), survey, map, list of locations, coupon, return response card, or in any other creative way.

Panel Six This final panel is most often used as a self-mailer. Located on the back middle panel, it can also be used to give more information. Leaving the panel blank is an option if all the information has been covered and the designer feels that more copy will just confuse the reader and muddy the message.

Folding techniques for brochures abound. Here are several.

Visual Quadrants

Western readers are conditioned to read from left to right and from top to bottom based on a reverse S-curve. Each individual panel has four **quadrants** that divide the paper into four equal squares and follow the reverse S-curve format. The first quadrant contains the hook, the second and third are supplemental in format, and the fourth may use logos, photos, ads, and coupons to gain the readers' attention.

There are no rules or regulations as to what style a brochure should follow. It is important, however, to create an optimum style for conveying messages to the proposed target audience.

Design Elements

Photographs, line art, and graphics help distinguish a brochure in many different ways. They help to supplement copy by conveying a message that words alone cannot accomplish. Many different design elements can be incorporated into a brochure.

The choice of **font** (typeface) in brochure design is much more flexible than it is in other publications. However, differences in fonts should be limited to two or three. The type should always be flush with the left margin of the page, and the same fonts should be maintained throughout the brochure. Font choices are serif and sans serif. Serif type includes a smaller line that finishes off the main strokes of a letter. The type in this book is an example of a serif font. **This is an example of a sans serif.**

Most brochures utilize a font size of ten or eleven points for the body copy and have one additional point of spacing, called leading, between lines. This spacing and size help to guide the eye and increase readability.

Using bold and italic type in moderation helps to accentuate important aspects of brochure copy. Overusing either of these elements may deter rather than attracting the reader.

Reverse copy is another element often used to emphasize important points. This process creates a dark background with light writing and can be extremely effective for short phrases within a brochure. Keep in mind, however, that large blocks of reverse copy cut down on the speed at which a person can read the information.

Headlines serve an important role in brochure design because they affect the overall appearance of the brochure. When used wisely and creatively, their brevity and power accentuate the message. Headlines that are in all uppercase letters slow reading and prevent messages from being conveyed. Using both upper- and lowercase letters is a better option. The use of bold, italics, and different-size fonts for headlines can create a sense of importance and distinction.

Subheads follow and amplify the headline, providing critical supplemental information. They also help to divide copy into smaller, more readable bits of information and highlight benefits. These smaller sections of information can stand alone or help the reader transition into the next section.

Lines, also known as rules, enhance understanding by breaking up copy into segments of information that can be more easily understood than large blocks. Lines can be used either vertically to separate the page into columns, or horizontally to underline, emphasize, or separate different ideas. Many designers mistakenly use lines that are too thick; these lines become overpowering and distract the reader.

Bullets help to maximize space by allowing the copy to be written in short phrases rather than long, complex sentences. In addition to maximizing space, they help to highlight the important features, ideas, or benefits by focusing the readers' attention. Bullets can be check marks, dots, solid boxes, asterisks, or even a reduced-size version of the company symbol or logo. When there is more than one line of information per bullet, the next line of that bullet is indented to help distinguish one thought from another.

Boxes help emphasize particular points within the overall text. All copy within a box is narrower than the column width in order to allow for a border around the box. A strong page border can also provide a frame for the brochure, resulting in an interesting visual. Boxes are most often found in Panel One but can also appear on other panels.

Columns provide a sense of familiarity with newspapers and create a comfortable reading environment. Columns usually are no more than 40 to 45 characters in width, and they are most effective when visible lines are created to separate the copy.

Screens, also known as "shading," consist of different-size dots of varying intensity. They give the suggestion of color and take up a large area. They are often used to highlight important information, such as in a box.

Pull quotes are used as a design element. Quotes that best summarize the intended primary message are "pulled out" in a highlighted fashion. They are usually placed within the body of the brochure. Space is a crucial part of every brochure and often the hardest element to master. Creating just the right amount of "white space" is a design element as important as font size or color choice. **White space** in a brochure is that empty or unused portion of the total space. There are two basic guidelines that designers should follow to prevent "white holes" and to maintain good white space. First, the smaller the paper, the smaller the margins should be; conversely, the larger the paper, the larger the margins should be. Second, the space above a headline should be twice as much as the space below the headline. If the artwork or text runs off the edge of the page, it is considered to be a **bleed.**

There are different color options for designing a brochure. The use of one color is by far the most inexpensive format. When only one color is used, it is most often black. In that case, printing on a colored paper can help provide a color accent to catch the reader's attention. A two-color brochure includes a second color that is a supplement to the basic black ink color. This two-color option, also known as **spot color**, is another less expensive color option and can provide highlights to borders, boxes, and titles. When a third color is added, it offers more color options, but you should be aware that a 3-color job is usually printed on a 4-color press and is significantly more expensive than a 2-color job. In effect, you are paying for 4-color printing without getting the fourth color.

A full-color brochure uses all four process colors—CMYK, which is an abbreviation of Cyan (blue), Magenta (red), Yellow, and blacK—to produce a much more vivid brochure. This **four-color process**, as it is also called, costs much more than spot color and is not always a necessity for effectively conveying the message.

Paper choice is another key element of the brochure. Papers come in three principal weights—writing, text, and cover—and two principal types—coated and uncoated. Uncoated paper can either be smooth or have a textured finish such as laid, linen, or felt. Coated paper is always smooth and has a clay coating that creates either a glossy or a matte finish. The coating causes the ink to sit on top of the paper rather than sinking in, resulting in brighter colors and sharper photos. Coated paper would be a good choice if your brochure uses photos.

It is important to choose the type of paper that best fits the style and function of the brochure. If the brochure will be a self-mailer, for example, a good choice would be a cover-weight rather than a text-weight paper. You should also familiarize yourself with the U.S. Postal Service's (USPS) regulations regarding sizes and weights for mailed items.

Another paper concern is the "curl" factor. This refers to the point at which paper will buckle as the result of excess moisture. **Curling** occurs when the cover stock is coated on only one side.

A paper stock's **ink affinity** is the speed at which ink will dry on one side of the paper. Porous paper like newsprint allows for a faster absorption in exchange for a duller image. Less porous paper (coated paper) dries slowly but produces higher-quality images.

The color of the paper stock affects the clarity and brightness of the images. Type is best read on soft white stock—paper with a yellowish tint. Because four-color brochures utilize numerous tints and hues, type is more easily read on neutral white stock.

Reproduction

There are four methods used to produce a printed piece. The **letterpress** uses images from raised surfaces (similar to a rubber stamp). It is efficient and regarded as a good option for times when a lot of printing needs to be accomplished. The second method is **offset**, which uses lithography to create a soft, smooth color transition and is also the least expensive option. **Gravure**, the third type, uses recessed images instead of raised ones to create the highest-quality color reproduction.

The fourth method is **digital** printing. Since the advent of computers, almost everything that will be printed is created by the graphic designer as an electronic file. Today's digital presses are able to output these files directly to a finished printed piece without negatives or plates, thus eliminating one of the costliest elements of four-color process printing. Some digital presses are so advanced that they can print the four process colors plus three spot colors (up to seven colors) at once. In effect, digital presses are super-high-quality color copiers! At this time, digital printing is an excellent solution for short runs (less than 1,000). This segment of the printing industry is changing at the speed of light and the quality of the output is getting better and more affordable all the time. The only drawback to digital printing is that while you can see a PDF color proof before a job is run, any changes have to made to the original file by the designer, which sometimes may delay the final output.

Where Should They Go?

Brochures are distributed in many different ways. A brochure can be sent as a self-mailer when a complete address, return address, and postage indicia (markings that are substituted for stamps) are printed on Panel Six. Direct mail is often sent in this fashion to avoid the cost of buying envelopes. Again, it is crucial to research the USPS rules and regulations when sending anything through the mail. A brochure can also be sent in a traditional envelope or as an enclosure in a specially designed direct mail package. Both methods require postage, so you should consult the USPS to ensure that proper postage is being applied.

The second option is called direct distribution. This method distributes brochures in racks that are located in a variety of public places, including grocery stores, colleges, and travel agencies. For direct distribution, it is important to know the size of the rack and the display fixture to ensure that the brochure will fit.

Did They Work?

A successful brochure is one that conveys a message in a clear, concise, and organized manner. Vivid graphics, streamlined copy, and color choices are all implemented to help inform and persuade the reader. After we have conceived, written, designed, and distributed the brochure, we must do an evaluation to determine its success. Many brochures include a return response card. Return responses can take the form of a survey or a request for more information. We can statistically evaluate the success of a brochure by evaluating the rate of return on that card. Other options are to do telephone surveys of people who received a brochure or conduct focus groups.

Putting PR into Practice

Based on the information about public education in Emerald Heights given below, use the following four steps to outline a six-panel brochure.

1. Indicate the objective of the brochure and the target audience.
2. Briefly state the overall message and why you chose the message.
3. Use the panel descriptions on page 23 to create a bulleted list for each panel, describing the proposed copy ideas and design elements. Be as specific as possible.
4. Use a computer software brochure template such as Microsoft Publishing to "mock up" the brochure you are creating.

Facts for Brochure Exercise

- Recently the high school dropout rate in Emerald Heights doubled from 20% at the beginning of the decade to 40% by 2011.

- Unemployment has increased, as there were too few college or high-school graduates to train for job openings.

- Research with Emerald Heights dropouts indicated that students lose interest in school in the eighth and ninth grades as they fall behind and cannot catch up academically.

- Research in the field of education indicates students in urban public middle schools need mentors and tutors in order to succeed.

- The mayor of Emerald Heights, Judith Gold, and the Emerald Heights Public Education Foundation are joining forces to create a community coalition, Project Graduation.

- Project Graduation's goals include creating a college-going culture in Emerald Heights, increasing parent involvement in the schools, recruiting 3,000 volunteer mentors and tutors from the community committed to at least two years of service, and enlisting business support for the coalition and the school district.

An *Example Gallery* for Brochures begins on the following page.

Example Gallery
Brochures

EachOneTeachOne
1836 Jefferson Square, NW
Washington, DC 20036

Mr. John Doe
2000 Anywhere Street
Washington, DC 20001

A Call to UNarms

Getting involved can be as easy as volunteering a few short hours of your time per week, making a donation to help fund the cause, or even working to help build coalitions among local and national businesses. To find the closest Each One Teach One chapter or to establish a chapter in your community, simply log on to our Web site or call the contact number located in this brochure.

("Imagine schools without guns. Envision communities without hate. Live in a future without violence.")

A six-panel brochure from a nonprofit organization designed to persuade and inform.

1 PANELS: Sides to a brochure that are designed for presentation of the desired information. In a six-panel brochure:

2 PANEL 1: First panel the audience sees; identifies the organization and grabs the reader's attention.

3 PANEL 6: The "self-mailer."

4 PANEL 5: The "wild card" panel; used as a return response card, a survey to fill out and return, or for other purposes.

Example Gallery
Brochures

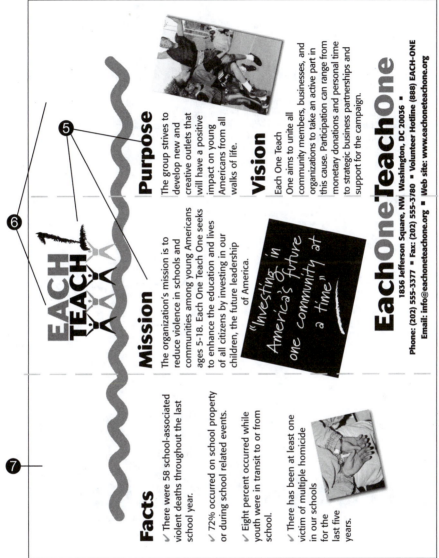

Page 2 of 2

❺ HEADLINES AND SUBHEADS: These attract readers' attention.

❻ PANELS 3 AND 4: The middle and right interior of the brochure; treated as one large page or two separate pages; give more specific information.

❼ PANEL 2: On the left inside the brochure; indicates the intent of the brochure and gives background information.

Example Gallery
Brochures

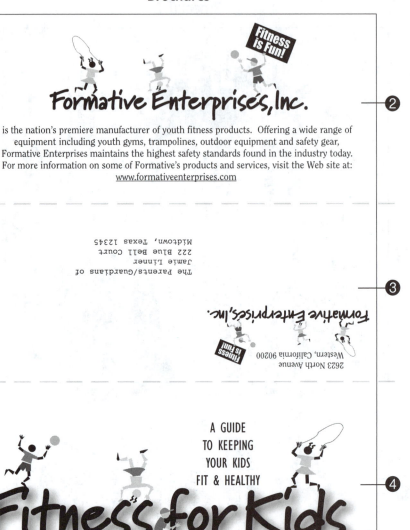

*A horizontal six-panel company brochure designed
to inform parents about child fitness.*

❶ PANELS: Sides to a brochure that are designed for presentation of the desired information. In a six-panel brochure:

❷ PANEL 1: First panel the audience sees; identifies the organization and grabs the reader's attention.

❸ PANEL 6: The "self-mailer."

❹ PANEL 5: The "wild card" panel; used as a return response card, a survey to fill out and return, or for other purposes.

Exercise & Your Child

Many parents and families fail to recognize the importance of their child's fitness until it is too late. By incorporating fitness and exercise into a child's life early on, the groundwork for a lifetime of fitness will be set.

Regular exercise is an important tool for children and adolescents to strengthen bones, improve their cardiovascular system, sustain good mental health, as well as maintain a healthy weight. It is important to tailor exercise for each individual child or adolescent to make fitness fun!

This guide is designed to help parents create a healthy exercise routine for their children (as well as the parent). It will provide parents with age-appropriate regimens as well as some suggestions for fun exercise activities.

Aerobic Activity

There are many aerobic activities that appeal to children and adolescents. It is important to find a few that are interesting to them. It is not necessary to exercise at a maximum capacity. Instead, 30 minutes of moderate aerobic activity nearly every day of the week is a more realistic goal. Some aerobic activities may include, but not be limited to, jumping on a trampoline, swimming, skating, and bicycle riding. Be sure to find an activity that is age appropriate and enjoyable for the child.

Strength Training

While strength training has become more popular, even among children and adolescents, proper supervision is essential to maintain proper form and technique. Children should avoid lifting maximum weights or attempting ballistic movements until their skeletal growth is complete.

See Formative Enterprise's brochure on exercise safety

Safety is the Key

There are many activities that children and adolescents choose to engage in that are a safety concern to parents. Activities such as skiing, hiking and skateboarding may be exciting for the child but may prove to be intimidating for the parent. Although exercise-related accidents are common, a careful evaluation of potential hazards may help reduce serious injuries or trauma. It is important to encourage the child while taking sensible safety precautions to minimize injuries.

Formative Enterprises, Inc.
800-555-5597 ▫ Fax: 800-555-5599
2623 North Avenue
Western, California 90200
www.formativeenterprises.com

Page 2 of 2

⑤ HEADLINES AND SUBHEADS: These attract readers' attention.

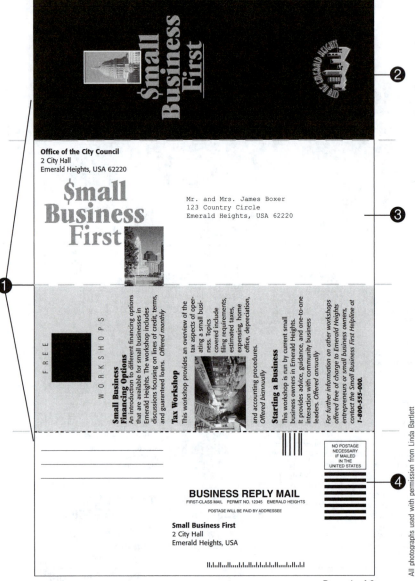

Page 1 of 2

An eight-panel brochure from a city government designed to inform the business community.

❶ PANELS: Sides to a brochure that are designed for presentation of the desired information. In an eight-panel brochure:

❷ PANEL 1: First panel the audience sees; identifies the organization and grabs the reader's attention.

❸ PANEL 8: The "self-mailer."

❹ PANEL 6: The "wild card" panel; used as a return response card, a survey to fill out and return, or for other purposes.

Page 2 of 2

All photographs used with permission from Linda Bartlett

⑤ HEADLINES AND SUBHEADS: These attract readers' attention.

⑥ PANELS 3 AND 4: The middle and right interior of the brochure; treated as one large page or two separate pages; give more specific information.

⑦ PANEL 2: On the left inside of the brochure; indicates the intent of the brochure and background information.

⑧ PANEL 5: This is the back of the return response card.

Chapter 4

Communication Audits

What Are They?

As managers in our field, we perform or review communication audits for our organization or for clients who request an audit. As public communication practitioners, we can learn a lot about the communication needs of our organizations through a communication audit. And as writers, these audits are helpful to us in the research phase of message development.

A comprehensive report detailing the positive and negative aspects of an organization's overall communication strategy, a communication audit examines the organization's structure, hierarchy, communication programs and products, publics, and strategic partnerships with other organizations. It also examines, analyzes, and assesses past communication efforts in order to determine their effectiveness.

Communication audits can review the work of the entire organization, or they can be limited to specific departments or other subdivisions of the organization. Regardless of the scope, an audit focuses on both the internal and external communication efforts of an organization. Internally, a communication audit examines communication that occurs within an organization, including the organization's structure and culture, employees' levels of job satisfaction, their impressions of the organization's communication efforts, how effective they believe these efforts to be, and how they believe that their work helps to achieve the organization's objectives. Externally, a communication audit examines how well an organization reaches its target audiences by reviewing the organization's communication products and messages and by interviewing its contacts with other organizations in order to determine whether the communication tactics and vehicles have reached audiences effectively.

An organization's in-house public communication practitioners may conduct an audit to gain an internal perspective, or the organization may hire consultants to perform an audit to obtain an external perspective. Either option is acceptable; however, employees auditing their own organization must take care to remain absolutely objective, fair, and open to providing constructive criticism when conducting the audit.

A communication audit involves three major steps. Our first step is to find out as much as possible about the organization and how it communicates to its internal and external publics. To conduct the research or fact-finding phase, we use a wide range of research techniques, including in-depth interviews, focus groups, surveys, reviews of organizational documents, and observation to determine the organization's processes of internal and external communication.

Step two is analysis. During this phase of the audit, we analyze the data collected during the fact-finding phase. This process involves exploring every aspect of the data, looking for cause-and-effect and correlations among the findings. The analysis outlines the quality, strengths, and weaknesses of the communication program elements.

The third step is evaluation and reporting, during which we prepare a written report for our organization. This report summarizes and draws conclusions based on the findings and analysis in steps one and two. Here, current communication programs and products are individually evaluated in terms of their strengths, weaknesses, and overall effectiveness. Lastly, we write a final report that delineates the scope of the work, the tasks performed, the research conducted, an overall evaluation, and recommendations for actions to be taken by the organization.

Who Gets Them?

Clearly, the audience for a communication audit is the organization's management team. The executive who commissioned the report should receive a complete written final report. It is wise for the public communication practitioner to write or request an executive summary of the report for management to use to brief stakeholders.

What Do They Do?

As diagnostic tools, communication audits identify areas that require attention in order to improve an organization's communication to its internal and external publics. They evaluate the effectiveness of the existing communication programs and products.

Internal communication audits should *not* be conducted during organizational restructuring, shortly after a change in management, or during other large projects, as these are times of stress for employees and findings may be skewed. Auditors should allow adequate, but not excessive, time to conduct the audit. A thorough and comprehensive internal audit tells an organization how well information is flowing and points to areas in need of review or change.

An effective audit of external communication provides valuable information to public communication professionals. It can serve as a guide for developing strategies for future communication campaigns. The audit tells us if communication strategies are effective, accurately targeting audiences, relevant to audience needs, and coordinated with established organizational plans and evolving organizational structures. This information allows the organization to revise its communication plan when necessary and thus operate more effectively.

A thorough communication audit supplies a broad overview of an organization's communication plan. In order to obtain such a detailed report, an auditor must thoroughly examine six areas: history and background, organizational issues, situational analysis, product service description, implementation issues, and evaluation issues.

First, an audit describes an organization's history and background. To do so, the auditor must determine when, how, and why the organization formed, the organization's key players, how the organization's goals have evolved over time, and what role the organization's history plays currently.

Second, to describe existing organizational issues, an auditor must determine the issues that surround an organization, including its vision, mission, goals, and priorities. An auditor must evaluate the type of environment in which the organization operates, including whether the organization is a formal or informal environment, the balance of organizational power, employees' satisfaction regarding their positions in the organization and the organization's objectives, and the position the organization holds in the community.

Third, an audit includes a detailed situation analysis, which describes the current problem or issue the organization hopes to overcome. An auditor must determine the organization's interpretation of the problem, the scope of the problem, and the public's interpretation of the problem. The situation analysis also attempts to analyze the organization's competitors and its position among competitors.

Fourth, an audit must describe the organization's products and services. This includes a determination of the products and services that exist, what the organization *believes* it is accomplishing with these products and services, and what the organization is *actually* accomplishing with these products and services.

The fifth area of examination for an audit is the organization's implementation process. An auditor must determine the distribution and implementation methods the organization employs, why it employs these methods, and how it works with available resources during implementation.

Finally, an audit must explore the organization's systems and strategy. An auditor must determine whether the organization believes that it is accomplishing its goals, how it has come to this conclusion, and how the organization communicates with its audiences to gain feedback about its products and services.

Overall, a communication audit must provide an organization with information about the effectiveness of its communication strategy and techniques. To do so, a communication audit should address questions in four areas:

- **Message Quality** Does the organization present audiences with clear and consistent messages? Are there discrepancies between the message the organization wants to send and the message it actually sends?

- **Message Delivery** Does the organization send its messages through appropriate, effective communication vehicles? Is the organization's message delivered in a timely manner with a minimal degree of distortion? Did the message reach the appropriate target audience?

- **Relationship Quality** Do the organization's employees understand and support the messages the organization attempts to send? Are there open lines of communication between all levels of employees? Are the organization's partners satisfied with the partnership? Do they support and understand the messages?

- **Audience Communication** Finally, the auditor must examine how the audience interprets the organization's messages. The auditor should attempt to discover whether the audience understood the organization's messages in the manner the organization intended. He or she should also learn what the audience wants to know and whether this corresponds with the information the organization is actually providing. In addition, the auditor should find out if the organization's messages are of interest to the audience. Thus, if the organization is sending messages that contain information that is not of interest to its audience and fails to provide them with the information they wish to receive, the auditor should address this problem.

How Do They Help?

Communication audits result in research data that provide organizations with feedback so that they can develop more effective communication programs and products. They help organizations to gauge how accurately they are meeting their stated communication goals and objectives, to focus on the strengths and weaknesses of their communication programs and products, and to make necessary adjustments to increase effectiveness. These adjustments help the organization develop a better relationship with its audiences, resulting in an improved internal and external image.

What Are the Pitfalls?

Communication audits can be time consuming and expensive because the process is very detailed and requires in-depth research. A full-scale communication audit can take up to six months and cost upward of $25,000. While a less extensive audit can reduce the cost and time commitment considerably, such audits often lack the information necessary for an organization to get a clear picture of the effects of its communication.

Internal communication audits cannot provide a full report of an organization's daily functions. Although auditors may spend several days in an organization to gain understanding of the work environment, they don't always get an accurate representation of the nature of daily life within the organization. Obviously, employees may behave differently when auditors are observing the organization.

How Should They Look?

Style Notes

A final report should clearly and concisely present the methods and results of the communication audit. The auditor should use business writing style to summarize the important findings. Because this report is the product of research, it should be written much like an academic research paper. A manual on scholarly writing is a helpful guide for style.

Format

A communication audit report is divided into several sections.

Title Page

The title page includes a report title, the name and affiliation of the author of the report, and the date of the report.

Table of Contents

The table of contents is the readers' guide to what is included in the report. It should therefore clearly list the titles and page numbers of each of the sections and subsections contained in the report.

Executive Summary

An **executive summary** is a two- to three-page summary of the contents of the entire report. After reviewing this summary, the reader should have a basic understanding of the audit's findings. The executive summary should include a brief list of the report recommendations.

Introduction

The introduction provides the reader with a brief overview of the organization and the purpose of the audit. This section of the audit report should clearly state the basic facts about the organization, including its mission and purpose, location, key figures, competitors, and any other important information.

Methodology

The methodology section describes in one to two pages the research instruments used to conduct the audit and how these instruments were used. This includes surveys, observation, questionnaires, interviews, and other audit instruments.

Audit Diary

An audit diary is one page in length and describes the activities throughout the period of time that the audit took place. This section explains what was done and where the activity took place. For example, the audit diary would include such information as when, where, and to whom a particular survey was administered.

Results of the Audit Process

The results section is 10 to 20 pages in length and discusses the information gathered through the use of the audit instruments. All research instruments and the information gained from each one should be discussed here. The report should provide as much information as possible, backing up assertions with statistical data. The auditor should express the results in a manner that is both statistically accurate and reasonably comprehensible so as to make the results completely understandable to the intended audience. The results section should include necessary graphs, charts, diagrams, and tables within the text. It should also refer readers to the appendix to view other, less essential visual representations of the collected data.

Conclusions and Recommendations

This section is three to five pages in length and summarizes the conclusions drawn based on the analysis of the collected data. This section carefully lists and discusses the organization's strengths, weaknesses, and opportunities in reference to its overall communication program. The auditor should list recommendations for the organization's communication program, separating the sections into things that must be done immediately, things that should be done soon, and things that should be done when time and money allow. These recommendations do not have to be specific but should be detailed enough to suggest a plan of action that the organization should implement to improve its internal and external communication. In addition, the conclusions and recommendations section should be substantive enough to stand alone, as it is often the only section that may be read.

Appendix

The appendix includes all items used to perform the audit, such as questionnaires, surveys, interview transcripts, and analyzed products. It should also include the raw data gathered.

Where Should They Go?

The complete final written report should be submitted to key figures within the organization following an oral presentation. This face-to-face presentation will allow for discussion during which any questions and confusion about the auditor's findings may be discussed. It is highly recommended that the employees who participated in the research process be given a brief written report that summarizes the audit findings.

Did They Work?

A successful communication audit is one that presents an organization with an accurate evaluation of its communication program. An audit should specifically list and explain the organization's strengths and weaknesses and provide solid suggestions about how the organization can further develop its internal and external communication in order to be more successful.

We can measure how successful a particular audit has been by determining whether or not the audit achieved its primary purpose. If the audit succinctly and accurately identified the organization's communication strengths and weaknesses and then pointed out opportunities that provide openings for organizational change, the audit was successful.

Putting PR into Practice

As indicated in this chapter, a communication audit can be a complicated and intricate task, but you can conduct a mini-audit to get the look and feel of an organization before you have a first meeting with a client or to better understand how the organization presents itself through its PR products. For our practice purposes, visit your university or college Web site and admissions office and ask for materials. Alternatively, you could go to the Web site of any organization with which you are familiar or with whom you want to be more familiar, and if possible visit its office.

1. Identify the PR products through which the organization attempts to communicate.

2. What appears to be the primary target audience for the materials?

3. What appears to be the primary purpose of each?

4. List the consistent or inconsistent messages.

5. Is the graphical identity consistent? List the inconsistencies.

6. How would you describe the tone? Are the products formal or informal?

7. Is the organization's mission stated clearly and concisely?

8. What recommendations would you make regarding revising the products?

9. If you are a member, employee, or volunteer of an organization, conduct a mini internal communication audit by asking the following questions of others in the organization:

   a. How do you describe our organization to others?

   b. How do you describe what our organization does or how we serve?

   c. Thinking of our organization, what adjectives come to mind when I say communication?

   d. Looking at how our organization communicated with you during the past year, describe your reactions. Both negative and positive reactions are helpful.

   e. What did we communicate effectively? What was not communicated effectively?

   f. Did you understand the purpose and content of the communication you received?

   g. How can we improve our communication with you? With our customers or the people we serve?

   h. Write a list of questions you would use to conduct a communication audit of an organization's customers or recipients of its services.

Direct Mail Campaigns

What Are They?

Direct mail, also referred to as direct marketing, is all forms of mailed advertising, including letters, postcards, booklets, brochures, circulars, catalogs, CDs, DVDs, email, and other collateral material. Direct mail campaigns are marketing and public communication tools used by organizations to contact the target audience/customer directly. With a direct appeal, the organization can sell or persuade a target audience from a particular mailing list of potential customers, donors, or volunteers.

Direct mail communicates a feeling of urgency, encouraging the audience to take an immediate action. Direct email can be very effective, as the target audience can respond instantaneously with just a click of the mouse. It goes straight to the source, bypassing the media to disseminate messages and giving the organization complete control over what is being conveyed.

It is highly unlikely that we, as public communication practitioners, will be asked to develop a direct mail campaign. These campaigns are usually left to firms that specialize in doing them. However, it is important for us as PR professionals to understand the elements of a simple direct mail appeal. It is highly likely we will be asked to work closely with product and e-marketers in developing strategy.

The **offer** is the most important element in a direct mail campaign because it entices the audience to respond to the organization, which is the main goal of the campaign. Like all advertising, direct mail targets an audience and sells the benefits that can be derived from using a product or taking an action. A critical element of the offer is stressing value and importance. The offer must be as specific as possible, explicitly stating what the audience will receive as a result of accepting the offer. This will help increase audience response. A successful tactic often used with the offer is the inclusion of a **premium**, or something free, in the package to entice the audience.

A targeted and accurate mailing list is critical to the success of direct mail campaigns. The mailing list should be representative of the organization's target audience and can be categorized in several ways, including demographics, psychographics, in-house customer or member lists, and geographic areas. *Demographic* information refers to an individual's ethnicity, income, age, and educational level, whereas *psychographic* information refers to a person's lifestyle, such as reading and viewing habits, organization or club memberships, and political party affiliation.

In-house customer or member lists are usually kept in a database and track the members or customers of an organization. State, city, county, region, and/or ZIP codes are used to organize mailing lists that are categorized by geographic location. Although not every direct mail package will be read, a good mailing list and a strong message increase the possibility that the recipient will read the package.

Who Gets Them?

The target audiences for direct mail campaigns can be wide ranging and include current or potential donors, product customers, organization members, and volunteers. Although the audience segment may vary from campaign to campaign, a clean and current mailing list helps ensure that the direct mail will reach the appropriate audience. In the case of direct email, audiences can click a link that will take them to the organization's Web site, where they can preview or purchase a product, sign a letter, make a donation, accept an invitation, or register for an event.

What Do They Do?

There are several reasons to use direct mail campaigns, but the main purpose is to get the audience to take action immediately. The actions come in many forms, including answering a survey, sampling a product, attending an event, buying something, and sending money.

As you have probably noticed by now, the organization's objectives are the driving force behind any communication strategy and message. It is important for the organization to clearly define its objectives for conducting the campaign at the outset, because those objectives will guide the direct marketing process.

Direct mail campaigns are also used to garner additional publicity and to generate news for an organization. Demographics and psychographics collected from direct marketing campaigns are very valuable to public communication professionals. This information can lead to good story ideas, news hooks, and local news angles. News releases citing statistics, such as survey results and percentages of responses compiled from marketing analyses, can generate additional news coverage for an organization and help establish credibility with the media and other publics.

The direct mail campaign is also a good research tool to use when analyzing and identifying audiences. Responses provide a better understanding of the targeted audience. Audience responses segmented by demographic, psychographic, and geographic information can assist in message development, positioning a product, building long-term customer relationships and loyalty, receiving feedback from an audience, testing new ideas with selected audiences, and analyzing results by market segment.

How Do They Help?

The key advantage of direct mail campaigns is that they allow us complete control over the message and to whom the message is sent. Because the media is not relaying the message, it is not subject to additional filters and only the intended audience will receive the communication message. Direct mail campaigns also allow us to position our organization positively by recycling publicity. For example, reprints of the best feature articles and media clips can be excerpted and included in a direct mail package, reminding some recipients and exposing others to the organization's positive publicity.

One of the most attractive features of direct mail campaigns is their cost efficiency. Organizations can reach a mass audience with adequate results at a reasonable cost. Public communication professionals can pretest a direct mail campaign by mailing packages or emailing messages to a small segment of the target audience. By pretesting campaigns, we can avoid flawed packages or messages that turn into costly mistakes, because we are able to garner a general idea of the type of response that can be expected and how successful the campaign will be.

As a research tool, direct mail campaigns can inform public communication methods used by an organization's communication professionals. The insights gained from audience responses can assist in the implementation and evaluation of communication strategies and campaigns, help an organization save time and money by avoiding costly mistakes, and assist organizations with communication campaign decision making.

What Are the Pitfalls?

Nothing can guarantee that your direct mail will be read. Direct mail packages and email messages often end up in the trash before being read because audiences perceive these packages as "junk mail." PR professionals in charge of direct mail campaigns must be aware of factors that will entice their audience to respond to direct mail. This requires appropriate audience research at the outset of the campaign. Again, the offer should be compelling and should highlight the benefits and value to the audience. The most difficult aspect of the campaign is generating the response intended. Also, it is difficult to predict responses and therefore the success of direct mail campaigns.

Another challenge facing organizations and communication professionals is obtaining mailing lists that represent the target audience. If direct mail packages are mailed to individuals outside the target audience, the effort has ultimately been wasted. Also, lists must be clean and up to date. Most companies specializing in direct mail guarantee their address lists, and the software that manages direct email is smart. The software manages the lists, monitoring bounce-back, click-through, and opt-out rates and understanding receiving computer capability for text and HTML.

Lastly, though less costly than many other communication tools, postal direct mail campaigns can become quite expensive, depending on the number of people receiving the package and how much it costs to mail each package.

Collateral materials such as envelopes, brochures, booklets, CDs, postcards, and other materials needed in the package can drive the costs above initial estimates if they are not included in the budget at the outset.

How Should They Look?

Process

Creating effective direct mail requires adequate planning and direction. First and foremost, objectives and goals of the campaign need to be established and the target audience should be clearly defined. Next, a timetable should be developed to assist with the accomplishment of stages in the campaign. A budget helps inform the organization what can and cannot be produced. Developing a compelling and clear statement of the offer will increase the response rate. Lastly, time needs to be allotted for the production of creative materials and the actual mailing.

In general, simple direct mail packages incorporate five printed elements: the **outer envelope** (carrier) containing the package, which usually has teaser copy on front to entice the individual to open the package; the **letter**, which emphasizes the offer and benefits; the **brochure** or data sheet, which re-emphasizes the benefits; the **reply vehicle**, which allows the recipient to respond; and the **business reply envelope** (BRE), which is a way for the recipient to mail back the reply. Clearly, these are components of an uncomplicated direct mail package. There are many types of more intricate packages that include some of the elements discussed earlier. Email, of course, can use a compelling message with a link the audience can use to take an action.

Format

- **Email Message Format**

    From Box—Clearly identifies your organization to the audience. This is very important for first-party opt-in audiences who know your organization because they willingly and purposely signed up for the mailings while they were on another Web site. This box is more problematic if the addressee is a third party receiving the email as a result of someone else's relationship.

    To Box—Your audience's address.

    Subject Box—More than the message itself, the content of the subject box is the most important element of direct email. An effective subject line that resonates with the target audience can mean the difference between opened or trashed email.

    Salutation—The salutation should be friendly and personal. *Hello, Hi,* and *Dear* are acceptable beginnings. Sometimes salutations are left out and the message begins with a headline.

    Body Copy—Presents the offer or states the issue in the most compelling and convincing terms.

Tone—The manner in which the copy is written is crucial. Because an email cannot benefit from layout and design as hard copy materials do, the manner in which the copy is presented is very important. The information should be organized well, presented in active voice, and speak directly to the target audience.

Personal Pronouns—Talk directly to your audience. Use the pronoun "you" to make your message conversational. When referring to your organization, use the pronoun "We."

Use an Action Closing—Thank your audience for taking the desired action as you close the email. For example, "Thank you for ordering."

Links—Embedded links are provided to take the target audience to where it can take the desired action.

- **Outer Envelope** The outer envelope (also known as a **carrier**) serves as a promotional piece that entices the audience to open the letter. It should incorporate **teaser** copy—a few lines of copy written on the front envelope. Teaser copy should be focused and precise and include a good hook specifically targeting the reader. Besides the letter, it is the most important element of the direct mail package. It determines whether the letter will get opened and read—or thrown in the trash. Phrases like *"Free Gift Enclosed!" "Free Gift Offer"*, and *"Please Open Immediately"* included in the teaser copy encourage readers to open direct mail packages. Another tactic used to entice people to open the letter is a first-class stamp and an individual's name (not the organization's name) and address in the upper left-hand corner of the envelope to make the letter appear to be personal correspondence.
  It is important that the materials fit easily inside the envelope. Standard sizes are #10 business envelopes, 6" × 9" and 9" × 12". Odd-size envelopes are costly to produce and mail and *may not* attract more attention than regular-size ones. Some organizations use envelopes that mimic the overnight envelopes used by shipping companies.

- **Printed Letter Format** A personalized letter will potentially increase the response rate by 30 to 40%. The letter is considered to be the most important and most powerful part of a direct mail package. The writer should use the letter to sell the benefits of the product, cause, membership, or event and ask the audience to take some form of immediate action. Remember, the benefits can be tangible or intangible. You may want to delineate the main points of the letter if it is going to be written by an outside firm. It is the job of the public communication professional to make a compelling offer to garner the response desired and to incorporate a mechanism that will make it easy for the audience to respond. The letter should be readable, with short sentences and paragraphs, indentations, and subheads. For maximum effectiveness, the direct mail letter should look like a standard business letter. These are the elements of the letter:

Letterhead—The letterhead should reflect the image of the organization and tone of the campaign and may appear at the top or bottom of the page.

Salutation—The salutation should be friendly and personal.

Signer—The signature should be legibly written and signed.

Typeface—The typeface should be easy to read.

Tone—Previous research should be a guide to how to talk to the members of the target audience and to the appropriate tone for conveying the message.

Opening—The opening paragraph should be an attention-getter with no more than two lines.

Johnson box opener—This is an indented, boxed, and introductory block of copy that introduces the product or third-party endorser.

Body—The body should clearly state the features of the offer and benefits to the recipient. The most powerful benefits are stated first.

P.S.—Studies show that audiences look at the signature and "P.S." first, so the P.S. should confirm and repeat information from the body of the letter.

- **Brochure/Data Sheet** The brochure or data sheet illustrates the features, demonstrates the uses, and provides facts and interesting background information. It can come in a variety of forms such as a circular, flyer, folder, or booklet. This piece should be visually pleasing and, if the budget permits, should incorporate photos and graphic art and be more than one color. In most instances, however, the audience will not read the brochure unless they are interested in the product or cause.

- **Reply Vehicle** The reply vehicle includes a *summary* of the offer and benefits—nothing new is introduced at this point. It is important to make the reply vehicle as simple as possible. It should be easy for the recipient to fill out the form, using a mailing label in the window envelope on the reply card. Reply envelopes should include prepaid postage.

- **Reply Envelope** The BRE or business reply envelope is pre-addressed back to the sender of the direct mail package. It is usually postage-paid, making it easy to send back. The BRE must conform to U.S. postal regulations; templates are available from the U.S. Postal Service. A #9 envelope is a standard size for a BRE.

Where Should They Go?

Except for direct email, which is distributed electronically, the main method of distributing simple direct mail packages as described above is through the U.S. Postal Service (USPS). Generally, postage can be categorized by first or third class, and as metered mail, printed indicia mail, and mail with a real stamp. Research has shown that metered mail receives approximately the same response as a stamp, except when dealing with personal appeals; printed indicia mail will not do as well as metered mail in eliciting the desired action; and real stamps generate the greatest response and are usually placed on high-ticket items and invitations.

Did They Work?

The best ways to evaluate the success of direct mail campaigns are to track and compile the responses received and/or determine the number of people who took the action step requested. Based on the number of packages mailed, an organization can determine the percentage of responses, or rate of return. Rate of return varies greatly depending on the campaign. These data can be used to help refine and update the direct mail campaign as needed. In addition, if surveys are included in the package or if there is a built-in mechanism that will allow organizations to track comments from their audiences, these data can help in tailoring future campaigns to meet the audiences' needs.

Another evaluation method is to track media coverage and placement. If the direct mail campaign was used to garner additional publicity, the number of media hits (including print, radio, and television) is a determining factor of the campaign's success. Because the media is relaying the information or news, the organization has to decide whether or not the information and message in the news story was conveyed in a constructive manner to the right target audience. As mentioned above, email software monitors and tracks responses to direct email campaigns.

Putting PR into Practice

1. Select a direct mail letter from the plethora of direct mail you receive every week. Rewrite and reformat it to become an email.

2. Draft a direct mail letter from your college or university to you on the day of your graduation, asking you to make a donation.

3. Consider the client you chose for this course.
   a. If a direct mail campaign is an appropriate strategy, who should sign the direct mail letter?
   b. Who is the best spokesperson for the audience?
   c. What would be the appropriate appeal to your primary audience?
   d. What should be the call to action?

An *Example Gallery* for Direct Mail Campaigns
begins on the following page.

Example Gallery
Direct Mail Campaigns

EachOneTeachOne

1836 Jefferson Square, NW / Washington, DC 20036

Ms. Jane Doe
5500 Maryland Place, SW
Washington, DC 20000

February 26, 2012

Dear Ms. Doe,

We would like to take this opportunity to update you on the progress of *Each One Teach One*, and show you how your thoughtful donation is being spent.

The purpose of creating *Each One Teach One* was to combat and reduce school and community violence among youth and adolescents in the U.S. Healthy lifestyles for thousands of D.C. children are hindered by environmental and societal realities such as poverty, drugs, gangs and child abuse. Programs initiated by *Each One Teach One* are designed to promote children's skills, to show self-control and to curb the use of violence and aggression.

Since September of 1999, *Each One Teach One* donors and volunteers have succeeded in creating a monthly newsletter, a functional Web site, and several workshops and retreats. Volunteers are working to make this a productive year of seminars, counseling sessions, retreats and workshops to provide our children with the tools necessary to deter violent behavior.

In order to make this vital procedure happen, we depend on the donations and gifts of volunteers and concerned citizens like yourself, Ms. Doe. We thank you for your continued support and service as a citizen of this country. We hope that through donations, *Each One Teach One* can help to effectively diminish the alarming crime statistics among youth today.

Sincerely,

Willis Bennett

Willis Bennett
Executive Director

A direct mail package letter from a nonprofit voluntary organization asks audience to donate to the organization.

❶ LETTER: Personally addressed, one-page call to action on company letterhead.

Example Gallery
Direct Mail Campaigns

Yes! I want to help Each One Teach One combat youth violence in D.C.!

Name _____

Address _____

City _____ State ____ ZIP _____

I have enclosed:

☐ $10

☐ $25

☐ $50

☐ $100

☐ Personal Check Number_____

(Make check payable to *Each One Teach One*)

☐ Money Order number_____

Please send donations to:

EACH 1 TEACH XXXX

EachOneTeachOne

1836 Jefferson Square, NW
Washington, DC 20036

❶

A direct mail package response card from a nonprofit voluntary organization designed to fit into a reply envelope to help an audience make a contribution.

❶ RESPONSE CARDS: For target audience to take action.

A direct mail package envelope from a nonprofit voluntary organization designed to help an audience make a contribution.

❶ ENVELOPE: #10 business envelope with a teaser to persuade the consumer to open.

❷ INDICIA: Special permit issued to nonprofits must appear on the envelope to get the special mailing rate.

Example Gallery
Direct Mail Campaigns

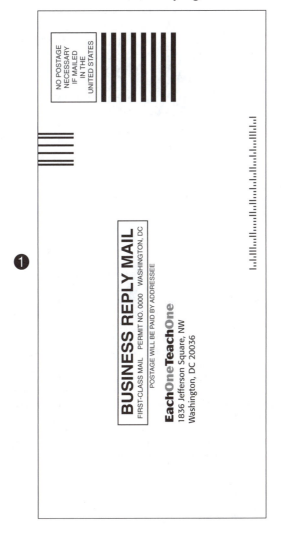

A direct mail reply envelope (BRE) from a nonprofit voluntary organization designed to help an audience reply with a contribution.

❶ REPLY ENVELOPE: This envelope was created using a U.S. Postal Service template. The envelope size is a #9 that will fit inside the carrier of the direct mail package.

Example Gallery
Direct Mail Campaigns

Committee for the Reelection of Mayor Judith Gold

55 Democracy Avenue
Emerald Heights, USA 62220 1111

Mr. and Mrs. Robert Smith
7906 Dale Corner
Emerald Heights, USA 62220

April 5, 2012

Dear Mr. and Mrs. Smith,

As you already know, the Emerald Heights mayoral election is only six months away. Just four years ago you helped us to elect Judith Gold as this city's most popular elected official. What a great few years it has been!

During Mayor Gold's tenure in office, she has focused on such issues as family and education initiatives, environmental protection laws, and crime deterrent projects. During these short years, Mayor Gold is already making a positive difference to improve the quality of life for all the citizens of Emerald Heights. But we need your help to continue the crusade.

We need your help to reelect Judith Gold as Mayor of Emerald Heights to continue her fight for the residents of this great city. We depend on contributions from private citizens like you to keep our city a safe and pleasant place to live and raise our families.

Enclosed you will find a donation card; we hope that you will continue to support Mayor Judith Gold and her quest for reelection by returning the card and a contribution in the amount of your choice. We thank you for your generosity during this critical election.

Best regards,

David Semmons

David Semmons
Campaign Manager for the Judith Gold Mayoral Campaign

A direct mail package letter from a reelection campaign committee asks audience to help by donating money.

❶ LETTER: Personally addressed, one-page call to action on campaign letterhead.

A direct mail package response card from a reelection campaign designed to help an audience make a contribution.

❶ RESPONSE CARDS: For target audience to take action.

Example Gallery
Direct Mail Campaigns

From: "Staci Kaufman"   skaufman@formative.com
To: soccermom@nsn.net
Subject: Discounted Child Fitness Equipment
Date: May 1, 2012

**AWARD-WINNING CHILD FITNESS EQUIPMENT
OFFERED AT 40–60% DISCOUNT!!!**

With the summer season approaching, Formative Enterprises is having its Sale of the Season!!!! For the month of May, every item will be discounted 40–60% through this special email offer.

Formative's child fitness equipment ranks as the top exercise equipment on the market today. This direct link will bring you directly to the savings.

Click on the products that most interest you for full descriptions.

FITNESS BALLS	EXERCISE SWINGS
TEEN GYMS	WEIGHTS
YOUTH GYMS	OUTDOOR EQUIPMENT
TRAMPOLINES	SPORTING GOODS
JOGGERS	

The Formative Guarantee—Simply try one of our award-winning youth fitness products for 30 days free of charge. If you and/or your child are not fully satisfied with the equipment you have purchased, just send it back within those 30 days and we will refund your money including shipping expenses.

CLICK HERE TO ORDER NOW!!!

Direct mail via email.

Media Kits

What Are They?

As a public communication practitioner, you are—or will become—well acquainted with media kits. They are a staple in our field. A media kit is a public communication tool used to generate news stories about an organization's newsworthy initiative, campaign, special event, major-announcement news conference, product launch, or trade show. It provides the media with the research, facts, perspectives, and historical context that they need to understand in order to write about an event or announcement. If we view a media kit as a reference guide and a good source of information for potential story ideas for journalists, we will develop effective kits.

Most media kits consist of a two-pocket folder containing hard-copy news releases, media advisories, feature stories, photographs, slides, backgrounders, biographical sketches, fact sheets, and position papers. Many media kits now appear in online press rooms where journalists can have immediate access to the materials. They can include streaming video and audio, interactive materials, photos, logos, charts, and slide shows. Media kits also incorporate visually pleasing graphics and text to capture the media's attention. It is important to prepare the contents of a media kit with the news media in mind. The contents will vary according to the use and purpose of each media kit.

Do *not* confuse media kits used in public communication with those provided by mass media sales representatives that describe advertising rates, circulation, the editorial calendar, and closing dates for advertisers to purchase.

The public communication media kit contains a unified theme, style, or message throughout to meet the goal of conveying a cohesive message to the media. Materials provided in the media kit should support the message being conveyed. Maintaining consistency throughout the kit, such as using the same fonts, colors, and graphic designs in all components, also enhances the opportunity for media coverage.

The goal is to convey a cohesive message to the media. The media kit represents the campaign, event, or organization, and all materials in the kit support the overall message. As well, we must be sure that all materials in the kit are relevant and useful to journalists.

Who Gets Them?

The target audience for this public communication product is clear because there is only one—the news media. Within this audience, the actual gatekeeper you target may vary: business editor, food editor, metro reporter, television or radio news or talk-show producer, to name just a few. But while the primary audience is the reporters who cover the news, we know that they have target audiences. Clearly, we want them to communicate our organization's message to those target audiences.

Media kits are also distributed at news conferences. News conferences are generally held for two reasons: to provide access to a celebrity or expert, or to provide access to a spokesperson during a crisis, when announcing a major breakthrough, or when involved in a controversy. In the first case, the kit should include biographical information; photographs of the celebrity, politician, or expert; and information about the relationship between the celebrity or expert and the organization. Media kits distributed during a crisis should be readily available and updated to provide the media with the most current information and updates on new developments. Online media kits are especially helpful to journalists during crises. They can be updated and accessed in a matter of minutes, keeping journalists informed 24 hours a day.

What Do They Do?

The primary function of a media kit is to disseminate information or a unified message about an organization to various media outlets. The media kit provides extensive background information to the news media in an attempt to generate coverage. Most media kits are used to introduce or announce a special event, highlight a product launch, provide information about an organization or recent developments within the organization, or to supply important information during a news conference or time of crisis.

While media kits are specifically designed for use by the news media, including reporters, editors, news directors, and producers, the purpose can change slightly depending on how and where the media kit will be distributed. The following are the three most widely used types of media kits:

- **Special-event media kits** provide explicit details, logistical information, and background material. They offer specific details about the event itself and don't focus much attention on the organization.

- **Promotional media kits** often include such materials as brochures, advertisements, quotes from critics, and reviews from third-party sources. In some instances, reprints from newspaper articles are included in this type of kit as well.

- **Crisis media kits** provide journalists with up-to-date facts, background data, and relevant supplemental information in a timely manner. To best communicate the most current news, media kits used in crisis situations are often distributed by PR professionals at news conferences and usually include background information about the organization, biographical details about key figures involved in some way with the crisis, visual materials, and a detailed description of the organization's facilities.

Although several elements can be included in a media kit, we must decide how much and what information is appropriate for the packet. Because media kits are intended for journalists, it is not necessary to provide a lot of copy or many photographs. It is important to determine which materials are necessary to effectively communicate the information being presented. Materials included in the kit should be newsworthy, timely, clear, and concise.

How Do They Help?

The media kit provides a good opportunity to relay an extensive amount of information to the news media at one time. It is one of the most comprehensive tools used to generate news coverage for an organization, to answer potential questions journalists may have regarding the organization or event, and to provide new perspectives on the organization. Media kits also allow an organization to provide new and original material in a creative, innovative way.

Online media kits are beneficial because they save time and money for an organization. Online distribution of media kits will cut the costs associated with hard-copy media kits such as reproducing the materials, mailing, faxing, and using a messenger service. After the media kit is uploaded on a server, the names and email addresses of journalists visiting the site can be compiled for future reference. Once a distribution list is compiled, information can be disseminated instantaneously. Online media kits can also be updated and accessed on a 24-hour basis, and they allow for two-way communication.

Using a CD for the media kit offers the news media flexibility and much more information than a traditional media kit. A CD holds a great deal of information and, with a good access menu, is easy to use. The journalist can review only the information that interests him or her to construct a story.

What Are the Pitfalls?

One of the biggest obstacles we must overcome when developing a media kit is getting the members of the news media to review the materials and information enclosed in the kit. Journalists are inundated with public relations materials on a daily basis, so it is the job of the PR professional to develop a media kit that is appealing and innovative to increase the odds of its being used.

Budget constraints are another factor to consider when developing a media kit, as assembling hard-copy media kits can be expensive. Postal fees, reproduction of media kit components—shell folder, news releases, photos, and other elements—and graphic designs and layouts can cost thousands of dollars.

Although compressing a media kit onto a CD offers more flexibility and allows more material to be stored, there are some drawbacks to using this form of distribution. First, a team of professionals with expertise in computer development, including programmers, graphics specialists, multimedia designers, and audio engineers, is needed to develop an effective CD program. This can become costly, especially if the creators are contract workers instead of employees. It is important to identify the journalists who regularly utilize CDs so that the kits can be distributed to the appropriate outlets. The benefit of a CD media kit over a printed one is that the CD can be easily and economically updated.

The Internet has become a popular way to disseminate information, making online media kits increasingly available. But there are some limitations to using an online media kit, as well. Once the media kit is online, the PR professional must properly promote it so that the intended media representatives will know when and where to get the information. Although the use of graphics can enhance the appearance of the online media kit, they have to be used sparingly because they slow down the user's loading, reading, and downloading of the site. Lastly, the use of software programs or other plug-ins such as animation should be an option, not a requirement, to view the site. These programs may delay journalists' search for basic information and ultimately cause them to leave the site without obtaining the information they were seeking and that we wanted them to have. The simplest and most effective media kit would probably be a downloadable PDF file. It would be accessible to everyone with a free Adobe Acrobat® Reader, would require no printing or mailing by the client, and could be easily updated.

The success of media kits relies heavily on the media relations work that precedes the distribution of the kits. We should know which journalists report on particular beats or topics. We also need to develop and cultivate effective media lists that identify the media who may be interested in the information included in the media kit. Tailoring the media kit to the specific needs of individual news media outlets also improves the chances for successful media placements.

How Should They Look?

Style Notes

A media kit must provide newsworthy information, which means incorporating a news hook into the materials provided. Enclosed news releases and supplemental materials should be well written, accurate, timely, and unbiased. Adhering to these concepts helps get the appropriate news coverage. Some elements of a media kit are standard, but the contents can vary depending on the purpose, the objective, and the targeted media.

Process

The basic stages of preparing a media kit include research, planning, organization, distribution, follow-up, and evaluation.

Research

During the research stage, we gather and compile pertinent information, identify target audiences, and prepare a list of news media that reach these audiences. It is very important to keep a media list current because contact information changes frequently. It is imperative for media kits to be received by the appropriate person. Sending important news and information to reporters who do not cover your organization's industry or field—and failing to send it to those reporters who do—is a formula for a media relations disaster.

Planning

The planning stage of the media kit encompasses three steps. First, we need to identify the purpose of the media kit. Second, a budget must be established. Because it is easy for media kit planning to get financially out of control, it is essential during the planning stage to determine a realistic budget that fits the organization's overall fiscal plan. The final element of the planning stage is deciding which key components to include in the media kit. This includes development of the shell, fact sheets, news releases, and any other printed materials that need to be created.

Follow-Up and Evaluation

After the planning is completed, the media kits have to be reproduced, organized, assembled, and distributed to the appropriate media outlets. Immediately after distribution, it is essential for the PR professional to follow up with the media to answer any questions, further pitch story ideas, or offer additional assistance. Finally, one of the most critical stages is the evaluation. This measures the success or failure of the media kit and its components.

Format

The contents of a media kit will vary depending on its purpose and/or the circumstances in which it is distributed. In general, media kits are developed to provide basic information about an organization, special events, major newsworthy announcements, crisis situations, and news conferences.

At the bare minimum, a media kit should include news releases, fact sheets, biographical information, backgrounders (detailed information about the organization), and visuals. A standard media kit used to introduce the organization to the news media can be developed and updated as needed. The following gives a brief description of materials that may be included in media kits for different occasions.

Shell

Usually a two-pocket folder, the **shell** holds all of the items contained in the media kit. The front cover must clearly identify the company, event, or theme and provide any other pertinent information. One of the most important steps is producing an attention-grabbing shell that expresses the style and overall message being conveyed. This calls for the careful integration of words, visuals, and designs. In the case of media kit shells, presentation is everything. The style can be simple or elaborate. The shell should be visually attractive, incorporating themes, slogans or tag lines, colors, graphic designs, and logos. The inside right pocket contains the primary information such as news releases, features, and fact sheets. The inside left pocket contains the supplemental information such as photos, backgrounders, newspaper clippings, position papers, and additional information regarding the organization, event, program initiative, or product.

Cover Letter/Kit Letter

When media kits are mailed, it is important to enclose a cover letter or kit letter. Typically, media kits are mailed if someone from the media list is unable to attend the event or if mailing is the best distribution method for the kits. This letter must clearly identify the contents of the media kit, state why the event deserves coverage, give the names of persons to contact for further information, and explain why the information is being sent. The letter should be written in a way that will entice readers to review the contents of the media kit. The first paragraph of the letter should be an attention-grabber. The subsequent paragraphs should offer interesting information that demonstrates why the individual, product, or topic is appealing. Media kits designed to pitch television producers for guest appearances on talk-show programs should include a cover letter that explains why the individual, product, or topic should be featured on the show and why it will appeal to the show's audience.

The Right Pocket

News Release Depending on the purpose of the media kit, the primary news release provides pertinent information about the organization, event, program initiative, or product. This information should focus on the *principal* news related to the media kit. It should also provide logistical information, such as time constraints, access limitations, directions, security, and what media credentials are required. More than one news release may be necessary in some media kits. For example, a community organization holding its annual gala fundraiser would include a news release about the event. If the organization uses the affair to announce a local celebrity as the new spokesperson, a release about the new spokesperson would also be included.

The primary news release should be the first item seen in the right shell pocket. Fact sheets that amplify that news release must immediately follow. All subsequent news releases should be placed in order of importance. Any supplemental news releases should provide only information that was *not* previously mentioned in the primary release. By focusing on different messages, supplemental news releases will not sound redundant or repetitive.

Fact Sheet There are many different styles and purposes for fact sheets. Generally, **fact sheets** are information that is broken into bulleted or numbered items. They are rarely written in paragraph form. Fact sheets should follow some identifiable order and organization. A basic fact sheet contains basic information about an organization, such as names of officers, locations of offices (with addresses, telephone numbers and Web sites), and a description of what the organization is or does. A historical fact sheet gives background information about the organization and historical milestones in its development, including when and where the organization was founded, when new activities began, and a list of annual events.

Special-events fact sheets not only explain the significance of the event, they also describe all activities and list the date, time, location, and duration for each. In addition, they list important participants and sponsors and provide contact information for the organization, including telephone numbers, addresses, and Web sites. This supplies the media with all necessary logistical information to cover the event in person. Event fact sheets often provide a brief history of the event (especially if it is annual), including when and where the event was first held, significant people who attended, and how many people were present. It should also describe milestones in the event's history.

There are several other types of fact sheets. Timelines incorporate a chronological list of key dates and events as they may relate to the current news. Another popular style of fact sheet is glossaries, which provide definitions of terms—industry jargon or language—that may be unfamiliar to reporters. FAQ fact sheets provide answers to frequently asked questions. Selected facts—also referred to as "Did you know?"—are additional isolated facts that may be interesting to the journalist and provide supplemental information about the organization. These provide quirky tidbits that can assist the reporter in including unique facts about the organization or event. Fact sheets are necessary components of the media kit because they give the media facts and information to reference when constructing news stories.

The Left Pocket

Visual Materials Visual materials are usually the first element found in the left pocket. Their purpose is to amplify the news element of the media kit, and they can be included in print and broadcast news stories. There are many kinds of visuals that can be included in a kit, such as individual headshots, product stills, graphics, or even photos of past events. Each visual element should include a **caption**, a brief description of the visual that identifies exactly what the visual is and how it relates to the news. Usually, the caption is part of the visual. However, when a caption must be attached physically to the visual, it should be printed on a separate sheet of paper, affixed to the back of the visual, and folded over the front of the visual. The caption should be removable without marring the photo.

Biographical Information Biographical information should be developed for officers, founders, celebrities, experts, or any other key players within the organization. In addition to providing background information, a **biography** might include headshot photos. All photographs should be reproduction quality for the print media. When this is the case, the biography should immediately follow the accompanying photograph.

Two types of biographies are used in media kits. The *straight* biography lists factual information in a descending order of importance, with company-oriented facts preceding personal details. *Narrative* biographies, on the other hand, are more creative and written in a descriptive fashion, paying more attention to personal details.

It is critical to keep updated biographies of key players in the organization, celebrities, and experts on hand. When a biography focuses on a celebrity, it should provide information about the celebrity's relationship with the organization, how the celebrity got involved with the organization, and the contributions made by the celebrity.

Biographies can take more than one form. Some mini-biographies, or **mini-bios**, are as short as two paragraphs and highlight only the information that is relevant to the subject of the kit. In this case, three or more biographies can be included on one page. Biographies for key newsmakers are generally written in a feature-story style and are lengthier.

Backgrounder A **backgrounder** is an expanded version of the history, mission, goals, and purpose of an organization. It is usually written in paragraph form and deals primarily with fact-driven information. It should anticipate questions about the organization that the media may have, and provide comprehensive answers. Backgrounders should be placed following any and all biographic material. Unlike fact sheets, the backgrounder provides more depth about the functions of the organization. It can include elements like the mission statement, organizational policies, and a description of daily operations. A backgrounder should fully define what the organization does. This provides reporters with a wealth of information about the organization that they can include in the news story.

Position Papers A **position paper** describes an organization's stand on a certain issue. This issue can be local, regional, national, or international in scope. Position papers are placed immediately following the backgrounder. Unlike the backgrounder, the position paper focuses mainly on opinions and is supported by facts. The position paper should include a sufficient amount of information that supports the organization's point of view, but it should also include opposing points of view. Position papers give the media insight into the organization's (or, in the case of election campaigns, the candidate's) viewpoint on issues. They can be a vehicle for image building and possible placement in the op-ed pages of newspapers.

Feature Story A **feature story** highlights a lesser-known human-interest story related to the news surrounding the media kit. It focuses on something that is not necessarily considered immediate or hard news. Features are often creative and emphasize the unusual, the dramatic, or the surprising. They should incorporate a specific angle or slant to capture the reader's attention. Feature stories often assist journalists by offering an alternative way of viewing the organization or principal spokesperson.

Organization Publications Magazines, brochures, or newsletters that the organization distributes to the public are often included in media kits. This type of information is optional, but it gives the media insight into the organization's audiences, especially if the publication is member- or employee-based. Interesting articles or facts from these types of publications may also provide a different news angle for reporters.

Cooperating Organizations List This compilation acknowledges outside organizations that contributed to and cooperated with the program initiative, new product development, or special event. It may garner media coverage for the organization's partners, as well as providing credibility to the organization. Information sheets should explain and describe the cooperative organization's support given to—or its partnering relationship with—the primary organization. The information should be factual and accurate and requires approval from the acknowledged organization.

Invitation If the media kit is publicizing a special event, a formal invitation sent to the media adds a personal touch. It should include all logistical information, such as time, location, and directions, and any special instructions, such as procedures for media credentials. If the event is in the evening or on the weekend, the invitation should state that members of the media are "welcome to bring a guest."

News Briefs During a crisis, the media want up-to-date information. News briefs can provide this information. News briefs regarding breaking or developing news should summarize what has happened in the past 24 hours. News briefs should stick to the facts and include relevant statistical information. It is critical to indicate who the designated spokesperson is and how that person can be contacted. Updated information relevant to the crisis should be regularly communicated to the media, and the news brief is an appropriate vehicle.

Statement From Spokesperson During a crisis, a statement from the organization's crisis spokesperson should be included, as well as contact information for further details and access as the crisis continues. Of course, this person needs to be well informed of the situation and a credible representative of the organization. The statement from the spokesperson provides quotes for reporters to incorporate in their news stories.

Where Should They Go?

A media kit can be distributed in several ways. After a target audience is identified (see the research phase under "Process," earlier), the PR professional compiles an effective media contact list to determine who will receive a kit. Special attention should be given to the format in which the news medium likes to receive information. Some journalists may like a mailed copy of the media kit, whereas others may want the media kit delivered electronically via email or the Internet. Traditionally, media kits are distributed at the event or at the news conference site before activities begin. Media kits are also mailed or sent by messenger directly to reporters, editors, news directors, and producers in advance of the event to help them prepare for coverage or for preparation of stories if they are unable to attend the event.

The purpose and objective of the media kit will determine who receives it. The media list includes names and contact information for the appropriate news media outlets. It is very important that this information remain current, so it should be updated frequently. It is imperative the media kit be sent to the appropriate gatekeeper. In general, media kits sent to the broadcast media should be addressed to the producer of a particular show or segment. When you are sending media kits to the print media, editors or departments should be targeted.

Of course, media kits can now be distributed online. Media kits can be posted to an organization's Web site, and news media can visit the site and download only needed information.

Did They Work?

Effective media kits should provide comprehensive and useful information for the appropriate news media outlets. Such effectiveness can be measured against the following criteria:

- Is the information factual, accurate, truthful, verifiable, and comprehensive?
- Does the media kit provide answers to journalists' most basic questions?
- Is there ample background information that allows the journalist to select a story angle, slant, or new approach to relaying the information?
- Is the media kit free of ads, sales materials, and promotional collateral?
- Are opinions and value judgments validated by quotes from credible third-party sources?
- Is the media kit visually impressive and eye-catching enough to grab the media's attention?

In addition, media kits are evaluated by the number of news media that attended a particular event (i.e., news conference, product launch, special event). An effective way to obtain immediate feedback is to distribute kits to credentialed media in person and use a checklist of names to determine who is present.

One of the best ways to evaluate the effectiveness of the media kit is to monitor, compile, and analyze any and all news stories or media hits generated by the media kit. There are several outside sources that can monitor broadcast or print information for an organization (see "Media Clippings" in Appendix A).

Web sites can accurately identify what media visited a media kit link, what pieces were downloaded, and when the information was obtained.

Putting PR into Practice

An effective media kit relies on the sum of its parts. It is important to think strategically about how those parts are developed. As always, consider your target audience. In this case, you should think about working journalists and the audiences they reach.

Consider the client you chose at the beginning of the course or one assigned to you.

1. Formulate a list of facts you think are most interesting and most important to your two audiences.

2. Reorganize the list in the order of importance to your client or your organization, being careful not to be too self-serving.

3. Use the list to write a fact sheet, backgrounder, and bio.

An *Example Gallery* for Media Kits begins on the following page.

Media kit cover for a for-profit organization event.

❶ SHELL: Folder with graphics, logo, organization, event, date, and theme.

2623 North Avenue
Western, California 90200
Phone: 800-555-5597
Fax: 800-555-5599
www.formativeenterprises.com

NEWS RELEASE

April 26, 2012
FOR IMMEDIATE RELEASE

Contact:
Staci Kaufman, Public Affairs Director
(800) 555-5597
SKaufman@formative.com

FORMATIVE ENTERPRISES INITIATES FREE YOUTH EXERCISE PROGRAMS
IN LOW-INCOME NEIGBORHOODS

The New Program will Kick off Today at the Western Youth Center

WESTERN, CA — The nation's premiere manufacturer of youth fitness products will introduce a new youth exercise program today, April 26th at 1:30 pm at the Western Youth Center on Plainview Avenue. Formative Enterprises is sponsoring these sessions free of charge in low-income neighborhoods.

The kickoff celebration will also include an informational talk and demonstration of the new programs which are set to be offered at youth facilities nationwide.

On hand to host the festivities will be the CEO of Formative Enterprises, Jamie Molack, Congressman Chad Lathem, State Senator Rona Jackson, and John Peters, the Athletic Director of the Western Youth Center.

"The members of our company felt a responsibility stemming from the recently passed National Fitness Initiative," explains Molack. "Since we develop and manufacture more youth exercise equipment than any other company, we were determined to pass on the importance of exercise to kids who cannot afford to purchase these products themselves due to a lack of resources."

-more-

Page 1 of 2

News release for an event news media kit.

❶ NEWS RELEASES: Should be one to three about organization and the event.

Example Gallery
Media Kits

page 2 of 2

Working hand-in-hand on this new venture with Molack is U.S. Representative Lathem. Besides being one of the sponsors of the original National Fitness Initiative, Lathem's home district is located in the same area as Formative Enterprises home office, Western, California.

According to Lathem, he believes this program can change the exercise habits of thousands of underprivileged youth in this country. "It is great to see a large company make such a major contribution to low-income families the way Formative Enterprises has done. They have and continue to make a difference in the lives and well-being of this nation's children."

Other individuals who will be in attendance at the demonstration include program participants, key executives from Formative Enterprises and a contingency of Youth Fitness Directors from across the United States.

Formative Enterprises is the nation's leading manufacturer of youth fitness products. Founded in 1994 by a former state fitness advisor, the goal of the company continues to be keeping this country's youth fit and healthy. For more information on Formative Enterprises visit the website at www.formativeenterprises.com.

For media inquiries or advance media credentials contact Staci Kaufman at (800) 555-5597.

-###-

Page 2 of 2

Example Gallery
Media Kits

2623 North Avenue
Western, California 90200
Phone: 800-555-5597
Fax: 800-555-5599
www.formativeenterprises.com

BACKGROUNDER

Founded in 1994, Formative Enterprises, Inc. is the nation's premiere manufacturer of youth fitness products. A 25-year-old fitness advisor, Jamie Molack, made it her life's work to bring exercise and fitness to the youth of America. Located in Western, California, Molack started her company in her family's basement with a few ideas and two very loyal and committed employees.

Today Formative Enterprises grosses over $20 million in annual sales while putting nearly 25% of its profits back into the community. Offering a wide variety of exercise and fitness equipment through retail and online sales, Formative Enterprises tailors all exercise equipment to fit the sizes and abilities of its young users.

Identifying the needs of today's youth has become a major concern for Formative. The company works very closely with youth centers across the country while developing a healthy and safe exercise regimen that kids find fun and invigorating.

The future of Formative Enterprises is brighter than ever now that Congress has passed the National Fitness Initiative. Hoping to work closely with federal and state sponsored youth centers, Formative's short term goal is to develop youth exercise programs that will be offered free of charge to children of low income households.

Contact: Staci Kaufman, Public Affairs Director
                    (800) 555-5597
                    SKaufman@formative.com

Backgrounder for a news media kit.

❶ BACKGROUNDER: Information about the organization.

Example Gallery
Media Kits

2623 North Avenue
Western, California 90200
Phone: 800-555-5597
Fax: 800-555-5599
www.formativeenterprises.com

Formative Enterprises, Inc.

KIDS & EXERCISE
FACT SHEET

• Physically active children are more likely to maintain healthy bones, muscles and joints, sustain lower blood pressure and healthy weight control, and enjoy improved psychological well-being.

• Fit children tend to do better in physical-performance tests. They have a stronger self-image, more self-confidence, and they demonstrate greater improvement in skill- and health-related fitness.

• Children generally need enough physical activity requiring regular participation in activities that increase energy expenditure above resting levels. Physical activity need not be strenuous to be beneficial. Emphasis should be placed on play (rather than exercise) and on activities that the child enjoys, that are consistent with the child's skill level. Children are remarkably able to adjust their levels of activity to their individual capability.

• Twenty-nine percent of American boys and 25% of girls six to 17 are considered obese, according to the National Exercise for Life Institute. These figures are up 54% for kids six to 11 (and 39% for ages 12–17) compared to 1965.

• Fifty percent of American children are not getting enough exercise to develop healthy cardiorespiratory systems according to the recent national Children and Youth Fitness Study.

• Studies by the American Academy of Pediatrics indicate that low physical activity by young kids is a primary contributor to excessive fat accumulation.

❶

Fact sheet for a news media kit.

❶ FACT SHEET: Numbered or bulleted information relevant to the organization and/or event.

2623 North Avenue
Western, California 90200
Phone: 800-555-5597
Fax: 800-555-5599
www.formativeenterprises.com

Formative Enterprises, Inc.

JAMIE MOLACK
PRESIDENT

BIOGRAPHY

As a young child, Jamie Molack was always playing sports with her older brothers. She left her dolls, tea sets and dress-up clothes inside the house. The first girl in her hometown of Western, California to play on an "all boy" Little League team, Molack knew that passion for exercise and sport would be her calling.

After graduating from California University with a Master of Science degree in physical education, Molack went to work for the Western California Schools as an elementary school physical education teacher. Not satisfied with the area's exercise curriculum, Molack developed a comprehensive physical education regimen for the area students to follow.

"We thought that Jamie was being a bit ambitious at first," explained Western School Superintendent Rona Browning. "When the teachers and administrators saw the students not just participating but leading their own regimens, we were confident Jamie knew her stuff."

Once word leaked to other California schools about the success of the Western School's physical education program, Molack was asked by the state governor to expand

-more-

Page 1 of 3

Biographical sketch for a news media kit.

1 BIOGRAPHIES: Background information about principals of the organization or event including presenters, celebrities, and participants.

Example Gallery
Media Kits

Formative Enterprises, Inc.

page 2 of 3

her curriculum to every California school. As Molack began to visit the different schools, she realized that many areas did not have age appropriate equipment to complement her physical activity regimen.

"I knew there was a void in the youth exercise market but I just had no idea how large that void had become," said Molack. "I wanted kids to enjoy all the nuances that physical activity had to offer and I knew it would be up to me to provide the equipment for them."

So at the same time that Molack was consulting with California educators, she was running a three person shop out of her family's basement to develop, create, manufacture and sell youth fitness equipment. And so Formative Enterprises, Inc. was born.

"We were never expecting the business to grow as quickly as it did," said Molack. "We realized that there indeed was a need to be filled and we were one of the few organizations with the drive, determination and know-how to do it."

Today, Formative Enterprises grosses over $20 million in annual sales. However, Molack never forgot about the kids. "I believe it is our corporate responsibility to give back to the community. So many children do not have the resources to purchase Formative equipment, therefore the company donates many of our most popular products to low-income community and youth centers for all kids to enjoy," explained Molack.

-more-

Example Gallery
Media Kits

page 3 of 3

    Donating almost 25% of Formative Enterprise's profits to low-income neighborhoods has gained the company, and more notably Molack, acclaim and notoriety among educators, community leaders and, of course, the children.

    "My goal is to reverse the trend of children who would prefer to watch television and play video games than ride their bikes and play sports," said Molack. "I look forward to the day when the children of today are the healthy and fit parents of the healthy and fit kids of tomorrow."

-###-

Example Gallery
Media Kits

Jamie Molack, CEO of Formative Enterprises ❷

❶

Publicity photos.

❶ PUBLICITY PHOTOS: One to three 5″ × 7″ or 8″ × 10″ photos to amplify a story.

❷ CAPTION: Description of accompanying photo.

Media kit cover for a nonprofit organization event.

❶ SHELL: Folder with graphics, logo, organization, event, date, and theme.

Example Gallery
Media Kits

EachOneTeachOne

1836 Jefferson Square, NW / Washington, DC 20036

NEWS RELEASE

March 15, 2012
FOR IMMEDIATE RELEASE

Contact Information:
Sarah Woods, Communications Director
Office: (202) 555-3377
Fax: (202) 555-3780
Email: swoods@eachoneteachone.org

EACH ONE TEACH ONE STUDENTS RECEIVE SCHOLARSHIPS
Participants Win College Funds for Aid in Curbing Youth Violence

WASHINGTON, DC — Five students participating in *Each One Teach One* activities were presented with $1,000 scholarships at an awards ceremony yesterday at the organization's headquarters in Washington, DC.

High school seniors who have participated in *Each One Teach One* events competed for five scholarships for assistance at the college of their choice. The criteria for this award include demonstrated leadership skills, impact of the program on everyday life, and the desire to continue the mission of the program.

-more-

Page 1 of 2

Announcement news release.

❶ LETTERHEAD: The logo and title of the organization on the first page only.

❷ DATE OF DISTRIBUTION: The date the release is sent to the media.

❸ "FOR IMMEDIATE RELEASE" or "EMBARGOED UNTIL [DATE, TIME]"

❹ CONTACT INFORMATION: Name, office telephone number (home number is optional), fax number, and email address.

❺ HEADLINE: Uppercase letters, bold and underlined; states summary of the news.

❻ SUBHEAD: Upper- and lowercase letters, bold and italicized; supplements news headline and does not paraphrase.

❼ DATELINE: Location of event or story in capital letters.

❽ LEAD: One- or two-sentence statement of the five "W's" of news—who, what, where, when, and why.

❾ PAGE SLUGS

Example Gallery
Media Kits

"These students exemplify the progress and development that *Each One Teach One* strives to accomplish in all children," said Executive Director Willis Bennett.

Each One Teach One receives funding for the scholarship, activities and events through the Presidential Safe Schools/Healthy Students Initiative and donations by individuals and corporations. The organization's plans include expansion of the scholarship fund to provide more college aid.

The honorees include Amanda Sheffield of Atlanta, Georgia; Bradley Lawrence and Paul Stevenson of Washington, DC; Terrell Jones of Chicago, Illinois; and Tanya Spelder of Miami, Florida. — 10

Attorney General Janine Redding, a member of the board of directors, recommended the creation of a scholarship to motivate the children involved in the program. According to Redding, "*Each One Teach One* wants to recognize students for their hard work and desire to reach their goals. This, I believe, is the perfect way."

For more information, please contact Sarah Woods at (202) 555-3377 or by email at — 11
swoods@eachoneteachone.org.

Each One Teach One is a nonprofit organization created in 1999 in response to the growing number of tragedies from youth violence. The anti-violence campaign includes seminars, workshops and retreats as well as counseling services and fundraisers. Volunteers — 12
have also created a monthly newsletter and a Web site for the organization. The mission of *Each One Teach One* is to encourage youth to help each other find alternatives to violence.

-###-   13

⑩ LEAD AMPLIFIERS: Two or more quotations from relevant sources, statistics, or other pertinent story information.

⑪ CONTACT INFORMATION: Contact name, telephone numbers, fax number, and email address.

⑫ BOILERPLATE: Summarizes the philosophy, goals, and purpose of the organization. Appears just before the end of the news release.

⑬ PAGE SLUG

EachOneTeachOne

1836 Jefferson Square, NW/Washington, DC 20036

BACKGROUNDER

Each One Teach One was created in September 1999 in response to the Inglewood tragedy that occurred in Akron, Ohio earlier that year, in which a 14-year-old boy shot and killed three of his classmates and his teacher. The nonprofit organization was originally spear-headed by Attorney General Janine Redding as a project for the Washington, DC metro area and is funded by the Presidential Safe Schools/Healthy Students Initiative.

With the motto, "It Takes a Village To Raise a Child," *Each One Teach One* strives to reduce school and community violence by identifying young children who demonstrate patterns of violent behavior and promoting skills that show self-control. Volunteers strive to develop activities that encourage alternatives to aggression. This includes providing creative outlets, workshops, seminars, retreats and positive environments to help children ages 5 to 18 reduce the use of violence. The organization also strongly encourages family members, friends, adults and teachers to take active roles in the lives of children and teach them skills that will help them become productive adults and citizens.

The organization's monthly newsletter, "Hand to Hand," and Web site provide useful information, including upcoming events in various cities around the United States, and contact information for members and students. Future plans include developing more events and outlets for troubled students, increasing the number of active participants in the program, and expand-ing the program to other urban cities.

❶

Backgrounder for a news media kit.

❶ BACKGROUNDER: Information about the organization.

EachOneTeachOne

1836 Jefferson Square, NW / Washington, DC 20036

FACT SHEET

- *Each One Teach One* was launched in September of 1999 in Washington, DC, in response to the growing number of tragedies from youth violence.

- The non-profit organization was originally spearheaded by Attorney General Janine Redding, and was organized by Willis Bennett, the executive director.

- The mission of *Each One Teach One* is to reduce school and community violence by identifying children who demonstrate patterns of violent behavioral problems. Volunteers and counselors promote skills that show self-control, curbing the use of violence.

- The organization's campaign includes seminars, workshops and retreats as well as counseling services and fundraisers. Volunteers have also created a monthly newsletter and a Web site, www.eachoneteachone.org.

- *Each One Teach One* currently has a staff of 35 full-time employees, 50 volunteers and 1,000 students who have been enrolled in the program and participate in the various activities.

- Funding is provided by the Presidential Safe Schools/Healthy Students Initiative, receiving an annual budget of $1.8 million.

- Goals for the next five years include increasing the number of students involved in the program and reducing not only the rate of violent activity, but also the dropout rate across the country.

Fact sheet for a news media kit.

❶ FACT SHEET: Numbered or bulleted information relevant to the organization and/or event.

Example Gallery
Media Kits

EACH TEACH 1

EachOneTeachOne

1836 Jefferson Square, NW / Washington, DC 20036

SENIOR STAFF BIOGRAPHIES

Willis Bennett,
Executive Director

Willis Bennett was appointed by the Board of Directors and is responsible for long-term strategic development of the various programs at *Each One Teach One*. He serves as spokesperson for the organization and is in charge of promoting and publicizing *Each One Teach One* across the nation.

Bennett has an extensive background working with the youth of America. For the past 15 years, he has worked as an acclaimed motivational speaker for at-risk students. He traveled across the nation speaking to students and with school administrators to develop techniques for handling problem students.

Rose Ward,
Vice-President of Operations

Rose Ward serves as vice president of operations for *Each One Teach One*. She is responsible for overseeing the day-to-day activities of the organization. She ensures that the programs run smoothly and troubleshoots any unforeseen problems that may arise.

Prior to working for *Each One Teach One*, Ward worked as program director of the L.A. School Association (LASA). LASA serves 17 schools with 8,400 high-risk students who are two or more years below grade level. It was her job to develop programs that would enable these students to rejoin their peers at their appropriate grade.

Patrick Smathers,
Director of Volunteers

Patrick Smathers is the director of volunteers for *Each One Teach One*. In this capacity he is responsible for appropriating all volunteer efforts for the organization. He develops training procedures and organizes counselors and mentors for the various programs at *Each One Teach One*.

Smathers worked as Director of Volunteers for Spanish America, a non-profit organization dedicated to helping Spanish-American students assimilate more easily into Florida schools. He recruited volunteers from all 50 states for mentor programs.

Composite of biographical sketches for a news media kit.

❶ BIOGRAPHIES: Background information about principals of the organization or event, including presenters, celebrities, and participants.

Example Gallery
Media Kits

EachOneTeachOne

1836 Jefferson Square, NW / Washington, DC 20036

FLORIDA STUDENT RECEIVES COLLEGE GRANT
Tanya Spelder Succeeds Through Each One Teach One Program

Each One Teach One recently presented a significant college scholarship to a graduate of the organization, Tanya Spelder. With the help of *Each One Teach One* volunteers in Miami, Florida, Spelder progressed from being a reluctant participant in the anti-violence program to her current role as the organization's youth spokesperson. This year, Spelder won a grant from the organization to defray the costs of a college degree in social work.

Spelder was born into a poor family in urban San Diego, California. From just after her birth, Spelder's family was troubled. Violence in her neighborhood and abuse in her home, taught Spelder violence and aggression. She learned early to take care of herself, no matter the consequences, and because of this, became a quiet, isolated child.

Early school years proved to be difficult for Spelder. She had few friends, and those she did have were accustomed to a hostile environment. Her school, located in the inner city of San Diego, was poor and most of the students were, like Spelder, living in single parent families or extremely impoverished households. Spelder often engaged in school fights with other students just to keep her lunch money. She did not excel in her classes because of this environment and was not motivated to succeed.

Spelder felt her life was going nowhere. She did not want to make new friends, and she was afraid to leave her home. She was afraid and yet she had to defend herself every day. So

-more-

Page 1 of 4

Feature story for a news media kit.

❶ FEATURE STORY: Human interest story about a particular person or event related to the main event of the kit.

Example Gallery
Media Kits

when her father left her mother and moved to Miami, she decided to join him. However, when she realized that he had left to be with another woman, she felt that she was not welcome in his new family. Although he continually suggested she move back home, her life dealing with a new mother and new sibling was seemingly better than being in San Diego.

Spelder adjusted to her home in inner-city Miami, but she found that her life was not significantly different than her California situation. Although her neighborhood was less violent, her school was still quite competitive and unfriendly. Students Spelder met had drug addictions, a common occurrence in the area, and she fell into the addiction in an attempt to make friends. After an incident between her gang and another during a drug trip, Spelder realized that she could not continue her path. She again rejected her friends and school and went to work. Her only understanding was that she needed to defend herself against the world.

When *Each One Teach One* volunteers visited Spelder's school, one of her friends mentioned to the speaker that Spelder had serious violence and aggression problems, and had recently dropped out of school to work and support herself. With the help of her father and counselors through the program, Spelder agreed to enroll in the program, "I felt like at that point, I had nothing to lose. I knew I wasn't happy, and I hated everything, including my family. When I realized that, I knew I needed to change," she said.

Once in the program, Spelder found motivation. She noticed that by talking to other students like herself, she felt better about herself and was more confident that she could succeed. Spelder progressed so well in the program that she moved from counseled to counselor. Volunteers noticed that she had a natural talent for talking to her peers and reasoning with them,

-more-

Example Gallery
Media Kits

and for some of the students, was actually more effective than some of the trained counselors. She said, "I think being able to talk to people in similar situations made me that much more self assured. And as we spoke, I was able to help them, which in turn helped me. It was a great experience." She has spent the last year working with students and helping them to grow just as she had.

Directors of the program witnessed Spelder's development and suggested that she join them in talking to local schools. When the group attends a school assembly, they discuss the importance of awareness about youth violence and the benefits of a program like *Each One Teach One* for aggressive or violent students. During the last six months, Spelder has spoken to groups of students at 11 local schools. She recounts her own struggle to gain self-confidence, and emphasizes the importance of goals and motivation in order to achieve success, the value of staying in school and the meaning of a supportive family.

This spring, Spelder won an *Each One Teach One* college scholarship. She received the prize not only for her remarkable progress while working in the program, but for her achievements and dedication to the community even after completing the program. Not only did Spelder dramatically improve her sense of self and motivation to succeed, but she did the same for many of her peers, and has encouraged and supported them in overcoming their own struggles. Her experience moved nearly 100 students to join the program this year.

Students have acknowledged being inspired and motivated by Spelder. As one student commented, "I always liked just beating up on people and things because it made me feel better, at least for a while. But I listened to her speak during school one day, and I thought maybe I could feel better all the time without the aggression. I figured I'd give it a try."

-more-

Example Gallery
Media Kits

Spelder is now finishing high school in Southern Florida and plans to attend college to earn a degree in social work. She feels strongly about continuing her dedication to *Each One Teach One*, an organization which she says saved her life and the lives of her peers and friends. She wants to reach out to troubled children around the country and perhaps internationally with motivational speeches and youth counseling. According to Spelder, "My personal experience may help children in similar situations and help them to overcome their struggles."

-###-

Example Gallery
Media Kits

1836 Jefferson Square, NW / Washington, DC 20036

SUPPORT OF GUN CONTROL
AND LIVE IN A FUTURE WITHOUT VIOLENCE

The *Each One Teach One* organization, its donors, volunteers and sponsors are in support of legislation and regulations favoring gun control. Thousands of children are killed each year by accidents related to the use of guns. With youth violence becoming a growing cause of death every year, it is even more important that the use and ownership of guns in the home is controlled, to protect our nation's future leaders. Youth violence is a real problem in America, and the ease with which children gain access to guns and other weapons needs to be controlled.

One of *Each One Teach One*'s primary concerns is the rate at which children are being killed each year as a result of youth violence, specifically by the use of guns and other firearms. Every day, about 75 American children are shot. Most recover — 15 do not.

The majority of fatal accidents involving a firearm occur in the home, and an adolescent is twice as likely to commit suicide if a gun is kept in the home. More teenage boys in America die from gunfire than from car accidents and gunshot wounds are now the leading cause of death for teenage boys in America (white, African-American, urban, and suburban). This is a serious problem that needs to be addressed by America's leaders.

According to a study published in the *American Journal of Preventive Medicine,* "access to firearms and other weapons has been cited as an important factor contributing to the rise in violence-related injury among adolescents in the United States." Children have a much greater ease of access today, and parents need to be alerted and cautioned about the risks of having potentially deadly weapons stored in the home.

Each One Teach One supports the *Educational Fund to Stop Gun Violence*, an organization founded in 1978 to stop "gun violence by fostering effective community and national action."

-more-

Page 1 of 2

Position paper on the issue of gun control.

❶ POSITION PAPER: Outlines a cause or issue and explains both the position on the issue and why the group is in support of it.

Example Gallery
Media Kits

With the help of such organizations, *Each One Teach One* and community activists can progressively curb the use of violence.

Every day ten children die, and many more are seriously injured by guns. In a study of gun death rates for children under 15 years of age in 26 industrialized countries, the overall gun death rate in the U.S. was nearly 12 times higher than in the other 25 countries combined. Gun-related deaths accounted for 22.5% of all injury deaths in children and adolescents ages one to 19. These statistics are particularly alarming to members of *Each One Teach One* whose primary goal is to alleviate the growing problem of youth violence.

Each One Teach One supports anti-gun use, controlled gun use and other weapon control related legislation that is being debated in the U.S. Congress. Political action and applied programming are necessary to ensure that the fight against youth violence is recognized as a serious problem in need of attention. Children in America do not see an active role being taken to prevent the use of weapons and violence to resolve problems, and this needs to be addressed.

Many anti-violence and anti-gun advocacy groups contend that adults bear the burden of responsibility for ensuring that young people grow up in safe environments, free from gun trauma. *Each One Teach One* believes that parents need to be actively involved in the lives of their children in order to guide them to find alternatives to violence. Youth violence is a grave problem in the United States. *Each One Teach One* was created in order to slow the growing trend of violence and aggression among children. It needs the help of organizations and individuals, including families to support its cause against the uncontrolled use of guns, for the safety of America's future.

-###-

Page 2 of 2

Chapter 7 — Media Lists

What Are They?

There is no point in developing creative and dynamic messages that resonate with our target audiences if the appropriate news media never receive them. Accurate and comprehensive media lists are critical to the success of an effective public communication campaign. They serve as a bridge between the sender and the receiver—a link between the organization that has information to give and the news organizations that disseminate information to audiences. At their most basic level, media lists are compilations of data about the news media that cover an organization's or a person's industry or field or topics that concern or affect the organization.

The information in a media list includes the name of the journalist, editor, or producer, the beat or topic(s) of interest, and the name of the affiliated media outlet and its address, telephone number, fax number, and email address. We can include side notes about the individual media contact in these lists. Individuals or specialty teams within an organization create media lists on behalf of the organization. Media list entries are usually compiled from personal networking, old media lists, and media directories. Media relations firms maintain enormous databases to target their clients' audiences.

Media lists and media directories are vastly different, although their purposes are often similar. Media directories are published sourcebooks that are available to the general public for a fee. These sourcebooks include complete contact information for a wide variety of news outlets and can be national or regional in scope. Guides such as *Bacon's Media Directory* and media map—an Internet resource—contain names of thousands of media outlets and contacts throughout the country. A media list, on the other hand, is comprised of the media contacts necessary for a specific campaign or industry or for a particular geographic region.

Media lists are often medium-specific. Many organizations choose to break up the lists into broadcast, print, and Internet. Broadcast media lists include local and/or national information on television, cable, and radio news and information programming, depending on the scope of the campaign. Print media lists include local and/or national information for daily newspapers and local weekly publications, as well as trade publications and other miscellaneous periodicals that may be relevant to the intended message. National magazines are sometimes included in print media lists, but in some cases magazines constitute their own category and therefore their own list.

Who Gets Them?

There is no external audience affiliated with media lists. Instead, it is an important tool for practitioners to use to contact the news media that reach their intended audiences. Internally, media lists are tools that can be used by the many departments that make up a communication division.

What Do They Do?

Media lists provide an easy and convenient way for an organization's media relations specialists to reach those who disseminate news and information to regular audiences, usually the news media. The media relations specialist is a public communication professional who contacts news media representatives, or is contacted by news media representatives, to **pitch**—offer or suggest—a story or to provide information to a journalist who is working on a story. An effective media list is both comprehensive and selective. It should include all the appropriate media representatives and their contact information without incorporating every reporter and every outlet. As public communication professionals, we can determine the appropriate media representatives for a media list by reviewing what audience we have targeted for the message.

Media relations practitioners must be aware of the list's strengths and weaknesses. A media list that is well developed is an asset because it includes people and organizations that will be most receptive to the information. A weak media list is one that includes too many contacts or the wrong contacts, leading to frustration, aggravation, and wasted energy and time for the practitioner and the media representative. What is more, a poorly developed list can lead to the collapse of a working relationship because both the practitioner and the media representative work in deadline-oriented environments where wasted time can be catastrophic. The goal of a media list is not to include every name but instead to include the names of the media representatives who best fit the objective.

In the quest to create a comprehensive media list, the most challenging task is making sure that the list is accurate. Because journalists and other media representatives are part of a transient industry, keeping a media list current is critical. Reporters and news editors and directors move around so frequently that sometimes a media list can be used for only a month before it needs some sort of revision. A media list may be in a constant state of flux, and every media relations practitioner will attest to the fact that these lists must be updated on a regular basis. Without correct and current information, an organization can be viewed as unprofessional, unprepared, and, most importantly, unable to properly disseminate its story. An outdated media list is both useless and harmful. It tells news media gatekeepers that the organization's communication staff has not taken the time to truly understand them so, in turn, they are not inclined to take the time to listen to the communication staff.

How Do They Help?

Media lists create a link between an organization and the news media. Communication campaigns with targeted audiences cannot survive without that link. A well-constructed, current, and focused media list helps ensure that the story an organization wants to tell will reach the proper target audience. Media lists are also a way to distinguish one campaign or one organization from another. Each list demonstrates a public communication professional's strategic approach and understanding of the ebb and flow of the news industry. An effective media list is our first step toward gaining positive publicity and increased visibility for our organization. If an organization can afford an outside media relations firm, it can depend on that firm's comprehensive list.

What Are the Pitfalls?

The single greatest limitation of a media list is inaccuracy. The many hours we spend constructing news releases, media kits, video news releases, and public service announcements are wasted if they never even make it out of the office—or if they are delivered to the wrong person and ultimately discarded. Failing to create an accurate media list—or choosing not to update a media list—is equivalent to never compiling one in the first place. An ineffective media list will ultimately cost an organization both reputation and revenue.

How Should They Look?

Process and Format

Creating a media list is a collaborative process. Because one individual may specialize in one area of media relations while another concentrates on an entirely different area, all parties must contribute to constructing a comprehensive media list. Most important is that everyone have a clear understanding of where to obtain contact information and how much of it to include in the list.

Identifying the best place to find contact information about the media depends on both the needs and budget of a campaign or an organization. Networking and personal contacts provide not only the most effective information, but often the most reliable as well. It is also important to use other sources such as the Internet, local or regional publications, and the public library. Keep in mind, though, that when a media campaign targets a larger or more fragmented audience on a national or international level, the task of compiling an effective media list becomes quite complicated, requiring more time, people, and sources.

Printed media directories like *Bacon's* are divided into different volumes, each focusing on a different medium: television, radio, newspapers, and magazines. Each listing includes the name, address, telephone number, fax number, and sometimes email address of the media outlet.

Computer software, also provided by sources such as *Bacon's*, allows the practitioner to select media by location or by the type of publication or broadcast station. The lists can be created, compiled, and printed with just a few simple keystrokes.

Software programs like *SpinWARE*, *Media Map*, and *Press Access* allow the user to track media lists and distribute news releases by mail, fax, or electronic wire services. These services are updated quarterly. Budgetary restrictions can be a factor in using these programs, however. There is a fee to obtain the software (about $1,400) and then a fee every time the service is used via the Internet.

Online media directories and fax services like Media Distribution Services (MDS) and Targeter System contain databases of more than 150,000 editors and reporters at more than 40,000 print and broadcast outlets throughout the United States and Canada. The advantage to systems like MDS is that the information is updated daily, but these systems are unfortunately quite costly.

If directories are too expensive, there are other options for creating a media list. The public library and the Web are great places to investigate and sample different types of directories. The library also provides access to trade publications and other media periodicals that may not be listed in directories. The **masthead** inside the trade publication is often used to create a specialized media list.

After the contact information has been gathered, the list is constructed. Adhering to a set of established guidelines for developing a media list will help ensure that all necessary data are incorporated:

- Media lists always contain first and last names. They can also include salutations, middle names, initials, nicknames, and job titles. Addressing envelopes properly—or calling reporters by their preferred, rather than formal, names—indicates respect and helps create a positive working relationship.

- Current, correct, and complete mailing and email addresses are imperative. A media kit or a public service announcement cannot reach its destination if the address on the media list is wrong.

- Telephone and fax numbers are often lifelines between media relations practitioners and journalists. An organization's media relations professional often turns to the telephone to inform journalists about a story. That conversation is usually followed by a fax containing preliminary information and news releases. Wrong phone numbers and incorrect fax numbers shut down communication campaigns.

Sometimes other items are included in a media list: important, specific editorial information such as style guidelines, deadlines, times of broadcast, use of actualities, and photo requirements.

Organization

After gathering all the information, the media relations practitioner must decide how to organize the contact list. Before computers, media contacts were recorded on index cards and kept much like a Rolodex. The Rolodex media lists gave way to database computer technology that allows for easy updating and consolidation of various lists for different purposes. These lists are most commonly created in formatted columns. There are numerous programs that help to create a document that is both organized and flexible.

NewsTrack is a database software program specifically designed for managing media lists. The program consists of preformatted records that can be expanded in order to assign special-interest and distribution codes for each record. Other options include using Excel or any other standard database management software package. Such programs should allow for categories and names to be added later and for information to be deleted or merged with future lists.

Many media lists are developed with the top horizontal axis for categories such as the journalist's name, his or her title, the news organization's name, and an address and telephone number. The actual data then go in the vertical cells. Each cell contains a different piece of information corresponding to the category and to the specific person. This method is very popular, but not necessarily the only choice. The format of a media list should be customized for the particular organization. What most media relations experts advocate is that the format of each new media list be consistent with that of existing lists. This is done in order to ensure that future and past lists can be combined and manipulated easily.

Where Should They Go?

Effective media lists are valuable and proprietary data for the organization that uses them as well as for the competition that may want to profit by them. You will find that professionals in this field do not share their media lists. Therefore, the communication specialist, organization, or firm that develops media lists usually keeps them confidential. They are rarely distributed to anyone inside the organization and never to competing or partnering organizations. Effective media relations are key to the distribution and dissemination of information surrounding almost every media campaign and organization. Confidentiality is critical to success.

Did They Work?

The most effective way to evaluate the success of media lists is to determine whether the proposed story that was pitched to the journalists on the media list actually disseminated the intended message. However, we can also evaluate a media list during the media pitch itself. If phone calls are being taken and faxes are being received, a media relations practitioner will know that the email and media list are correct and accurate. In addition, calls from journalists seeking additional information are indications that the list targeted the right individuals and that the contact information was accurate. The media list is only as good as the strategy behind its conception. A truly effective media list will include the right people and eliminate unnecessary contacts.

Putting PR into Practice

Consider the client you chose or were assigned for this course. Create or update your client's media list. Include all the relevant blogs you can find. If your client is in a major media market, you know how difficult it is to get attention, so be sure to include as many blogs and community, daily, and regional publications as possible.

An *Example Gallery* for Media Lists begins on the following page.

ORGANIZATION	NAME	TITLE	ADDRESS	PHONE	EMAIL
PRINT					
DC Today	Bob Hamil	National News Editor	120 DC Way, Washington DC 20071	202-555-1231	hamil@DC2Day.com
Capitol Post	Georgia Scott	News Editor	36 North Deer Road, Washington DC 20002	202-555-1255	scott@times.com
New York Standard	Diane Banding	National News Editor	555 West Park, New York, NY 10036	212-555-1266	Band@stand.com
New Yorker Gazette	Mark Crowing	News Editor	1 Power Place, New York, NY 10036	212-555-1277	crow@gazette.org
LA Post	Jennifer Noeler	News Director	55 Rampling Way, Los Angeles, CA 90012	213-555-1299	jenn@lapost.com
National Times	Cecily Joel	News Director	10 Bethesda Drive, Bethesda, Maryland 20814	301-555-9999	joel@nation.org
TELEVISION					
TBC	David Amster	News Director	1 West Park, New York, NY 10036	212-555-0099	amster@tbc.org
ABS-TV	Brian Davids	News Director	123 New York Street, New York, NY 20030	212-555-5111	Davids@ABS.org
NTV-News	Margie Allen	News Director	125 Power Place, New York, NY 10036	212-555-0522	Alans@ntv.org
BNN-News	Bradley Frazin	News Director	30 News Place, Tucker, GA 30084	770-555-2707	Fraz@BNN.com
RADIO					
CP News Wire	Norman Harris	National News Director	1 Capitol Place, Washington, DC 20001	202-555-0735	Harris@CP.com
APR-Radio	Mike Murphey	News Director	55 DC Station, Washington, DC 20018	202-555-0491	murphey@apr.org

Each One Teach One *National Media List*

❶ ORGANIZATION: Media outlet.

❷ NAME: Contact person.

❸ TITLE: Position of contact person.

❹ ADDRESS: Location and/or mailing address.

❺ PHONE: Direct telephone number of media contact.

❻ EMAIL: Personal email address of media contact.

Chapter 8

Media Tours

What Are They?

As students and practitioners, we know the value of creating a forum where a well-prepared spokesperson can interact with the news media, taking questions and providing answers. We also know that only really big news can justify calling reporters out for a news conference. Whereas news conferences occur when the media convene in one central location to hear a spokesperson or newsmaker, media tours bring an organization's spokesperson or newsmaker to the reporters. Media tours provide organizations an opportunity to promote their causes directly to news outlets across the world. They allow organizations to further expand their messages beyond written news releases and to communicate one-on-one with the journalists and analysts that influence the organization's target audiences.

The various types of media tours include talk-show interviews, interviews with newspaper reporters, visits to business and trade press offices, and satellite media tours. There are advantages and disadvantages to each type of tour. We have to work with our organization leadership, spokespeople, subject matter experts, and newsmakers to determine the type of media tour that is right for a particular campaign or news event.

Local and national talk shows and newspaper interviews usually occur when the organization's spokesperson or newsmaker travels to meet with the media representative in his or her office or studio. Some radio talk-show interviews and newspaper or magazine editorial board meetings can take place on the telephone and through conference calls. But the more traditional-style tours can require the spokesperson or newsmaker to spend weeks or even months traveling from city to city, being interviewed on local talk shows and by local print media. The cost incurred for an out-of-town media tour can be very high, but the payoff can be substantial because of the visibility it provides for the organization. The objective is to introduce the journalist to the organization while building a personal relationship with the journalist. The ultimate goal is to obtain news coverage and to promote the organization's key message(s).

If the organization has a narrow focus, public communication professionals may choose to target the particular business or trade press. These news organizations are primarily trying to provide news to individuals in a particular field. Much like a full media tour, the spokesperson travels to and is interviewed by relevant trade publications in order to build relationships and generate news coverage.

Satellite media tours **(SMTs)** are usually a series of news media interviews with a spokesperson in a studio or a remote location who talks to journalists during a period of two to four hours. The television interviews run about three minutes while radio and Web interviews can run as long as 10 minutes. An SMT provides a means by which almost any organization can get its message disseminated in person more conveniently. Satellite transmission can take a spokesperson or newsmaker to the international, national, or local news media, including television, radio and Internet shows. Prior to satellite media tours, newsmakers and spokespersons were forced to embark exclusively on traditional media tours in order to promote their causes, which meant logging many travel hours. SMTs make it possible to reach people all over the world while communicating from just one studio.

What Do They Do?

The goal of every media tour is to gain news coverage and publicity for an organization and to influence public perception of an issue, individual, or organization. In order to accomplish this, it is critical to know where, when, and how to conduct a media tour. Different situations call for different types of tours.

Traditional media tours are used for book promotions, movie openings, new product unveilings, and industry breakthroughs. These tours take a great deal of planning and preparation. The opening of a movie and the publication of a book are events that are planned and scheduled months in advance, giving public communication professionals time to plan and arrange a nationwide tour. Traditional media tours are also used in the wake of a crisis to reestablish trust and goodwill among the public. Unfortunately, because traditional tours take such a long time to prepare, they are not the ideal vehicles for dealing with an emergency situation.

When an organization has to deal with a crisis, an SMT is more appropriate than a traditional media tour. SMTs do what traditional media tours cannot—happen quickly. It is possible for a spokesperson of an organization to be speaking to news media outlets across the country within hours of a disaster.

SMTs are not used solely for emergency situations. These tours are now being used more frequently to replace traditional tours and promotions. They are also used to encourage fundraising, elicit sponsorship, address strikes and labor activities, and announce new products. SMTs are utilized by a variety of different organizations, including large corporations, communications firms, government agencies, and advocacy and nonprofit organizations.

Sometimes these organizations use media tours to promote issues that don't fit the definition of news. Successful media tours should always highlight newsworthy messages such as important announcements of public concern, new research, original inventions, or product launches. Organizations often develop a news angle to tie in to their issue to eliminate the appearance of a staged promotional event.

How Do They Help?

Media tours allow local news media outlets the opportunity to conduct interviews of international and national public interest—interviews that they most likely would not have the budget to conduct otherwise. These tours provide organizations the chance to reach out to communities and nations that they are often unable to reach on a one-on-one basis, gaining news coverage and reaching untapped markets. Media tours accomplish more than traditional video or print news releases because they allow reporters to ask questions and receive immediate answers from the spokesperson. Whereas some news directors are wary of prepackaged broadcast pieces such as video news releases or radio actualities, they are more comfortable with media tours because the tours allow news organizations to get the story for themselves rather than accepting the version provided by the sponsoring organization.

SMTs have the added benefit of being relatively inexpensive and timely. These tours commence as soon as satellite time is secured, which can happen in a matter of hours, and they are a much less expensive endeavor than traditional city-to-city traveling media tours.

What Are the Pitfalls?

Traditional media tours are constrained by time because they cannot be planned overnight, and they are expensive because of the amount of travel involved. A traditional media tour takes a lot of planning and manpower that exceed the budgets of many organizations.

While SMTs do not involve as much planning as traditional media tours, their spontaneity is sometimes a problem. If a spokesperson is not properly prepared, the interview can look unprofessional. Even well-planned satellite tours have limits: in a largely technology-dependent society, there are still some outlets that do not have access or funding to link to satellites in order to download images.

How Should They Look?

Process and Format

Prior to the logistical planning stage of a media tour, a budget must be prepared by a PR professional and reviewed by the client or management. Any media tour, traditional or satellite, involves substantial costs, although satellite tours are less expensive. A finalized budget that fits both the need for news coverage or publicity and the financial situation of the organization is critical to the planning stage. The cost of media tours depends on location, props, visuals, length of interviews, speakers' fees, hotels, rental cars, satellite time, studio times, and more. These costs are carefully calculated ahead of time to ensure that the media tour will be a success. After the costs are assessed and research has been gathered and analyzed, the sponsoring organization must narrowly define its key messages and target audience.

Next, the targeted media should be identified. The number of targeted media should be limited to strategically key markets. It is unrealistic to target any other media because the costs and logistical planning would be prohibitive.

The preparation of a spokesperson is one of the most important steps in any media tour. An effective spokesperson should be more a newsmaker and less an organization representative. In order to be effective, a spokesperson should be thoroughly prepared to answer difficult and probing questions on a wide variety of topics related to the organization's message. The best way to familiarize newsmakers and spokespersons with the media tour format is to have them participate in media training exercises, such as mock interviews that are recorded and played back for their review. This exposes them to a variety of situations that they may encounter during a tour. Media training also focuses on tactics that will make the newsmaker a more effective interview subject. Strategies focusing on body language, eye contact, dress, and message delivery can have a big impact on the success of the messages being conveyed.

Media relations professionals need to contact the targeted media to inform them of the upcoming tour. Making pitch and follow-up calls allows the communicator the opportunity to provide the media with relevant information. In the case of a traditional tour, the news media should be informed about the date and time the spokesperson is available to be interviewed. For a satellite tour, the media should be informed of available time windows and the allotted length for the segment. Final preparations for the tour can begin after the logistical plans have been outlined.

The goal of every SMT is to make it seem as if two people are in the same room having a discussion. This is accomplished by setting up a spokesperson or newsmaker in one central broadcast studio to be interviewed by reporters from potentially all over the world. Usually these interview sessions are scheduled into five- to fifteen-minute windows. During these allotted segments, the video and sound image of the spokesperson are transmitted directly to the news station through a satellite transponder. Simultaneously, the reporter's questions are transmitted through the telephone lines into the earpiece of the spokesperson. What the viewer sees is an uninterrupted dialogue between the reporter and the newsmaker, as if they were actually having the discussion in person.

If the representatives of an organization decide to use an SMT, there are many additional elements that they can use to supplement the tour. **B-roll**, or raw video footage, usually accompanies the SMT hookup. The receiving news organization can use such components to enhance the interview and resulting stories. B-roll should be sent to stations prior to the interview in order for reporters to be able to coordinate the footage and the questions.

An organization must always remain flexible when trying to reserve satellite time. As more and more organizations are using SMTs, the number of windows is becoming limited. International times vary, so flexibility is key.

A traditional media tour also requires a great deal of flexibility. Traditional tours involve a spokesperson going to various news media outlets to participate in face-to-face interviews with reporters. Because the daily news agenda is always changing, it is possible for a spokesperson to get "bumped" from an interview in favor of important breaking news. In this case, alternative times for an interview should be negotiated. Other important issues involved in a traditional media tour include city selection and scheduling, hotel reservations, and maintaining the agreed-upon time slot for the interview.

Did They Work?

Media tours can be successful only if they are well prepared and thoroughly planned. Organizations evaluate success by examining a number of different elements. For traditional media tours that include the print media, a good source for evaluation is how often and how in depth the media covered the issue. The number of column inches devoted to an organization's particular cause is most likely a direct result of how well its spokesperson delivered the message. Clipping services (see Appendix A) can be hired to help with this process. These services monitor newspapers from all over the world and clip articles that contain specific criteria selected by the organization.

Broadcast tours, both traditional and satellite, can also be monitored and evaluated. The number of times a story runs on air and the length of the segment, as well as the slant of the story, are all ways to measure the tour's success. Companies such as Nielson and Arbitron track audience size electronically, providing ratings for television and radio. These companies assess the number of people watching or listening to a program at a given time.

In addition to the amount of media coverage, organizations review various indicators after the tour. Indicators such as a rise in stock prices or significant increases in membership, sales numbers, telephone calls, or the number of people assisted will indicate that the target audience has received the intended messages conveyed through the media tour.

Putting PR into Practice

A historic, and perhaps transforming, event is happening in U.S. public education. For the first time, 44 states have agreed to adopt common core standards in math and English language arts (ELA) that will ensure that all American students who graduate from high school are college- and career-ready. That is, they will be ready to succeed in college or be trained for careers. These are not national or federal standards. The standards will reflect the work of the individual states, but, for the first time in the United States, if students leave one state to live in another or even one county to live in another, instruction will be comparable and students will not fall behind. Also, the standards are more rigorous, providing U.S. public-school students with K–12 schools on a par with their international competition. Some political entities see the states as a federal intervention while others say that not all students need to go to college.

Your client is a corporate foundation headquartered in Connecticut that is well known for its public education philanthropy and supports public school districts and the movement toward common core standards. The foundation wants to help families, communities, and businesses understand the importance of supporting the standards. The two principals of the foundation want to conduct a media tour. Although they are busy executives, they travel domestically and abroad, as well.

1. You could view the new standards as a new product launch. What steps would you follow to develop a media tour?
2. What would you need to know about the 44 participating states?
3. What media would you target? Why?
4. Where would you try to appear in person? On conference calls? Through SMTs? Why?

Chapter 9 — New Media

What Are They?

Want to learn about new media? Ask a tween. Young people have been quick to embrace the various new communication channels, even as a new one seems to emerge every day—often leaving it to PR professionals to play catch-up. But it is not just young people who are using new media. In 2011 more than 272,000,000 North Americans had access to the Internet—that's more than 78% of the population. Worldwide, almost 30% of the world's population is online.

New media, sometimes referred to as interactive media, is a rapidly evolving, loosely defined area of communication that has become increasingly important. As opposed to traditional media, which encompasses newspapers, magazines, radio, and television, new media harnesses the power of various forms of electronic communication—most importantly, the Internet. Blogs, podcasts, online video, and social networks are among the most popular forms of new media.

New media are interactive because they give users the chance to add or manipulate content, provide feedback, and engage with others as part of a social network. New media has revolutionized the way many people think about and access information. People can access information at any time, using a variety of devices (e.g., computers, handheld devices). Those who wish to disseminate information have a vast array of options for the creation, publication, and distribution of content—often for minimal cost. The result is a media landscape dense with content from sources that range from trusted experts to outright liars and scammers. Your challenge as a PR professional is to cut through all the other messages and create a relationship with your target audience.

You should remember a few key characteristics when considering the use of new media:

- **Limited Control of Messages**—An important part of new media is user-generated content (UGC), which is content or material created by a user and uploaded to the Internet. This can include commenting on a product, responding to a newspaper article, posting a profile on Facebook, or posting a video on YouTube. While you may launch a profile on Facebook for your organization or client, your "friends" may not stay on message with their postings.

- **Content Matters**—Surveys of Internet users emphasize the importance of the quality and relevance of content. Content must also reflect the interests of users. The importance of quality content is a key concept that PR professionals should understand and convey to clients. Time, effort, and resources are required to create high-quality content. For example, a successful blog may require the services of a full-time writer. Stories must be carefully researched to ensure accuracy. While it is true that information can be uploaded to the Internet at no cost and that the production quality of videos and podcasts is not as critical online as with some other channels, use of new media is not necessarily a cheap option.

- **Make It Clear**—Transparency is important in the world of new media. When using new media for your organization or client, you should always fully disclose whom you represent. For example, if you are paying a blogger to write about your issue, this financial relationship should be disclosed. Failure to do so can seriously impact your online credibility.

- **It's Back—Postings Can Live Forever**—With new media, the 24-hour news cycle is irrelevant. Stories can "go viral," meaning that they can spin out of control. Online discussions can stretch out for weeks and resurface when you least expect.

- **Build Relationship**—New media is about relationships—building and maintaining relationships is extremely important to users. Successful networks, once established, can be leveraged in the future. Use of new media should be considered a long-term endeavor (with a corresponding strategy) and not a series of unrelated forays into the online world.

To varying degrees, businesses and organizations are using new media to reach their audiences. In 2007 the Society for New Communications Research, with support from the Institute for Public Relations, conducted a survey of "social media power users," who were identified as "communications professionals with a deep knowledge and heavy usage pattern of social media tools." Of those surveyed, 78% used blogs, 63% used online video, 56% used social networks, and 49% used podcasts in their communications efforts. Over half of those surveyed reported that new media were becoming increasingly valuable in their efforts. Use of new media was identified as a core element of their communication strategy by 27% of respondents.

Because the use of new media is evolving so quickly, you should consider working with someone who specializes in new media if you choose to use these communication channels to disseminate your messages. A specialist can help you to assess your needs, establish goals, and identify the most appropriate channels.

Who Uses New Media and Who Gets Them?

Because of the rapid changes that take place in cyberspace—something that is hot today can be totally passé tomorrow—it is important to keep up with the latest usage statistics. But as we know, there is always a lag in usage data. The snapshot provided will not necessarily reflect the current environment. This said, it is possible to get a general idea of the popularity of various new media channels.

Ketchum, in partnership with the USC Annenberg Strategic Public Relations Center, conducted the *Media Myths and Realities* survey each year from 2006 to 2008. The survey examined consumers' use of more than 40 different media channels. Of respondents, 26% reported using social networks, 24% used blogs, 11% used videocasts, and 7% used podcasts. Traditional media remained the predominant source of information—65% of respondents reported using major network television news and 62% reported using local television news—but these channels dropped in popularity from year to year. Notably, advice from family and friends is a major source of information relied upon by 47% of respondents. This credibility of family and friends has implications when one considers how many "friends" a person may have on Facebook.

The *Media Myths and Realities* survey in particular looked at the habits of "influencers," the 10 to 15% of the population who initiate changes in their community or society through a variety of activities. These influencers were more likely to use many of the new media channels.

What Do They Do?

Some of the major social media channels at the time of writing are listed below. There will no doubt be additions to this list in the time it takes to put this book into final production.

Social Networks

Social network sites (SNS) are forums for people with shared interests—be they personal (family and friends), professional (industry- or networking-focused), or reflective of a specific interest, such as a hobby or the work of a particular artist. Social networks such as Bebo, Facebook, LinkedIn, and MySpace are among the most well-known online networks. While SNSs are often perceived as most effective in reaching young people, this is not necessarily the case. More than 50% of MySpace users are older than 35, and LinkedIn reports an average user of 39 years old with an annual income of $139,000.

As the name implies, these sites are all about networks. Users post profiles that include a list of their contacts or "friends." Users can send messages to their friends, whether privately to individual friends or to the group as a whole. Beyond profiles, friending, and messaging, SNSs vary greatly in their features. Some allow users to share videos and photos, use built-in blogging technology, or instant-message other users.

Using SNSs can be a great way to promote your organization, issue, or product. There are some important rules to remember:

- **Engage**—the point of social networking is to participate in the conversation. Leave comments and make connections with other users. Those who observe but don't participate are known as "lurkers."

- **Contribute**—Share information that is of value. Don't just promote your product.

- **Monitor**—Track what is being said about your specific topic or organization. Google Alerts is a useful tool for monitoring content based on a query by specific topics (http://www.google.com/alerts). By tracking this information, you can work to ensure that it is accurate by participating in the discussion.

- **Be Productive**—Have a clear plan about what you want to achieve from your efforts. It is easy to get sucked into the networking process and devote (or even waste) a significant amount of time.

- **Be Interesting**—Think of ways you can provide users with something new. Consider using multimedia tools, such as webcasts or podcasts

Blogs

A **blog**, short for Web log, is an online posting. Blogs are often closely associated with the author. Some blogs are purely an expression of opinion while others blend facts with a personal perspective. Bloggers tend to post regular entries, which are often displayed in reverse chronological order. Readers are encouraged to add their comments. A Universal McCann study of social media trends conducted in April 2008 found that 73% of active online users have read a blog and 45% have started their own blogs.

Bloggers are a varied lot. For example, the executive director of an organization may use a blog as an advocacy tool to promote the priorities of the organization. Others use blogs to tell the world about their personal experiences. A new mom may write a blog about life with baby, and a person training for a marathon may regularly post about the training process.

There are several key elements to a successful blog. First, a blog should encourage dialogue. Expect both positive and negative comments and be prepared to respond to both. In terms of content, select topics that you are both passionate and knowledgeable about—care about what you write. Since building up an audience of regular readers is a goal of blogging, plan to post on a regular basis. People will lose interest if you are sporadic. Finally, from a PR perspective, it is important to remember that even though authors of blogs should let their personalities show through in their writing, they should stay on message. A blog is not license for the authors to say anything they want.

Wikis

A **wiki** is a type of Web site built through collaboration. Users contribute the content, via their own browsers, which is edited, updated, or even changed completely by successive users. Some wikis are open to all Internet users, while others require membership or specific qualification to participate. The technology behind wikis makes collaborative writing via the Internet relatively easy. Wikipedia (http://www.wikipedia.org), an online encyclopedia, is a wiki that has become extremely popular, with more than 3,370,000 articles posted in English.

Microsites

Microsites, also known as landing pages, minisites, or weblets, are a single page or cluster of pages that supplements the primary Web site. They usually focus on a single event, cause, product, or service. Microsites can be added to and removed from the main site as necessary, which makes them a useful tool for PR professionals who wish to keep journalists and other stakeholders up to date about an issue or event.

Microsites can be used to drive visitors to other social media for additional information. They also can provide an opportunity for the user to take action, such as by donating to a cause. Because they can be uploaded and removed, all while the primary site remains unchanged, microsites are popular with freelance writers, artists, and designers, who can demonstrate their projects, portfolios, and capabilities by adding and removing samples of their work.

Widgets

A **widget** is a small program that can be easily added to a Web site, blog, or profile page to add an element of interactive content. For example, the content-related ad that runs across of the top of a Web site is a widget. The use of widgets is more allied to traditional media, in that the content is controlled by the publisher but the user can put the content on his or her own page, such as a blog or social network profile. Technically, widgets are a form of content syndication. They are used extensively as a popular form of news distribution.

It can be a challenge to find widgets appropriate for the content on your site. Widget galleries are databases of widgets, searchable by category. They allow users to create, distribute, and find and install widgets on their start pages, Web sites, blogs, or profiles.

Twitter

Twitter is a social networking and microblogging service. The users of Twitter are called "twitterers." Twitter allows twitterers to "tweet" to one another. Tweets are 140 character messages—allowing twitterers to send a short update on any topic to their audience at any time. Since its creation in 2006, Twitter has grown in popularity and now has over 100 million users worldwide.

While Twitter has gained a reputation for being somewhat frivolous (e.g., users have been known to send tweets telling what they are eating for lunch), it can be very useful for keeping in touch with an interested audience and directing them to other sources for more information. For example, members of Congress use Twitter to keep their constituents up to date, sending tweets from the House or Senate floor to let constituents know how they voted or their reaction to an issue.

What Are the Pitfalls?

Some of the potential pitfalls related to using new media channels are mentioned in the discussion above. Loss of credibility is always a looming possibility when using new media. Most importantly, always be transparent and open with your audience. If you represent a client, let users know whom you represent and that you are being paid. If you pay or provide a sample to a blogger, make sure the blogger discloses this information. Failing to be forthright with your audience can result in a severe backlash that could undermine your Web-related efforts for many years.

As with all public communication efforts, choosing a target audience for your new media communications will depend on the organization's goals and the research conducted to gain insight into your audience's interests. It is important to carefully target your messages. Just as audiences loathe spam emails, users of social media do not want to be bothered by irrelevant information. You and your client will lose credibility and weaken your relationships if you fail to provide information that is interesting and useful to your audience.

Finally, one of the most important aspects of new media is the relationships that result. Even though you may never meet in person the people with whom you communicate, it is important to nurture the relationships that you develop online. Politeness, responsiveness, and dependability can go a long way in building and maintaining a useful and effective network of contacts.

Did They Work?

To assess the effectiveness of PR efforts, you must be able to relate cause to effect. Unfortunately, most PR professionals who are actively using new media acknowledge that this is a challenge. It is therefore all the more important to identify clear goals for your new media efforts and to establish a baseline measure.

There are social media analytics consultants and organizations that can help you track the impact of your Web site and your efforts on Twitter, Facebook, YouTube, and other new media channels. They offer a range of services at various price points. Just as with initiating your new media activities, you can benefit from consulting with professionals who specialize in new media in order to track the results of your communication efforts. These professionals will be up to speed on the latest developments in tracking new media efforts.

Putting PR into Practice

Establishing a new media strategy requires strategic thinking and the assistance of a new media expert. Using social media is not necessarily a strategy for every organization but can be used when an organization is coordinating a public event such as a conference.

1. Ask the following strategic questions.
   a. Is your client currently on the Web?
   b. Who are its online audiences?
   c. With what social networking sites (SNS) does your client currently engage? How regularly?
2. Create an online profile for your client.

3. List the opportunities available to your client to begin engagement in a social media strategy.

4. In what specific way can your client bring information and content to SNS?

5. Talk to your client about the possibility of talking to a social media expert to help create a strategy.

An *Example Gallery* for New Media begins on the following page.

Example Gallery
Social Networking Site

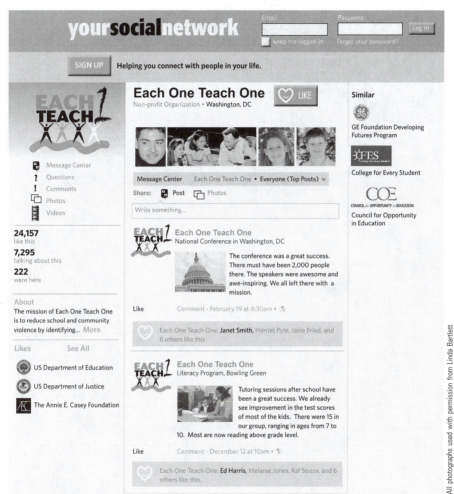

Example Gallery
Social Networking and Blogging Site

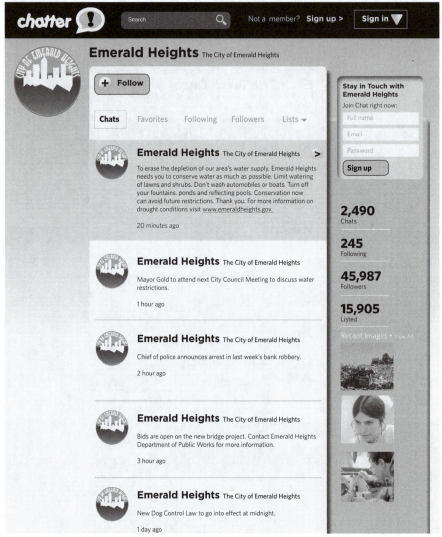

chatter

Search

Not a member? **Sign up >**   **Sign in** ▼

Emerald Heights The City of Emerald Heights

➕ **Follow**

Chats   Favorites   Following   Followers   Lists ▼

Emerald Heights The City of Emerald Heights   **>**

To erase the depletion of our area's water supply, Emerald Heights needs you to conserve water as much as possible. Limit watering of lawns and shrubs. Don't wash automobiles or boats. Turn off your fountains. ponds and reflecting pools. Conservation now can avoid future restrictions. Thank you. For more information on drought conditions visit www.emeraldheights.gov.

20 minutes ago

Emerald Heights The City of Emerald Heights

Mayor Gold to attend next City Council Meeting to discuss water restrictions.

1 hour ago

Emerald Heights The City of Emerald Heights

Chief of police announces arrest in last week's bank robbery.

2 hour ago

Emerald Heights The City of Emerald Heights

Bids are open on the new bridge project. Contact Emerald Heights Department of Public Works for more information.

3 hour ago

Emerald Heights The City of Emerald Heights

New Dog Control Law to go into effect at midnight.

1 day ago

Stay in Touch with Emerald Heights

Join Chat right now:

Full name

Email

Password

Sign up

2,490
Chats

245
Following

45,987
Followers

15,905
Listed

Recent Images • View All

Watching the School Board | Emerald Heights

by Willis Bennett on August 17, 2012

 ☆☆☆☆☆   (i) 30 Votes

The number one and two finishers in the Emerald Heights school board election this week have some interesting views about schools and education policy.

Patterson has the standard libertarian take and Bishop is known for launching a charter school. But the guy who didn't place at all has been regarded as something of a leader on education. When asked by education "experts" who has the best background for our schools, the answer was most often Chow, consistently leading the pack. What does this tell us about the school board we have now? What should we be on the lookout for in the future?

Remember: Many school board candidates don't care about the state of our public schools. They are launching political careers.

SUBSCRIBE

BLOG STATS

32,876 hits

SEARCH OUR BLOG

[   ] Search

RECENT POSTS

Jane + Fred | Emerald Heights

Maurice Chow |Emerald Heights

Candace Williams | New York City

Howard + Edna | Washington, DC

Vanessa Jones | Rockville, MD

Warren Brown | Richmond, VA

Bill + Denise | Washington, DC

Harvey + Zach | Washington, DC

Bootsie | Emerald Heights

Diesel | Ft. Howard, CO

AP Style — A Primer

This chapter is an introduction to AP style and a summary of some AP style rules. "The Associated Press Stylebook" is far more comprehensive than what this chapter attempts to condense. Its most recent edition includes more than 5,000 entries. For a complete guide to AP style, you should consult the most recent edition of the stylebook.

Introduction

"The Associated Press Stylebook and Briefing on Media Law" had humble beginnings as 60 pages of compiled suggestions; it has since undergone major revisions in 1977 prior to publication in 1978, more revisions in 1986, and complete updates annually since 2008. It is an indispensable tool for American journalists, public relations professionals and students of both fields. It is one of the most important tools a public relations professional can own. The foreword to its most recent edition says it well: "Far more than a collection of rules, the book became part dictionary, part encyclopedia, part textbook—an eclectic source of information for writers and editors of any publication." The "Stylebook" provides all of the writing conventions used by professional journalists, including abbreviations, definitions, capitalization, spelling, grammar, numerals and usage. Chapters on social media, food, business, sports and punctuation assist you in writing about everything from an avatar (no, not the movie) to zest and from acquisitions to yearlings—punctuated properly and with consistency and decorum.

No, as PR professionals, you are not expected to write news articles, but you are expected to follow the guidelines professional journalists follow when you develop PR media. Why? There are two very good reasons. Often, your ultimate target audience is reached through the news media. As strategic practitioners, you want to communicate with journalists in the manner that makes them most comfortable and most inclined to discover more and write about your projects. Also, frankly, it is a matter of respect. Respecting the culture and customs of others is something you should seek to do as a professional.

Secondly, PR products are often the result of many writers, editors and copyeditors. Having prescribed rules and guidelines helps limit the opportunity for mistakes and helps ensure accuracy, brevity, clarity and consistency of copy. As a PR professional, you have to care about good writing.

That said: Many journalists are not as concerned about the style question as others. The "Stylebook" acknowledges that some journalists have a passion for it, feeling that style questions are really important, whereas others think that consistency adds to reading ease and others debate the "official" rulings. While it is not the final arbiter of many style questions, the "AP Stylebook" is a definitive compilation of correct style for journalists.

There are, of course, other recognized stylebooks of great reputation. If you have not encountered them in undergraduate work, you will run into some them as graduate students: "The Chicago Manual of Style," now in its 16th edition; The American Psychological Association's guide ("APA Style," 7th edition); "The New York Times Manual of Style and Usage." Also, you can consult the "British Times Online Style Guide" and the Web-based "AP Stylebook." Despite its eccentricities, the one indispensable reference work for American PR professionals, journalists and journalism students remains "The AP Stylebook," updated annually and available in both print and electronic forms.

Organized alphabetically, "The AP Stylebook" is an easy reference guide. It also refers you to other sources. For example, under the entry **company name**, you are referred to the major stock exchanges, but it lists 125 major U.S. companies and 65 major non-U.S. companies. Here are some basic rules and important guidelines for writing well.

Abbreviations and Acronyms

As a general rule, "The Associated Press Stylebook" cautions against creating "alphabet soup," but it acknowledges the need to use "universally recognized" abbreviations and some others depending upon context. For example, Dr., Gov., Lt. Gov., Mr., Mrs., Rep., the Rev. and Sen. are required before a person's full name when they occur outside a direct quotation. Other acronyms and abbreviations are acceptable but not required, although many are easily recognizable, such as FBI, CIA and GOP. When used with dates and numerals, abbreviate A.D., B.C., a.m., p.m., No. and certain months when used with the day of the month (Sept. 11).

Abbreviate names of states when used after the names of cities and towns, but spell out when referring to the state generally ("He lives in Silver Spring, Md." and "She lives in Maryland"). Insert a comma between a city and state and behind the state unless it ends a sentence or is a dateline (Rehoboth, Del., is a small resort). States can be eliminated in the case of major cities when names alone are adequate (Atlanta, Boston, Chicago, Cincinnati, Cleveland, Denver, Dallas, Denver, Detroit, Honolulu, Los Angeles, Milwaukee, Minneapolis, Philadelphia, Seattle, etc.). Eight U.S. states are never abbreviated in headlines and text: Alaska, Hawaii, Idaho, Iowa, Maine, Ohio, Texas and Utah. All other states can be abbreviated:

Ala.	Fla.	Md.	Neb.	N.D.	Tenn.
Ariz.	Ga.	Mass.	Nev.	Okla.	Vt.
Ark.	Ill.	Mich.	N.H.	Ore.	Va.
Calif.	Ind.	Minn.	N.J.	Pa.	Wash.
Colo.	Kan.	Miss.	N.M.	R.I.	W.Va.
Conn.	Ky.	Mo.	N.Y.	S.C.	Wis.
Del.	La.	Mont.	N.C.	S.D.	Wyo.

All states have U.S. postal code abbreviations that should be used only when using a full address, including ZIP code.

Addresses

If a street name is a number, spell out and capitalize First through Ninth and use numerals for 10th and higher (8915 Second Ave. or 125th St.). Always use numerals for building and residential number addresses (5 Dale Drive). Abbreviate directional cues and Ave., Blvd. and St. only when used with a numbered address (2215 S. Woodside Ave.). If the street name or directional cue is used without a numbered address, it should be capitalized and spelled out (West Park Avenue). Always spell out other words such as alley, drive, court and road. Use periods for P.O. Box numbers.

Ages

Always use figures for ages, including one through nine. If the age is used as an adjective or a noun, it should be hyphenated (a 66-year-old woman; Social Security is for 65-year-olds). Do not use apostrophes when describing an age range (a woman in her 60s).

Capitalization

Proper Nouns

The names of people, places or things that uniquely identify should be capitalized (Celeste, Deborah, New York, France).

Proper Names

Capitalize common nouns such as association, foundation, north and party when they are an integral part of the full names of people, places or things (National Education Association, GE Foundation, North Dakota, Democratic Party).

Titles

Capitalize formal titles when they appear before a person's name, but lowercase titles if they are informal, appear without a person's name, follow a person's name or are set off before a name by commas (President Barack Obama; the governor from Georgia; Senator Harry Reid). Also, lowercase adjectives that designate the status of a title. If a title is long, place it after the person's name, or set it off with commas before the person's name (former President George W. Bush; Joel Klein, chancellor of the New York Department of Education, spoke first.)

Titles of Books, Periodicals, Operas, Plays and Other Types of Compositions

Capitalize the principal words in these titles, including prepositions and conjunctions of four or more letters. Conjunctions of fewer than four letters should be capitalized only if they are the first or last word of the title. Most Web sites and application names are capitalized.

Measures

Use numerals when writing about measurements such as height, distance or length, and spell out words such as feet, inches and yards. When writing about height, distance or other dimensions, use figures and spell out words such as feet, miles, etc. (She is 6-foot-1; She ran 35 yards; Her porch is 30 feet long).

Numerals

The figures 1, 2, 10, 101 and so on and the corresponding words—one, two, ten, one hundred one and so on—are called cardinal numbers. The terms 1st, 2nd, 10th, 101st (first, second, tenth, one hundred first) and so on are called ordinal numbers.

Never begin a sentence with a numeral, except for sentences that begin with a year (Six hundred people joined; Five of them were alumnae; 2011 marks 10 years).

Roman numerals should be used to designate wars and to show sequences for people (World War II, Elizabeth II, King Harold V).

Spell out the first through ninth ordinal numbers and use figures for 10th and above when describing order in time or location (second base, 11th stop). Some ordinal numbers, such as those indicating political or geographic order, should use figures in all cases (6th precinct, 8th District).

Consult individual entries in "The Associated Press Stylebook" for cardinal numbers. If no usage is specified, spell out numbers below 10 and use numerals for numbers 10 and above. (The movie was nominated for 11 Oscars and won five)

Use numerals when referring to money. Spell out cents in lowercase and use numerals for less than a dollar (10 cents, 99 cents). Use the $ sign and decimals for larger sums ($1.50, $3.25). For amounts of $1 million or more, spell the words million, billion and trillion and use only two decimal spaces ($8 million, $9.5 billion, $6.42 trillion).

Spell out the numbers one through nine. Use Arabic numerals for numbers above nine. For ages and percentages, always use Arabic numerals, even for numbers less than 10.

For large numbers, use a hyphen to connect a word ending in y to another word (twenty-seven, one hundred thirty-three, sixty-six thousand five hundred ninety-three).

Spell out casual expressions (Thanks a million).

Proper names: use words or numerals according to an organization's practice (3M, Twentieth Century Fund, Big Ten).

Punctuation Marks

The "AP Stylebook" has an entire chapter that presents guidelines for the use of punctuation marks. The use of correct punctuation is crucial to good writing. Incorrect punctuation can change meaning significantly. Below are just a few of the most commonly used.

Ampersand

Do not use it unless it is a part of a company name or a composition title.

Apostrophe

For possessives, add 's to plural nouns not ending in S (the men's restroom, the alumni's contribution). Add 's to singular nouns (the state's right, the woman's purse). Add 's even if the word ends in the sound of S (Xerox's profits, Buzz's car, justice's speech). Add only an apostrophe to plural nouns ending in S and proper names ending in S (the decision was based on states' rights, the United States' economy).

Colon

Use a colon at the end of a sentence to begin a list, texts, quotes, etc. (The foundation has specific interests: scalability, efficiency and economy). Capitalize the first word at the end of the colon if it begins a complete sentence (The foundation chairman was clear: There would be no new grants this year).

Colons go outside of quotation marks unless they are a part of the quotation itself.

When the time of day is important, use figures, but spell out noon and midnight and use a colon to separate hours from minutes, but do not use :00 (3 p.m., 3:30).

Comma

Use commas to separate items in a series, but do not use commas before a conjunction in a simple series (The car is red, fast and dangerous; He has been married to Susan, Eileen and Lenore). Use a comma before a conjunction in a complex series of elements (The foundation is interested in the scalability of the program, the efficiency of the use of data, and the economic impact on the district).

Commas must set off nonessential clauses and phrases. The same is true for introductory clauses. Essential clauses and phrases must not be set off from the rest of the sentence. Use a comma to introduce a direct, one-sentence quotation (Wendell said, "She was in no position to bargain"). Use a colon to introduce quotations of more than one sentence.

Quotation Marks

Use quotation marks (open-quote and close-quote marks) to indicate the exact words of a speaker or writer.

Use quotation marks in running dialogue, opening and closing the remarks of each person.

Use quotation marks around the titles of books, songs, television and radio shows, computer games, poems, lectures, speeches, operas and works of art ("La Bohème," "True Grit").

Do not use quotations around the names of magazines, newspapers, the Bible or books that are catalogues of reference materials.

Commas and periods go within quotation marks.

English Language Usage and Grammar

Accept, except: Accept means to receive, approve or agree, while except means to exclude.

Adverse, averse: Adverse means unfavorable. Averse means reluctant.

Affect, effect: Affect (v) means to influence. Affect as a noun should be avoided. Effect (v) means to cause. Effect (n) means results.

All right and never alright.

Allude, refer: Allude is to speak of something without mentioning it. Refer is to mention it directly.

Allusion, illusion: An allusion is an indirect reference. Illusion means an unreal or false impression.

Among, between: Generally, between introduces two items; among, more than two.

Average, mean, median, norm: Average and mean are the result of adding a series of numbers and diving the sum by the number of quantities/cases. Median is the middle number of points in a series: the median grade in the group 60, 65, 90, 98, 92 is 90. Norm implies the standard of average performance.

Awhile, a while: Awhile is an adverb and a while is a noun.

Back up (v), **backup** (n and adj)

Blast off (v), **blastoff** (n and adj)

Build up (v), **buildup** (n and adj)

Capital, capitol: Capital is the city where a seat of government resides. Capitol is a building.

Check in, check out (v); **check-in, check-out** (n and adj)

Complement, compliment: Complement (n and v) denotes completeness or a process of supplementation. Compliment (n and v) denotes praise or courtesy.

Every day (adv), **everyday** (adj)

Farther, further: Farther is physical distance. Further refers to degree.

Fewer, less: Fewer for individual items and less for bulk and quantity.

Forego, forgo: Forego means to go before. Forgo means to abstain from.

Incredible, incredulous: Incredible means unbelievable. Incredulous means skeptical.

Lay, lie: Lay (v) is the action and takes an object (I will lay the money on the counter). The past tense is laid (I laid the money on the counter). Lie is the state of reclining on a horizontal plane (I will lie down on the bed). The past tense is lay (I lay down on the bed all day yesterday). When lie (v) means to make a false statement, its past tense is lied.

Nonprofit not non-profit

Overall

Prime time (n), **prime-time** (adj)

Principal (n and adj) means someone or something is first in rank order. **Principle** (n) means a fundamental truth.

That, which: Both pronouns are used for inanimate objects or animals without names. That is used for essential clauses and without commas (Stop at the house down the street that has black shutters). Use which for nonessential clauses and use commas (The house down the street, which sold last year, is for sale).

Under way rarely underway

Who's, whose: Who's is a contraction for who is (Who's there?). Whose is a possessive (Whose coat is this?).

Who, whom: Who is a pronoun used to refer to humans or animals and is always the subject of a sentence. (Who left the door open? The child who lived next door left the door open). Whom is for objects of a verb or preposition (To whom did you address the letter? The child for whom she is waiting left the door open).

Word-of-mouth (n and adj)

Zero, xeros

Chapter 10

Newsletters

What Are They?

When an organization wants to start a newsletter, there is good news and bad news for those of us who get to serve as editors. There's good news? Yes. A newsletter is one of the most effective and versatile means of internal and external communication available to an organization. Isn't there always bad news? Yes. The newsletter rarely gets the priority—time and attention—it deserves from an organization's executives. And everyone wants to kill the messenger—or newsletter editor (again, that's us)—because we have to deliver the difficult message. There are rules about publishing a newsletter, and we have to adhere to them if we want the benefits. Newsletters must appear regularly and on time. This means that copy, quotes, photographs, and calendars have to be approved promptly.

These documents are creative outlets for organizations to convey a lot of useful and important information to a target audience. Employee, member, community, special-interest subscriber, and advocacy newsletters are among the most popular types.

- **Employee newsletters** directly address employees in a fairly informal and conversational tone. They are formatted like a short newspaper and include brief articles and features. Unlike internal office memoranda and organizational briefs, these publications disseminate information with a human-interest tone and quality. The job of the public communication writer is to give employees a sense of belonging while informing them about the inner workings of the organization. These newsletters cover a wide range of topics, including company finances, client and customer information, new program initiatives, employee accomplishments, and general news from within the organization.

- **Member newsletters** help to keep members of clubs, organizations, and associations informed about important news, upcoming events, educational opportunities, and other important membership information. Member newsletters encourage member participation and introduce new members into the network.

- **Community newsletters** are usually geared toward people who live in the same town, neighborhood, development, or building. The primary goal of these publications is to foster a sense of community and involvement among neighbors and to better their quality of living. Articles usually highlight important news that may affect the neighborhood, include a calendar of events, and provide other neighborhood information.

- **Advocacy newsletters** present information about a specific topic or point of view. While this type of newsletter can be produced as a single publication, it can be published in conjunction with employee, member, or community newsletters. The primary purpose is to promote a specific opinion and to gain and maintain public support and activism.

- **Special-interest subscriber newsletters** are designed for groups whose connections are based on common interests. These publications can be related to hobbies, trades, and political or religious affiliation. They often provide information on such topics as health, travel, economics, and computers. Special-interest newsletters are primarily purchased by the audience and should contain enough useful information for readers to feel the publication is well worth the money spent.

Newsletters provide an opportunity to convey a variety of messages to a target audience in a recurring format and are produced and distributed weekly, monthly, quarterly, or yearly. They usually carry the same overall themes and messages in every issue, but the story and feature focus should vary. The style and layout of newsletters remain consistent to ensure audience recognition. Maintaining newsletter identification by the target audience can occur only through extensive planning. Brainstorming and idea sessions happen months in advance to ensure that the final product gels with the previous issue.

The target audience depends on the type of newsletter. Target audiences include members of groups, associations, clubs, communities, and other member groups; employees of any organization; customers and clients; people who share special interests such as hobbies, political affiliations, or trades; and donors and philanthropists.

This chapter discusses format and style for hard-copy newsletters only. Electronic magazines and newsletters and other online publications are useful public relations and marketing tools. Many companies have developed software for creating electronic or online publications that can be found on the Internet.

What Do They Do?

Newsletters aim to reach a target audience and maintain that audience's attention in order to convey specific messages. Accomplishing this goal is not an easy task, but the task is much easier if the newsletter is carefully planned, has been extensively researched, and reflects and meets the needs of the audience.

Designers and writers must decide early in the planning stages whether the overall purpose of the newsletter will be to inform, entertain, or persuade the target audience. Sometimes these purposes are combined to create a multipurpose newsletter. The theme of the newsletter will be carried throughout the life of the publication. While newsletters can and must vary their ideas from issue to issue, the overall theme is always maintained.

Because of their size, newsletters often pick up where memoranda, letters, and bulletin boards leave off in providing information. They can explore a variety of topics in depth and focus on current issues in both a creative and insightful way. Also, unlike magazines, whose editorial calendars are often set in stone months in advance, newsletters can report on current stories and thus be more up to date because they are less restricted by editorial deadlines.

While information printed in newsletters can be found in other sources, newsletters provide the information in a uniquely concise but thorough manner. Newsletters provide many articles and features that are of interest to the target audience. Highly specialized newsletters are their audience's only source of information on the topics they highlight.

The objective of producing a newsletter is to create and maintain a lengthy relationship with the audience. Therefore, newsletters are serial publications. They are produced and distributed with the same frequency, whether it is weekly, monthly, quarterly, or yearly, and are generally assigned volume and issue numbers. Newsletters are expected to be reliable in terms of content, production, and distribution.

In addition to providing important information in a timely manner, newsletters incorporate a personal touch and human-interest element. This tone and style can be used in all types of newsletters. Including stories that identify with the human side of the audience helps the reader to better identify with the subject matter. Stories about fellow employees, members, and neighbors help the newsletter to gain credibility while creating an emotional connection between reader and newsletter.

How Do They Help?

Newsletters provide the optimum opportunity to relay lengthy creative messages to a target audience in a timely and recurring manner. They have the space it takes to delve into particular topics, allowing an organization to establish a relationship with its audience. A newsletter should be a predictable source of information that audiences can begin to depend on. Gaining the audience's trust with a newsletter also means gaining their trust with regard to the organization. Overall, a newsletter provides useful information in a unique way to a specific audience in a set time.

What Are the Pitfalls?

Newsletters are most successful when they are carefully planned. Their success may be limited if they are produced hastily and carelessly. The success of newsletters depends on timely production and delivery; design and content appropriate for the target audience; and accurate and well-conveyed messages.

Budget constraints also have an enormous impact on the effectiveness of newsletters. The budget is a critical factor when deciding on the frequency of publication, the length of the newsletter, graphics, paper stock, and the number of ink colors used.

Newsletters are generally not thought of as completely unbiased sources of information because they are commonly produced with a particular objective in mind. Therefore, fairness and presentation of the whole story are important to the success of a newsletter. If an audience begins to sense severely biased content and writing, it will lose trust in the newsletter content and stop reading.

What Should They Look Like?

Style Notes

Coming up with fresh new ideas while maintaining recurring themes and frameworks is one of the greatest challenges in designing an effective newsletter. This balancing act must take place amid a cast of writers, editors, designers, and printers—all trying to work together to create an effective document. There are a number of different stylistic elements to consider before the process can begin.

Hard-copy newsletters are produced in a variety of sizes. For organizations that want to encourage readers to maintain a reference file, the 8½″ × 11″ paper size is preferable because the sheets can be three-hole-punched in order to archive copies in binders. Hole-punching the newsletter prior to distribution can also send the nonverbal message that this document is important enough to preserve. For longer newsletters, organizations choose the 11″ × 17″ paper size, also known as tabloid. The tabloid size lends itself best to long articles, artwork, and photos.

Newsletters may be either horizontal or vertical in their direction, and they may use a two-, three-, or four-column format. Column choice is as much a nonverbal message as color or font size. Justified columns are more formal, while wider columns tend to give the newsletter a more relaxed feel. Photographs and other visuals within the columns need to fit the style of those columns and the theme of the overall newsletter. Big photos are limited to large formats, while small artwork fits small page sizes.

A newsletter should have a conversational or informal writing style. Complete adherence to journalistic writing styles is not required, but newsletter writers should borrow heavily from this genre. For instance, to avoid overwhelming the reader with a lot of type all at once, you should create short sentences and short paragraphs. This type of writing requires the KISS (keep it short and simple) method. It is important to use active voice and strong nouns and verbs—and to avoid the excessive use of adjectives, adverbs, and redundant phrases.

Newsletter articles borrow the **inverted pyramid style** (see Chapter 11) from journalism. This style puts key points in the **lead**, which is the opening one- or two-sentence paragraph. This allows for easy reading and editing. But this rule is not set in stone. Feature articles often utilize a delayed lead for effect. Newsletter editors should strive for a balance between news articles and feature articles in each issue to help create a well-rounded publication. Most articles are between 100 and 600 words, for a total of 2,000 words for a four-page newsletter.

Format

In the case of a standard four-page newsletter, each page has its own purpose, style, and characteristics. The following format describes the standard four-page newsletter; however, the descriptions can also be applied to longer formats. Generally, the front and back pages remain the same, while the inside pages follow the styles chosen for pages two and three.

Page One/Cover Page

This is the first element the audience sees. The goal of this page is to engage the audience with attractive visuals and catchy headlines. There are a few elements this page must include: the organization's logo, the volume number, the issue number, the date, and the title of the newsletter (also called the **banner**). Page one should also include a table of contents, or a teaser box, that indicates what stories are covered in the issue and on what page(s) they can be found. Two major stories should appear on the front page. These articles are usually the most important, relevant, and timely for the particular issue and can continue on additional pages so as not to overwhelm the reader with too much type at once. Page one often includes photos and graphics to pull in the reader and break up the text.

Inside Pages

The contents of the inside pages are largely left up to the discretion of the newsletter's editor. Both recurring features and news stories can be found throughout the inside pages.

Recurring features usually appear in every, or almost every, issue. They should appear in the same place in every issue. Maintaining the format can add to the reader's sense of familiarity with the newsletter. There are many types of recurring features that can appear in newsletters. They include:

- *A letter from the president, chief executive officer, founder, or director:* An opportunity for the leader of the organization to relay an important message to the reader. It also supplies the reader with a sense of direct contact with the leader.

- *Announcements:* Bits of information the reader may find interesting but that are too short or trite to sustain an article.

- *Job information:* Job openings and career advice.

- *Department/division news:* Brief synopses of the activities of each division of the organization since the last issue.

- *Questions and answers:* Questions from readers that are answered by a specialist in a particular subject area.

- *Spotlight sections:* Columns that focus on an employee, volunteer, or participant who has accomplished something special.

News stories appear throughout the newsletter. While the most important news stories, also known as "lead stories," are found on page one, they often continue on an inside page in order to entice the reader to open to the inside of the newsletter instead of just reading the cover. There are many other types of news stories included throughout the inside pages. Topics may include:

- an organization's stand on the issues
- information on community involvement
- financial information
- upcoming events
- a summary of past events

The inside pages should include visuals and text that balance out and create a smooth-flowing and easy-to-read document.

Page Four/Back Cover

This final page is the last point of contact between the audience and the newsletter. A good design idea is to split the page into two different panels. The panel above the fold can contain a calendar of upcoming events or general information. The panel below the fold can make the newsletter a self-mailer. A label can be used to address the newsletter so that no envelope is required. Other possible uses for the back page include extra articles or return-response cards. Page four is usually a bit more structured than pages two and three, but the final decision is left to you as editor to decide what will best resonate with the audience.

Heads

Like newspapers, newsletters have **headlines** throughout the body. An effective headline must communicate the essence of the story in an enticing yet brief form. Also similar to the standard newspaper format, headlines should always be written with a proper sentence structure that includes a subject and a verb. Headlines are generally used for cover stories and other important articles within the newsletter. The headline font is larger and bolder than the font for the text, giving emphasis to the story.

The **deck head**, or subhead, appears below the headline and is known as the introductory line. It is often italicized and in a smaller font than the headline, but it is still in a larger font than the story text. The deck head usually offers supplemental information not included in the headline while properly amplifying the headline. Also like the headline, it should be written in proper sentence structure.

The **masthead**, often found on page two or three, contains the publication information: the names of the publisher and editor and the address.

The **banner**, often called the nameplate, promotes the name of the newsletter. This is where a newsletter may demonstrate its editor's artistic creativity and keen sense of wording. Creative wording and interesting font choices can produce a name that stands out and demands attention—a critical element, since the banner is the first thing the reader sees. The banner is key to the success of the newsletter because it becomes the distinguishing focal point for the publication and is the element readers identify most with the newsletter.

Design Elements

Numerous design elements help to make the words of the articles even more appealing to the reader. Some of the elements that should be considered in order to produce a lively newsletter include the following:

- **Color** sends a message to the reader. Pure white, ivory, and light-gray paper stocks are considered businesslike, whereas light brown is viewed as casual or informal. The use of more than one ink color can often be expensive, but there are several tricks that can make your money go farther. To achieve a two-color look with just one color, newsletters can be printed with a single ink color, generally black, on colored paper stock. Screens create different-size dots of varying intensity to produce different shades of a color.

- **Paper stock** itself is also an important element when producing a newsletter. The length of a newsletter often determines the stock of the paper. Heavier stock may encourage the reader to hold on to or catalog the newsletter, whereas thin stock may make the newsletter seem less important and more disposable.

- **Pull quotes** can be used within the text. A pull quote is a section of copy from the article that is set in larger, often italic, type and sometimes boxed. It is used to highlight, emphasize, or draw attention to certain important points in the article. This design element is also used as a space filler when an article runs too short.

- **Rules** are solid lines that help separate the editorial material. They can be used vertically to divide columns or horizontally to separate headlines from text or paragraphs within text.

- **Sidebars**—blocks of copy—give a unique perspective on the article they accompany. They are often boxed for a highlighting effect.

Some organizations struggle with the cost of producing a newsletter and turn to outside advertisers to help subsidize the expense. This offers outsiders the opportunity to publicize their goods and services in the newsletter for a fee. While advertising revenues may take a great deal of the financial burden off the organization, the editor must determine whether the target audience will tolerate the inclusion of advertisements before the space is sold.

Where Should They Go?

Distributing a newsletter can be a daunting task. A newsletter should not just be distributed as a handout similar to a leaflet or a brochure. These documents have a specific audience, and in order to reach that audience, companies and organizations consistently update their mailing lists to ensure both accuracy and validity. If a newsletter is new, it is important to create a comprehensive mailing list comprised of a target audience with the appropriate demographics. Creating and maintaining lists takes both money and time. The other large expense in distributing a newsletter is, of course, the mailing costs. Many newsletters are also self-mailers; they help keep costs down by avoiding the expense of an envelope. Whether the newsletter is in an envelope or is a self-mailer, the design must always meet U.S. Postal Service (USPS) specifications for domestic or, if relevant, international mail.

Many newsletters are now developed and distributed via the Internet or via an Intranet, a system viewed only by in-house personnel. Electronic publications have many appealing characteristics. Besides having the immediacy that goes along with posting something on the Web or sending it via email "blasts," a method for immediately distributing an email or attachment to a large number of recipients at one time, electronic newsletters tend to be much less expensive than print newsletters. Not only do electronic newsletters bypass all printing costs because they are produced online, they also do not require postage fees. But, as with mailed newsletters, a good mailing list is the key to success. Organizations need to maintain accurate email address lists to guarantee documents are reaching the correct audience. If the target audience is unfamiliar or uncomfortable with the use of a computer, the standard printed version must be reconsidered. Another concern that arises from the electronic posting of newsletters is privacy. This concern can be addressed by implementing a password or by placing the newsletter on an Intranet system.

Did They Work?

Newsletters are most effective when designed, written, and distributed properly and when they evoke the desired response from the target audience. The most effective means of evaluating the overall newsletter is to conduct telephone, online, or mail surveys to confirm that the intended receiver actually received and read the publication. The survey can also include probing questions about what the reader does or does not like about the publication. Tracking how many people take part in the events highlighted in a newsletter is another way to measure its success. Other evaluation tools include newsletter response cards from readers seeking additional information and reader mail and feedback.

Putting PR into Practice

1. Consider the client you chose for this course or an organization with which you are very familiar. Answer the following strategic questions about a newsletter for this organization.
   a. Who is the primary audience for the newsletter?
   b. What type of news will the organization have to share with the primary audience?

  c. How will you determine the news value of the articles?

  d. Will there be enough news and other information to share regularly with your audience?

  e. How often will you publish the newsletter?

  f. How will you disseminate the newsletter?

  g. How will you evaluate the newsletter's effectiveness?

2. Draft a timely and relevant news article for the cover page of the newsletter. Remember to use an inverted pyramid style for the article, decide who the primary spokesperson will be, and enhance the article with quotes.

3. Draft a feature article for the newsletter. This should be soft news. Make an attempt to relate it to a larger news story in the newsletter or in the news locally.

4. Use a computer software template to create a sketch of a newsletter for your client organization before deciding on all of the elements. This will give you the opportunity to think about graphics, banner, and other elements.

An *Example Gallery* for Newsletters begins on the following page.

Hand Hand

VOLUME 1 ■ ISSUE 3 ■ SPRING, 2012

THE NEWSLETTER OF EACH ONE TEACH ONE

Each One Teach One Awards Student Scholarships

Participants Earn Money for Helping Curb Youth Violence

Five high school students were presented with $1,000 scholarships each courtesy of Each One Teach One on March 14th at an award ceremony held at the Each One Teach One headquarters in Washington, DC.

Students from across the United States vied for the prestigious scholarships. Each year they are awarded to participants of the Each One Teach One program who exemplify leadership skills, and active participation in anti-violence youth programming, along with the desire to continue the mission of the program.

"These students truly exemplify the progress and development that Each One Teach One strives to accomplish in all children," said Executive Director Willis Bennett.

The scholarships were developed as an opportunity to award the youth involved with the program who continually strive to eradicate violence in society.

For more information on how to apply for future scholarships contact: Sarah Woods (202) 555-3777.

This year's honorees (from left to right) are Amanda Sheffield of Atlanta, Georgia; Bradley Lawrence and Pam Stevenson from Washington, DC; Terrell Jones of Chicago, Illinois; and Tanya Spelder of Miami, Florida.

Annual Fund-raising Dinner Hailed as a Success

The Third Annual Each One Teach One Fund-raising Dinner, held at the Washington Hotel in Washington, DC, raised more than $25,000 on Saturday, April 8.

After raising more than the $15,000 goal, Fundraising Chair Avery Atlas pointed to the growing interest in the mission of Each One Teach One. "We were anticipating about 500 attendees but when we heard that nearly double the amount were planning to attend, we realized that Each One Teach One was successful

Continued on Page 3

Each One Teach One (EOTO) is a professional nonprofit organization for students, teachers, and educators, founded to develop and disseminate information on the nationwide problem of school violence.

Page 1 of 4

A nonprofit voluntary organization newsletter designed to inform its target audience of the organization's activities.

❶ BANNER: Name of newsletter.

❷ VOLUME AND ISSUE DATE.

❸ CONTENTS: Listing of where stories are found inside.

Letter from the Director

Spring 2012

This quarter, Each One Teach One has come such a long way in communicating the message of anti-violence to our nation's youth. It seems that our mission of encouraging our nation's youth to help one another find alternatives to violence has really begun to make an impact.

Since many of our young participants are from at risk backgrounds, our anti-violence campaign was a very risky venture from the onset. However, over the last few months the attendance at most of the Each One Teach One seminars, workshops, and retreats has skyrocketed. It seems that our participants have spread the word that programming at Each One Teach One is fun, beneficial, and rewarding.

We have also seen many of our early participants return to become leaders and advisors in some of our programs. This is a very exciting time for all of us here at Each One Teach One. We hope that you continue to support our programming by offering your time and/or financial commitment to help in our new program, "Turning Points of Life."

Willis Bennett

Executive Director,
Each One Teach One

If you are interested in being a part of the fall fund-raising effort, contact EOTO Vice President of Development Susan Pierce at (202) 555-3377.

Spotlight on: Tanya Spelder
Student Leader of the Quarter

At the recent Each One Teach One Award Banquet, Tanya Spelder of Miami, Florida was presented with a college scholarship for her current role as youth spokesperson.

After spending her younger years in San Diego, Spelder experienced violence both at home and in her neighborhood. Early school years also proved to be difficult for Spelder. She failed to excel in her classes and often engaged in fights with other students.

Spelder moved with her father to Miami only to find that his new wife was not interested in making her feel welcome. Hoping for a fresh start, Spelder once again faced a social environment not so different from San Diego.

When volunteers from the Each One Teach One program visited her school, Spelder saw other individuals who were not unlike herself. Only now, the people seemed to be on the road to success. Spelder cautiously enrolled in the program. "I felt like at that point I had nothing to lose. I wasn't happy and I hated everything including my family," said Spelder. "I knew I needed a change."

Once in the program, Spelder found the motivation she needed. By talking to other students like herself, she felt more confident that she could succeed.

Spelder progressed so well at Each One Teach One that she moved from being one of the counseled to being a counselor. Volunteers noticed that she had a natural talent for talking to her peers and reasoning with them.

The directors of the Miami program witnessed Spelder's development and suggested she join them in talking to local schools about the benefits of the EOTO program. During the past six months Spelder has spoken to nearly one dozen schools recounting her own struggle to gain self-confidence while emphasizing the importance of goals and motivation in order to achieve success.

Spelder is now finishing high school in South Florida and plans to attend college to earn a degree in social work. She feels strongly about continuing her dedication to Each One Teach One, an organization which she says saved her life.

"My personal experience may help relate to children in similar situations and help them to overcome their struggles," said Spelder. "I hope I can have a similar influence on a child in need."

Susan Pierce Named Vice President of EOTO Development

Willis Bennett named Susan Pierce, the former Director of Development for Safe Retreat USA, to the position of Vice President of Development at Each One Teach One in March of this year.

Already off to a successful start, Pierce has been able to increase major contributions by more than 40% for the first quarter.

"I was very excited about working with Each One Teach One because it is an organization with such great potential," said Pierce. " When a cause is received as well as EOTO, it makes my job seem easy."

Pierce will address the Board of Directors in June with preliminary estimates for the second quarter.

❶ STANDING FEATURE.

More Than 1,500 Participants Gathered for Annual Each One Teach One Retreat

The Appalachian Mountains played host on March 3-7 to the largest retreat ever sponsored by Each One Teach One.

Every year leaders, counselors, participants and volunteers gather for four days to exchange ideas, learn about new programs, and meet with other Each One Teach One participants from all over the country.

Noting the attendance was nearly double the size of last year's retreat, organizer Stuart Smith attributes the turnout to the success of EOTO's grassroots programs.

"A few of us came last year and we had the best weekend of our lives," said participant Michael Gooding. "This year almost our whole chapter wanted to take part in the retreat."

The weekend is set up not only to inform the attendees, but to establish friendships that can cross state lines as well as regional chapters. Included in the weekend camping trip are hikes, ropes courses, survival training, rafting and other activities.

Due to the large turnout, organizers are planning a late summer retreat to accommodate those who were unable to attend the March trip.

Annual Fund-raising Dinner
continued from Page 1

in spreading the words of anti-violence." This year's theme was "School Days" as it highlighted the importance of anti-violence in schools today.

Guest Speakers for the evening included Each One Teach One Executive Director Willis Bennett, Attorney General Janine Redding and actor/activist Maxwell Tyler.

Also on hand to help raise money for

Each One Teach One was comedienne Betty Better and musical sensation The High Tones.

"I was so proud to be a part of this Each One Teach One celebration," said Better. "The future safety of our country falls on the shoulders of our youth and it is our responsibility to set the foundation for them."

If you are interested in being a part of the fall fund-raising effort, contact EOTO Vice President of Development Susan Pierce at (202) 555-3377.

Who's Who at EOTO

Willis Bennett
Executive Director

Janine Redding
Founder,
Board of Directors

Rose Ward
Vice President,
Operations

Susan Pierce
Vice President,
Development

Sarah Woods
Communications
Director

Nathaniel Mitchell
Program Coordinator

Each One Teach One
National Headquarters
1836 Jefferson Square, NW
Washington, DC 20036
(202) 555-3377
www.eachoneteachone.org

Page 3 of 4

Example Gallery
Newsletters

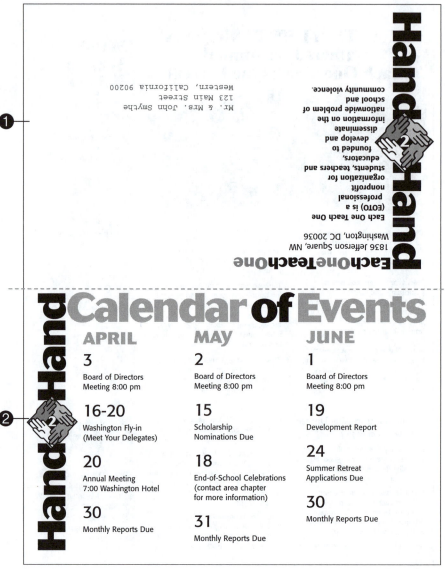

Each One Teach One (EOTO) is a professional nonprofit organization for students, teachers and educators, founded to develop and disseminate information on the nationwide problem of school and community violence.

EachOneTeachOne
1836 Jefferson Square, NW
Washington, DC 20036

Mr. & Mrs. John Smythe
123 Main Street
Western, California 90200

Calendar of Events

APRIL

3
Board of Directors
Meeting 8:00 pm

16-20
Washington Fly-in
(Meet Your Delegates)

20
Annual Meeting
7:00 Washington Hotel

30
Monthly Reports Due

MAY

2
Board of Directors
Meeting 8:00 pm

15
Scholarship
Nominations Due

18
End-of-School Celebrations
(contact area chapter
for more information)

31
Monthly Reports Due

JUNE

1
Board of Directors
Meeting 8:00 pm

19
Development Report

24
Summer Retreat
Applications Due

30
Monthly Reports Due

Page 4 of 4

❶ SELF-MAILER: Address of reader and organization's return address.
❷ CALENDAR.

Example Gallery
Newsletters

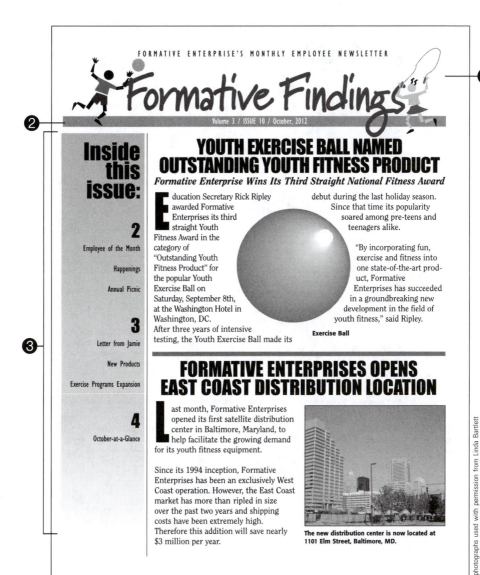

A corporate employee newsletter designed to keep employees informed about company activities and other company employees.

❶ BANNER: Name of newsletter.

❷ VOLUME AND ISSUE DATE.

❸ CONTENTS: Listing of where stories are found inside.

Example Gallery
Newsletters

Formative Findings Employee of the Month: *Staci Kaufman*

Prior to the hiring of Public Affairs Director, **Staci Kaufman,** Formative Enterprises focused primarily on the manufacturing, sales, and distribution of its line of youth fitness products. It was Kaufman who first developed our community relations, public affairs, and public relations divisions.

Originally hired strictly to handle public relations needs, Kaufman recognized the importance of being a good corporate citizen. So she started a campaign that offers free youth exercise programs in low-income neighborhoods called *Get Fit, It's Fun!!!*

With more than a dozen of these programs now in place, Formative Enterprises is being nationally hailed as a leader in community service.

Congratulations Staci!!

Annual Summer Family Picnic Is A Huge Success

On Friday, August 30th, Formative Enterprises held its Fifth Annual Summer Family Picnic at Meyer State Park for all employees, staff, and their immediate families.

This picnic had the largest attendance in the history of the company. More than 250 people enjoyed the barbeque food, games, and boating.

"This was my first picnic," said **Leon Staples**, who was hired just six weeks before the picnic. "It was a great time for me and my kids. I already feel like part of the Formative family."

> **"It was a great time for me and my kids"**
> — *Leon Staples*
> *Product Designer*

This was the first year that the picnic was held at Meyer State Park in order to best accommodate the significant increase in attendees as well as to best thank them for their dedication to Formative Enterprises.

"I'm so pleased that everyone enjoyed themselves at this year's picnic," said CEO **Jamie Molack**. "It was a pleasure to meet all of the wonderful families of our great employees. I can't wait until next year!"

Formative Happenings

What's New With You?

■ **Trisha Clark** of Human Resources gave birth on September 4th to her first child, Brett Noel.

■ **Jonathan Magack** in the manufacturing division announced his engagement to Tabitha O'Neal, his girlfriend of two years.

■ **Eric Moronz** in distribution received his B.A. in English from California University.

If you have any news you would like to share, send an email to: findings@formative.com

Page 2 of 4

① STANDING FEATURE.

Example Gallery
Newsletters

"Get Fit, It's Fun" Expands Its Horizons
Formative Adds 20 Youth Exercise Programs to Midwest

Following the success of the "Get Fit, It's Fun" program which sponsors youth exercise programs free of charge to low-income neighborhoods, Formative Enterprises has added 20 programs to youth centers across the Midwest.

Currently, "Get Fit, It's Fun" has more than 75 programs set up throughout California, Texas, Florida, and the Mid-Atlantic states. Nationally recognized as the leader in youth exercise equipment, Formative Enterprises is now gaining similar recognition for its youth exercise programs.

"I love coming to the Youth Center after school to participate in their teen fitness class," said 15-year-old Marcus Minor. "Before I learned how much fun exercise could be, I used to stay home and watch television. Now I am getting fit and looking fine."

Plans are in the works to expand the youth exercise programs to northern and southern states by next year.

New Products Are On The Way!!!

Jumping seems to be the activity of the month since both of the new products being released in October involve hopping.

The new pre-school trampoline called the Tike Tramp will debut in stores by the end of the month. This product is designed to meet the safety and fitness needs of our youngest customers.

The new adjustable jump rope (still unnamed) will also make its debut at the end of October.

From the President...

Jamie Molack
President,
Formative Enterprises

This has been the most fantastic month that Formative Enterprises has experienced in quite some time. Following last spring's passage of the National Fitness Initiative by Congress, it became very obvious to all of us that we should lead the way in introducing fitness to the youth of America. Now, nearly six months later, Formative Enterprises has become a corporate model for community involvement.

Once the "Get Fit, It's Fun" program was initiated last April, a study conducted by the National Fitness Association has noted that children, pre-teens, and teen-agers have been exercising more than 25% more often than they were this time last year.

It is with the help and guidance from Formative's employees and staff that we have come so far in such a short amount of time.

Thanks for all your help.

① STANDING FEATURE.

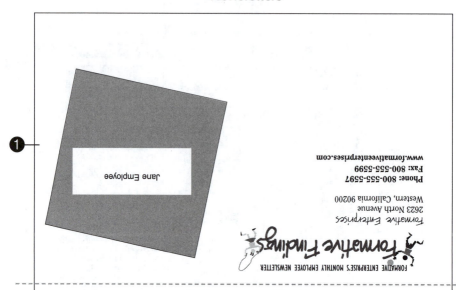

www.formativeenterprises.com
Fax: 800-555-5599
Phone: 800-555-5597

Western, California 90200
2623 North Avenue
Formative Enterprises

Formative Findings

FORMATIVE ENTERPRISE'S MONTHLY EMPLOYEE NEWSLETTER

Jane Employee

October-at-a-Glance

Sunday	Monday	Tuesday	Wednesday	Thursday	Friday	Saturday
	1	2	3	4	5	6
7	8 **Columbus Day Offices Closed**	9	10	11 **Baltimore Center's Open House**	12	13
14	15 **Senior Staff Meeting**	16	17	18	19	20
21	22 **Tike Tramp Product Debut**	23	24	25	26	27
28	29 **Jump Rope Product Debut**	30	31 **Employee Halloween Costume Party**			

❶ SELF-MAILER: Address of reader and organization's return address.

❷ CALENDAR.

News Releases

What Are They?

With the notable exception of brochures, news releases are probably the most highly recognized of all public communication products. Unfortunately, they are also the most misused. Daily, thousands of news releases with no news are distributed to the news media. As a public communication practitioner and writer, you will write, edit, and/or approve news releases throughout most of your career. You should know when one is needed and how to write one well.

A news release is a communication tool used by public communication practitioners to convey a particular message to specific news media outlets. When news releases are properly planned, formatted, and executed and contain genuinely newsworthy information, the media will incorporate the information into the framework of an original news story and disseminate it to audiences. News releases often represent the perspective of the organization that is sending them but should present a full and complete picture of the news they are reporting.

There are many different types of news releases. They cover information relevant to the sponsoring organization and may relate internal or external changes or events. It is customary for the public communication practitioner to distribute a news release in advance of the "news." The idea, of course, is to alert the media to a story so that they can report on it in a timely manner. Releases are also sent to follow up on a news item or event, offering additional information that may be related to the organization that is disseminating it.

An **announcement release** highlights changes that have occurred within the organization that may be of interest to a targeted audience. News such as internal promotions, upcoming or past events, fundraising information, introduction of new products and services, new hires and appointments, honors and awards, mergers and acquisitions, earnings, and the like are often the primary focus of an announcement release.

Spot announcements are written when an external influence or action has an effect on an organization. Again, it is critical that the information in a spot announcement be related to the organization and relevant and newsworthy to the target audience.

A **reaction release** is often used to counter or respond to something that was said or done within the public domain that has an effect on the organization and should be answered or redirected so that the organization can be on record regarding the issue. This type of release is most effective for an organization when the reaction is incorporated into a related news release that highlights additional information about the organization. The reaction release is a primary tool of political candidates and elected officials.

The **"bad news" release** provides the truth about a bad situation. The organization should release the bad news, including all information and facts, quickly and honestly. A major element of a successful image campaign is maintaining honest relations with the media at all times, even if the news is not good. The thought behind this philosophy is that if an organization is always honest and straightforward with information, it will be considered a reliable source by the media.

A **hometown release** focuses on a local angle to a bigger news story. It often highlights individuals or organizations that are located in the same area and/or community as the media outlets covering the story. As an example, if the president of the United States appoints a new commission, the White House press office will disseminate announcement news releases to the national media explaining the purpose of the commission and providing the names of the members of the commission. If a woman from Hometown, USA, is a member of this newly appointed commission, the press office will send a release with a local angle to the news media in Hometown.

Finally, the **feature release** offers an alternative news perspective to a larger news story. Considered "soft news," these releases are not necessarily time-sensitive and usually focus on the human-interest side of the larger news story. To expand our previous example, the woman from Hometown, USA, may have made an impression on the U.S. president because of a question she asked about the issue the commission will explore during a town meeting in Hometown last year. This fact could result in a feature release about the commission and the woman's role.

Who Gets Them?

At the risk of being redundant: As writers, we must not begin the writing process without first identifying and understanding our target audience, and then we write about what interests that audience. We use print news releases for the same reason we use audio and video news releases and emails to bloggers: We are trying to disseminate a message to the audiences that some of the news media reach through their articles and programs. In order to accomplish this, we have to direct our release to the news media so that they will produce stories that reach audiences we have already targeted. We have to know where that target audience is and what they read. Again, the target audience can be as narrow as boaters in Annapolis, Maryland, or as broad as people who suffer from type 2 diabetes.

What Do They Do?

News releases are an organization's most often used tool for gaining news coverage and exposure. The information presented in a news release is designed to arouse the curiosity of the reporters—who may choose to further investigate the story. The successful news release includes important and newsworthy information written in clear, concise language, and it provides contact information for reporters who want to know more. The goal of a news release is not necessarily to have the news media run the release verbatim (though some newspapers do); instead, it is to draw attention to the message so that a reporter will be interested in writing a story and an editor will be inclined to let the story run.

A news release also establishes the framework for discussion on issues concerning an organization and its related issues, activities, and philosophies. Because news media outlets spend a great deal of time processing information for stories, it has become common practice for them to use information from public communication sources to help create story ideas, supplement existing stories, and access information that may be difficult to otherwise obtain. When prepared correctly, news releases can save the media time, money, and effort.

As an integral part of a strategic public communication campaign, news releases help explain our organization's important objectives and messages to the public. Providing timely, accurate, and newsworthy information about current topics can also help to position an organization as a trustworthy authority on a set of issues.

The ultimate purpose of a news release is to inform the public. It is not the function of a news release to stroke the egos of senior management. Instead, senior management should work to ensure the development of an effective news release campaign. They must be included and consulted regarding the intended messages and goals.

News releases should *never* be the sole component of a public communication campaign. They are effective only when used in conjunction with other public communication tools. News releases should always be the result of an overall communication and media relations strategy. They should accompany media kits and annual reports and complement other message vehicles.

The primary element of an effective news release is *newsworthiness*. If the information is not newsworthy, it should not be released. If the release does not contain news, placement by the media is unlikely. News is not always what the public communication practitioner or the organization's management thinks it is. It is critical to examine all elements of newsworthiness and weigh them against the proposed message. As you become more experienced in working with the news media and learning to think like a news director, you will learn to judge newsworthiness and know when you see it. Meanwhile, there are specific elements to help public communication professionals gauge the newsworthiness of a message or story:

- *Timeliness:* relevance to current events or issues or relatedness to an important event that has just taken place
- *Magnitude:* the degree to which the story or issue has an effect on people
- *Impact:* the effect the story could have on the public
- *Human interest:* an appeal to readers' emotions
- *Celebrity:* the involvement of a well-known person, or of someone in the public eye, in the story

- *Proximity:* when a story hits close to the local coverage area and has relevance for people in a specific community or industry
- *Novelty:* an interesting angle that makes a story significant or unique

There are many news hooks that engage news media outlets and, in turn, targeted audiences. They include:

- tie-ins with daily news events
- cooperating with another organization on a joint project
- tie-ins with a media outlet on a mutual project
- conducting a poll or survey
- issuing a report
- an interview with a celebrity
- significant speeches
- making an analysis or a prediction
- formation and announcement of names for committees
- holding an election
- announcing an appointment
- celebrating an anniversary
- issuing a summary of facts
- tie-ins with a holiday
- developing an award
- releasing a testimonial
- taking part in a controversy
- staging a special event
- writing a letter of significance
- releasing a received letter of significance (with permission)
- adapting national reports and surveys for local use
- tie-ins to a well-known week or day
- organizing a tour
- inspecting a project
- issuing a commendation
- holding a protest
- conducting a contest
- passing a resolution
- appearing before public bodies
- honoring an institution
- staging a debate

How Do They Help?

When news releases generate news coverage by the media, an organization's credibility is increased and the public becomes more aware of the organization and its message. The news media provide third-party credibility.

Public communication professionals often underestimate another benefit of news releases: the creation of a platform to introduce and discuss issues relevant to an organization. Also, releases provide context for an organization to convey key messages to its target audience. Using credible, timely, accurate news releases over time as part of a public communication program will help to position an organization as a credible authority on issues pertaining to the business or interests of the organization. Often, the organization's spokesperson on these issues becomes a source for the news media to consult and quote as an expert on the topics.

What Are the Pitfalls?

Using news releases certainly can have drawbacks. In fact, releases are often misused by public communication professionals and thus are not used effectively by the news media. Failing to target appropriate news media outlets, providing information that is not newsworthy, and distributing information simply to please upper management will position the organization as an unreliable source to the media.

Even when a release is newsworthy and properly targeted, timeliness remains a cause for concern. Releases that highlight past events are taboo. Providing out-of-date information can lead not only to the immediate demise of an intended story but also to the certain demise of the organization's future news releases.

The language in a news release should be directed toward news directors, editors, and journalists, not toward the public. It is a mistake to write a news release as though you are writing a finished news story. Also, it is important never to raise questions within the body of the release; instead, news releases should anticipate the audience's questions and supply the answers.

When writing a news release, you will need to be familiar with the style, format, and audience of the targeted news media outlets. A news peg that interests one audience may not interest another, so it is important to tailor all messages appropriately.

While news releases should be tailored to the news media outlet's individual style, there are still some general rules of style to remember. First, it is not necessary to get the name of the organization into the first sentence. It produces a boring lead and leaves little room to tell the actual news. Second, it is also not necessary to use the name of the company president or other company figurehead in the lead. Leads tend to get cluttered when they try to include the date, time, place, and name of an event all in the same sentence.

The issue of libel is a major concern to news release writers. It is very tempting for a company to trumpet the good news and try to ignore or whisper the bad. However, doing so has serious legal consequences. All information released by a publicly traded company may be examined by parties who claim to have been misled to determine if the materials combined to create a misleading representation of the company. Such a finding means that a corporation may be held liable even if each *individual* release or statement is completely truthful when examined separately. The courts have found that a corporation, a corporation's officers, and the PR firm that handles its news releases may all be held accountable when the releases are found to contain misleading and/or false information. All organizations—not just corporations—must also take responsibility for the content of any news release or public statement.

Public communication professionals, including PR practitioners, should take careful measures to be truthful, accurate, and complete in their releases. If the situation does not warrant a rosy picture, then one should not be created. Withholding negative information, misleading the public, making extravagant claims, and making unfair comparisons can get the public communication professional, the organization, and the organization's officials into a losing legal battle. However, this does not mean that every news release that announces something positive must contain bad news as well.

How Should They Look?

Style Notes

A news release should be written in the traditional **inverted pyramid style,** with the most important or interesting information conveyed first, followed by information that is increasingly less important. Sentences and paragraphs should be kept short. The first part of a news release includes the most important information. The following section contains secondary information like attribution or background material. The third part elaborates or amplifies items mentioned in the first part. And the fourth and final part is supplemental information that may be related to, but not necessarily critical to, the intended message.

The **headline** of a news release should be concise, informative, yet eye-catching and intriguing. The **subhead** should incorporate supplemental information not highlighted in the headline. An effective news release **lead** should contain the who, what, where, why, when, and how of the story in one or two sentences. Most news release leads are found in the first paragraph; however, many feature releases incorporate a delayed lead to entice the reader.

The body of the release should contain facts that are clearly and concisely stated. A good release avoids the use of overly descriptive language, superlatives, jargon, and inappropriate quotes. The release reflects the practitioner and the sponsoring organization. Misspellings and grammatical errors can lead to credibility problems, so the release should be carefully proofread. This guide and a recognized news stylebook should always be consulted.

A news release should always try to explain the organization's viewpoint. A story is more likely to get picked up by the media when reporters have access to the newsmakers themselves. Additionally, when reporters request elaboration, information should be provided willingly and quickly.

Quotes are another very important aspect of any news release. They provide a personal perspective on the story and amplify certain elements of the lead. Quotes can be from experts, firsthand accounts, and reviews. Try to incorporate a minimum of two different quotes from two different individuals; when appropriate, the quotes should be from people whose perspectives are not identical. This gives the media the opportunity to "pick and choose." Just as all the sentences written within the news release should be succinct, so should the quotes. Write quotes that sound conversational and contain information that is relevant to the story.

Finally, many organizations rely on a well-written **boilerplate** to provide the necessary background about who they are, their mission, and other relevant information that they may want to convey. Usually found at the very end of a news release, the boilerplate is still considered to be one of the more important and indispensable elements.

Format

There are elements all news releases should contain in order to make them successful. First, news releases should be printed on the organization's standard letterhead including the organization's name and logo, address, telephone and fax numbers, Web site, and email address.

Writing "NEWS RELEASE" in the top left corner of the page will make it obvious to even the most novice journalists what they are about to read. Immediately following the date that the release is being distributed on can appear an embargo date if one is necessary. An **embargo** is a future date and time the media can release the information. If the embargo differs from the date of distribution, the news media understand that the information should not be released to the public until the date and time specified. Caution: not all journalists honor embargo dates, and only unusual circumstances call for embargoed releases. If a release is intended for dissemination on receipt, then the phrase "For Immediate Release" must follow.

Another very important part of the release is current and accurate contact information, found at the top right corner of page one. This information includes the name and title, address, telephone number, fax number, and email address of the individual who should be contacted by the media with any questions or concerns related to the release. Of course, this information is very important to the news release's success.

We should strive to make the headline of a news release effectively summarize the news contained in the body of the release in an intriguing way. The headline should be centered in the middle of the page, formatted in all uppercase letters, boldfaced, and underlined. Directly under the headline, the subhead incorporates supplemental news information and should be written in uppercase and lowercase and italicized.

Following the subhead is a **dateline**, or the city and state where the news originated. The lead directly follows the dateline and, as mentioned earlier, tells journalists who, what, where, why, when, and how.

The body of the news release includes **lead amplifiers**, which are quotes and supporting information that expand on the lead information. A boilerplate paragraph at the very end of the release summarizes the philosophies, goals, and purposes of the organization sponsoring the release.

If a news release runs more than a single page, a **page slug** should appear at the top, flush left (e.g., page 2 of 2). The word "-more-" should appear at the bottom of each page when another page is to follow. At the end of the news release, there should be some indication that no more pages will follow. Symbols such as -30-, -end-, or -###- centered at the end of the text are commonplace.

News releases are usually written in a twelve-point Times New Roman font. Double-spaced, they rarely exceed three pages in length; however, there are always exceptions. Once all the news is conveyed within the headline, lead, and body, you don't need to include more information.

Where Should They Go?

The success of the distribution of the news release depends significantly on the thoroughness of the media list (see Chapter 7). News releases can be disseminated to the media through fax blasts (a mass faxing to a large number of media outlets at a single time), mail, email, and individual media calls.

To obtain maximum placement, many public communication practitioners include pitch letters (see Appendix A), captioned photographs, and other materials with news releases. News editors value images they cannot readily obtain, and pitch letters help to clarify story ideas while explaining why readers will be interested in the story.

Embargoes are typically used to give reporters a chance to digest complex issues or lengthy pieces of information or to provide fair access by multiple news outlets. News organizations tend to dislike—and sometimes break—embargoes, so it is advisable to use them with caution.

Did They Work?

The best way to evaluate the effectiveness of a news release is to measure the number of hits or story placements that the news release created. Many monitoring services can obtain news stories from various forms of media, including print, television, radio, and online. Many smaller or nonprofit organizations rely on their own staff to research media placements resulting from news releases.

Once placements are established, news releases can be measured against the desired criteria. Such criteria include:

- circulation numbers
- target audience reached
- value compared to the advertising dollar (often done by converting print inches and air time into dollars)
- audience response (often measured by quantitative and qualitative data research)

Putting PR into Practice

As you read, news releases can be very powerful tools in the practice of public relations, but their use should always be driven by strategy.

1. Consider the client you chose for this course or an organization with which you are closely affiliated. If the client has asked for a news release or if you think an action or event merits one, ask and answer a few strategic questions.

    a. What news media is appropriate for the news release?

    b. Aside from the news media, who is your primary audience?

    c. What do you want the news release to accomplish?

    d. What is its purpose?

    e. What is the primary message?

    f. Why is your primary audience interested in the topic and message? Use the list on pages 139 and 140 to determine the newsworthiness of your topic.

    g. Whom will you quote?

    h. Who will be the best spokesperson for the news? Is there a contradictory side to the news that you need to consider?

2. List the important facts surrounding the topic, issue, action, or event. Include how the subject of the release affects the primary audience reached by the media you selected, keeping the inverted pyramid style and an effective lead in mind.

3. Draft the news release.

An *Example Gallery* for News Releases begins on the following page.

Example Gallery
News Releases

EachOneTeachOne

1836 Jefferson Square, NW / Washington, DC 20036

NEWS RELEASE

February 11, 2012
FOR IMMEDIATE RELEASE

Contact Information:
Sarah Woods, Communications Director
Office: (202) 555-3377
Fax: (202) 555-3780
E-mail: swoods@eachoneteachone.org

EACH ONE TEACH ONE KICKS OFF 2006 ANTI-VIOLENCE CAMPAIGN
Awareness Against Youth Violence

WASHINGTON, DC — *Each One Teach One*, a nonprofit organization dedicated to reducing youth violence, will begin its 2006 anti-violence campaign, "Breaking Down Anger" with a seminar on the prevention of youth violence on Saturday, February 18, 2012.

The seminar, to be held at the *Each One Teach One* headquarters, 1836 Jefferson Square, NW, will include presentations on youth violence and recent developments in the effort by Willis Bennett, the executive director of *Each One Teach One*, Janine Redding, the U.S. Attorney General, and Rick Ripley, the U.S. Secretary of Education. "These activities are vital to helping our children grow and learn about productive ways to resolve problems. There is too much violence in our youth today to let this continue," said Ripley.

The seminar will also include interactive activities for children and parents on controlling and curbing the use of violence and group discussions on how to effectively practice self-control and conflict-resolution techniques. Students and their mentors can discuss what provokes anger and together they can create possible alternatives to the use of violence. Counselors will assist in fostering creative, productive solutions to everyday conflicts.

-more-

Page 1 of 2

Announcement news release.

1 NEWS RELEASES: One to three pages about the organization and the event.

Example Gallery
News Releases

Willis Bennett, the executive director of *Each One Teach One*, spends much of his time talking to students and teachers in the Washington, DC area, planning and promoting *Each One Teach One* activities and events. "We want to provide our youth with the tools necessary to avoid violence. If the youth then begin to teach each other, they become involved and committed to the process. If they are committed, then we are successful," says Bennett.

For more information, please contact Sarah Woods at (202) 555-3377 or email at swoods@eachoneteachone.org.

Each One Teach One was launched in September of 1999 in response to the growing number of tragedies from youth violence. The organization's program includes seminars, workshops and retreats as well as counseling services and fund-raisers. Volunteers have also created a monthly newsletter and a Web site for the nonprofit organization.

-###-

Chapter

12

Opinion-Editorials

What Are They?

Opinion-editorials (or op-eds) are one of the most powerful tools available for influencing the opinion of a target audience. Clearly, for an op-ed to be effective, your target audience has to be readers of the editorial and op-ed pages. If they are and you can get an op-ed placed, your organization's viewpoint will be heard in one of the most credible sites in the marketplace of ideas.

An opinion-editorial is a form of opinion writing that addresses current issues and public policies. Unlike an editorial, which expresses the views of the publication, op-eds are vehicles that allow writers who are not employees of the publication to have their views on a particular subject published and shared with the community. Op-eds usually appear on the page opposite the editorial page in newspapers, magazines, and trade and online publications, and their topics may be local, regional, national, or even international in scope.

As a media relations tool, the op-ed is used to influence opinion leaders, sway public opinion, and effect change in society. In general, it is an essay that takes a stand or position on a particular issue and sometimes provides solutions to problems. This 700- to 800-word piece allows an organization to have complete control over its message. It is very important that it be well written and factual to avoid confusing and misleading the target audience.

To avoid writing misleading and manipulative op-eds, writers must be clear and concise, getting to the point at the outset, advocating a point of view, supporting the point of view with facts and figures, and suggesting a call to action. As public communication professionals, we must make sure our op-eds are well researched, balanced, and anticipate readers' questions and provide answers. They should stimulate the reader, explain issues, and advocate a position or solution. Op-eds should not only inform readers, but persuade them as well.

What Do They Do?

The primary purpose of op-eds is to influence public opinion or motivate attitude or behavior changes within a community or even the nation. When op-eds are used effectively, they have the potential to reach and persuade a large target audience, influence opinion leaders and "influencers (people who have the ability to shape public opinion because of their greater knowledge regarding the issue at hand), support a candidate, or gain support for a particular cause or issue. Op-eds are also used as a platform to present the ideas, views, and opinions of a particular organization or person.

Op-eds are unique because they can serve as a forum for readers and allow an organization to create, frame, and shape public opinion. They are one vehicle of expression in the marketplace of ideas and public dialogue. Op-eds provide target audiences with enough information and guidance to help them form an opinion, make a sound judgment on an issue, or take an action. An op-ed is meant not only to inform, but also to recommend, persuade, and even advocate.

Garnering widespread visibility for an organization, or for an organization's stance on a particular cause or issue, is the primary job of the op-ed. When op-eds are published in the national news media, they not only reach the publication's large readership but have the potential to reach readers of other publications, as well. If the op-ed is distributed over news wires, other publications may reprint it, expanding the reach and effect of the article. Permission from the author is usually obtained before the op-ed is reprinted.

How Do They Help?

Op-eds give organizations control over a message. Unlike typical news reporting, op-eds are subjective writing. In fact, the article should clearly and explicitly state an opinion. Because the op-ed has the capability of reaching a large audience at once, it is a very cost-effective public communication tool. If published in the right news medium, it can be distributed nationwide or even globally. Unlike "advertorials," text-heavy ads that promote or advocate ideas or points of view and cost thousands of dollars to publish, op-eds are published free of charge. In fact, the usual practice is for the publication to pay the author if it publishes the op-ed.

In addition, op-eds are a good way to address public policy issues, sway public opinion, and reach opinion leaders and influentials. Opinion leaders and influentials often pay attention to op-eds and inform their own opinions at least in part through op-ed messages. They can persuade the people they have influence over to take the same or similar position that the op-ed advocates, thus generating much-needed support for a campaign or organization or influencing public opinion. Reaching opinion leaders with effective messages may be the most persuasive method in public communication. As communication practitioners, we sometimes find it is easier to influence a select few, who in turn influence or persuade a larger audience.

What Are the Pitfalls?

Ethics Notes

Some critics argue that getting paid for a published op-ed article is unethical. Depending on the publication, a public communication professional can receive as much as $250 for each published piece. Concerns arise because there appears to be a conflict of interest or goals. It may appear that practitioners who receive payment for published op-eds are using their power of persuasion for their own personal benefit or monetary gain, instead of using it for the best interest of the organization or client. When this occurs, the professional's credibility and trustworthiness are diminished. Practitioners need to explain op-ed articles and industry norms to clients if the communication planning calls for this strategy. This will diminish opportunities for misunderstandings as the media strategy is implemented.

It is highly competitive, and at times difficult, to get successful placement of op-ed articles. Some news outlets, especially national news publications, receive hundreds of op-ed articles each day. Ultimately, it is up to the editor of the editorial section to decide which articles get published. Because there is no guarantee that the piece will be published, the communication professional should be familiar with the news organization to which the op-ed is submitted. Each news publication has its own set of rules and guidelines governing the op-ed page. Adhering to these rules and guidelines will increase the chance of publication.

Depending on the timeliness of topic, it may take weeks before an op-ed appears in print, and the public communication professional must ensure the piece will not appear in a publication before "shopping it around" to another one. Submitting an op-ed to competing publications at the same time is not acceptable practice and is a good way to damage a relationship with the media.

How Should They Look?

Style Notes

First and foremost, the information in the op-ed should be timely and direct. An outdated op-ed will never get published. The news media and public have short attention spans, so it is important for communication practitioners to keep up to date on current issues. The savvy practitioner takes a proactive approach in identifying current relevant issues. Monitoring trade magazines, public policy issues, daily news stories, and the editorial section of newspapers will help keep the public communication professional up to date. In addition, studying the op-eds that are published in a particular publication will help you gain insight into the format and issues the publication usually covers.

An op-ed piece begins with an explicit statement of the author's opinion and primary information. The reader should know from the opening paragraph what the author's position is. It is important to keep the target audience in mind when drafting the op-ed article, as it should speak directly to that audience. The article should be supported by facts and not be one-sided. It is necessary to consider both sides of an issue and present all viewpoints, including the opposing ones. The writer who ignores opposing views is guilty of using a propaganda device called card stacking, in which all the supporting arguments are given and no opposing points are mentioned. The author should write honestly and state opposing viewpoints, refuting them to prevent card stacking and bias.

The op-ed article should be clear, easy to read, and not use any jargon. It should be no more than 800 words. If possible, it is good to include graphs and statistics to illustrate and reinforce the important points. Citations and footnotes should *not* be used, as they are not journalistic in style and will not be published.

Format

The format for op-eds varies with each publication. However, it is widely accepted that submissions be typed and double-spaced. Part of the research process is to thoroughly review previous issues of publications to get familiar with their format. It is wise to talk with the op-ed editor for guidance as well. Generally, the op-ed must include the usual contact information: the writer's name, title, telephone number, and email address, as well as the organization's name.

Where Should They Go?

Never consider sending an op-ed to more than one publication/news medium at a time. If you get an op-ed placed in two competing publications, you will lose credibility with the media. It is the responsibility of the practitioner to determine whether or not an op-ed will be published by one publication before submitting it to another.

It is also best to check with the news organization to see how the op-ed should be delivered. Depending on preference, it can be faxed, mailed, emailed, hand-delivered, or uploaded to the Web. Op-eds regarding national issues should be submitted to national news publications. If the op-ed deals with a local issue, it is best to submit it to community and weekly newspapers. Op-ed articles on academic and research-based topics are appropriate for journals. Articles based on current issues or trends in a given industry should be sent to trade magazines.

Did They Work?

The most obvious way to evaluate the success of an op-ed is to track media coverage and placement. If the article was published in the appropriate news outlet, it will convey the intended message to the right target audience. In addition, the published op-ed might garner additional coverage on radio and television. Monitoring services can be engaged to monitor publications and broadcast and cable.

An additional evaluative method is to determine whether the desired outcome was achieved as a result of the op-ed. Clearly, it is difficult to make a direct correlation between a published op-ed and a desired outcome. But other news media coverage might mention your organization and its viewpoint regarding an issue and connect them, indicating your organization's role in helping to change the public's attitudes or behavior, to get a bill passed, to gain support for a particular cause or issue, to influence an opinion leader, or to get someone elected.

Putting PR into Practice

As we discussed, the audiences for op-eds are usually regular readers of the editorial page. Unlike a letter to the editor, an op-ed is written by an expert in the subject matter or topic who has intrinsic credibility with the reader. Consider the client for this course or an organization with which you are closely affiliated.

1. Identify an event, issue, or action that has appeared in the news recently and is relevant to your client's issues and audiences. How does it affect your organization?

2. Who is your primary audience?

3. Who is the best voice/spokesperson to write/byline the op-ed? What medium is best for this op-ed?

4. Outline the three major points you want to make and the evidence you have to support each. What is the action you want your audience to take? Be very specific.

5. Define the opposing or competing views on the issue. Delineate points to refute the opposing view.

6. Draft the op-ed.

Chapter 13

Public Service Advertisements and Announcements

What Are They?

Because of the expense of advertising time and space and the high cost of production, many nonprofit organizations consider adding public service advertising (PSAs) to their strategic communication campaigns. When placed in print media and online, PSAs are called public service ads, but when they run on radio or television, they are called public service announcements. You will find that PSAs can be very powerful tools if you can get the right free time and space.

PSAs are public communication messages created by or for nonprofit organizations. Executed well, they persuade, inform, or advocate for the public good. And they can boost an organization's visibility and create awareness about issues, events, and programs. The media run them free of charge on behalf of the nonprofit organizations. But therein is the challenge for you as a writer: Because they are placed at no cost, the competition is high and you have to write advertising copy and use visuals that are interesting, attention-getting, and suited to the medium. If this is not done, the PSA will not get placed.

Aside from cost considerations, the primary difference between PSAs and paid spot advertisements is that PSAs contain information that is intended to benefit the target audience. Messages conveyed by PSAs must include information that is beneficial to the community without being self-serving, and they should *not* contain a controversial or political slant. Topics for PSAs are as varied as the nonprofit sector itself. They include health and fitness, mental health, safety, environmental issues, quality-of-life issues for the poor and underemployed, community events, and, of course, nonprofit fundraising and volunteer and relief efforts. Nonprofits also use PSAs to advocate and to inform and influence public opinion.

The three main types of PSAs are print, radio, and television. Each type has a distinct style of development, format, and distribution. Target audiences and budget need to be considered when deciding which type to use. Depending on how the PSA is being produced, the choice of medium is also contingent on access to equipment to print, record, or film the announcement.

Who Gets Them?

Target audiences for PSAs are as varied as the topics and subjects mentioned earlier. Key, of course, is the research to determine the appropriate target audience. For years, public communicators in the nonprofit sector were less strategic about their advertising messages than commercial advertisers were. Now, nonprofit organizations use the proper research to identify and understand their target audience and to design a communication campaign strategy. Audiences include donors, volunteers, teenage smokers, populations at risk for many physical and mental diseases, the senior population, immigrants, and students. There are many, many more.

What Do They Do?

Public service announcements and ads can convey socially conscious messages or convey information about public services. The three primary purposes of PSAs are to inform, persuade, or advocate. In the end, because the goal is to get the audience to take an action, all PSAs are persuasive tools. Effective PSAs persuade by emphasizing a particular interpretation of information and arranging the message so that it has maximum impact on the audience. A PSA can position ideas in a unique way so that its message impacts what people understand, reject, or feel about the subject matter.

PSAs can also take the form of community calendars, listings that air throughout the day to promote community events. The calendars are often aired during talk-show programs and newsbreaks. Community calendars provide the time, date, and location of local community events sponsored by nonprofit organizations.

Publications and broadcast stations allot space and time free of charge to promote the messages, special events, and services of nonprofit organizations. These media outlets are inundated with hundreds of PSAs each week; therefore, they must be selective when choosing which will run. Due to the heavy volume of PSAs, organizations must remain competitive in order to get their announcements placed.

How Do They Help?

Like paid advertising, PSAs can successfully sell the public on an idea or a vision. PSAs raise awareness, inspire individuals to act, and influence public opinion. When produced and executed correctly, PSAs can reach a broad target audience. When a public relations practitioner can work directly with a community relations or public service director at a news organization, the news organization may sometimes donate production, spokespersons, and other resources.

The biggest advantage of PSAs is that publications and radio and television stations run them free of charge. This makes PSAs extremely appealing to organizations with small budgets.

What Are the Pitfalls?

While PSAs offer many advantages to organizations, there are also some draw-backs to using them. Because organizations do not pay for the dissemination of PSAs, they do not have much control over when or where the PSA is run. Radio and television stations and print publications derive their profits from advertisers that pay for time or space; therefore, the majority of prime placements go to these advertisers. In contrast, PSAs are placed wherever there is available time and space, and often this is not the most desirable time or position. This limitation of PSAs may result in messages reaching the wrong audience and miss-ing the target audience altogether. Public communication professionals must work closely with stations or publications to get the best placement possible.

Another limitation of PSAs is the cost of production. Talent, production fees, editing, and distribution can cost a great deal of money, and it is not always possible to include PSAs in every public communication campaign. Strategic planning of communication campaigns requires evaluating the budget constraints *before* finalizing the campaign.

How Should They Look?

Style Notes

Effective PSAs include a strong theme and message, logical reasoning, and emo-tional appeal. As with all public communication products, you should determine that the benefits offered to the audience are tangible and meaningful and that they attempt to satisfy an emotional need. The communication strategy should consider the target public and its desires, needs, and values. An effective PSA campaign has evaluated existing and potential competition and reviewed all the pertinent facts about the intended message and issues from both the position of the organization and the position of the organization's competition.

A PSA should be simply stated with short sentences that are no longer than 12–15 words. Clichés, slang words, and jargon should be avoided. Using the active voice, rather than the passive voice, offers a sense of immediacy. A con-versational tone and a strong opening and closing help make a lasting impression on the audience.

Several structural components are critical to the success of a PSA. In general, you should include the most important information in the first paragraph in order to be "up front" with the audience about the purpose of the PSA. The message should be credible, avoiding exaggerated claims. Repetition is also an important strategy; it reinforces facts that the public needs to remember such as dates, times, and telephone numbers. All PSAs should explicitly state how the information and requested action help the audience. Lastly, the PSA should motivate the target audience to act by telling them where they can go, what they can do, or whom they can call.

PSAs can take many forms, including testimonials, interviews, jingles, and the mini-drama. In a testimonial, a credible spokesperson talks about how the organization's message worked for him or her. In contrast, interviews consist of an announcer speaking with a representative of the organization. Jingles use music and words to make copy more interesting, entertaining, and memorable. Finally, the mini–drama presents a dramatization of a situation that the audience may be able to relate to from having had a similar personal experience.

A PSA needs to identify key elements of the message in the order of importance, beginning with who, what, when, where, and why. This information must be conveyed clearly and concisely in order to have a successful play. Lastly, the copy for a PSA has to be written to suit the medium for which it is intended. Each medium requires a different writing style.

Format

Print PSAs

Print PSAs rely solely on visuals and written copy to attract the reader's attention. The copy should convey to the audience why the issue, message, or public service is both desirable and necessary for the reader. The most important element of print PSA copy is the headline. It is responsible for grabbing the reader's attention, while making a lasting impact. The remaining copy and any visuals should expand on the headline and heighten interest. Credible statistics and specific examples are often used to supplement the information provided in the headline. The copy should close with a call for the reader to take a specified action.

After its initial production, a print PSA is printed out as camera-ready art that can be processed into a negative to fit into any publication's format.

Radio PSAs

The first step in producing a radio PSA is to contact the public service directors at target stations to determine their preferred format and length. Typically, radio PSAs are produced in 10-, 15-, 30-, or 60-second lengths. On average, 10-second PSAs are 25 words, 15-second PSAs are 38 words, 30-second PSAs are 75 words, and 60-second PSAs are about 150 words. Longer PSAs are not necessarily more effective than shorter ones. Even a 15-second spot is enough to convey a message. The shorter the time allotment, the simpler the PSA needs to be so as not to confuse listeners with too much information during a short timeframe. In contrast, longer messages need to repeat key information for reinforcement. Organizations often produce the same PSA in varying lengths to accommodate different stations' time slots.

A radio PSA script is usually written in all uppercase letters and triple-spaced, which makes it easy for an announcer to read. It should also include a **header** with the organization's name, telephone number, and contact name, plus the title and length of the spot. Printing the script on paper with the organization's logo adds credibility.

Due to limited time, radio PSAs must focus on one or two important points. Similar to print PSA headlines, radio PSAs need to begin with a hook to attract the listener's attention. The organization's name and telephone number should also be included in the message.

If your organization can afford to do so, you may want to ask members of the intended target audience to review and comment on the completed script before production begins. This process may be conducted in focus groups or on a more informal basis, such as central-location intercept interviews or mall intercepts.

Once the script is finalized, production can begin. Most public communication executives audition voice talent. No more than two or three voices should be included in a PSA; any more participants might confuse the listener. It is commonplace to provide different versions of the same PSA to offer variety.

Some organizations opt to have the radio station produce the PSA. This means that the organization's script is read by the station's on-air talent during regular programming. The benefit of this approach is that the message receives more credibility because the announcer already has an established relationship with the audience. But such announcements are usually aired exclusively on that station. If the PSA is written on a local agency level, you will likely write the script. If the national office produces the PSA, it will provide you with written scripts with a space for local **tag lines**, copy added to the end of the PSA that gives local information related to the PSA.

Television PSAs

A television PSA script should have clear objectives and focus on the most important points of the intended message. As with other types of PSAs, the communication practitioner will need to check all facts for accuracy. Because the audience both sees and hears a television PSA, camera directions must be included in the script along with dialogue. A television PSA script is usually formatted with two separate columns. The left column is dedicated to the visual elements, and the right column includes all audio elements. The script should be double-spaced, with a header similar to a radio PSA header.

If the sponsoring organization has the appropriate resources, it should consider making two or three different versions of the PSA so that the same spot will not be played over and over. Television PSAs can range from 10 to 60 seconds in length; stations should be asked for their preferred length.

After the script is completed, a detailed production plan should be developed. The strategy should include details about the filming, editing, music, and graphics. Special effects and graphics should be used sparingly because too many of these may distract the audience from the message. However, one good way to reinforce key messages is to utilize character generation (often called CG), which is the display of printed words on the screen.

Television PSAs should remain simple in content. Once the PSA is filmed and edited, it is a good idea to test it with representatives of the target audience and other important community members before it is accepted for television. Many organizations leave room in their PSA for a tag line to be added at the local level. Television PSAs are also produced directly for local stations. Other organizations may provide video footage to stations, which will edit it. A station announcer or local celebrity can then volunteer to "voice" for the audio. It is important to work with the station's community relations or public service director from the outset to make sure you have an outlet for this expensive tool. As well, this is a good way to build a new relationship and perhaps get the production assistance you need.

Where Should They Go?

Distribution of PSAs can be one of the most challenging tasks facing public communication professionals. However, there are several steps you can take to help ensure success. The first thing to do is to compile a complete media list, including newspapers, city and regional magazines, local trade and business publications, news operations at local radio and television stations, local cable television stations, and public broadcast stations. Then you need to research the demographics of each media outlet to determine access to the target audience.

Again, it is best to contact the person in charge of PSA placement before the PSA is developed. If your PSA has been produced without contacting media outlets, you should write a letter to the appropriate contact person in charge of PSA placement at each media outlet prior to distributing the PSA, introducing the organization and the communication campaign and the importance of the campaign to the media outlet's audience. The letter should describe the campaign and its implications for the community. Accompanying the letter should be the organization's introductory media kit and fact sheet. You should follow up the letter a few days later with a request for a meeting. At the meeting, emphasize the importance of the campaign to the station's or publication's audience.

You should contact the community service or advertising department at a publication to express interest in obtaining a print PSA placement. Some organizations also provide a tag line that gives credit to the publication for the donated space.

Again, it is important to identify the publication's primary audiences in addition to confirming its style and format. Weekly newspapers, pennysavers (free weekly shopping guides), and college newspapers are more inclined to print PSAs than daily papers. National newsmagazines place PSAs for national organizations and their campaigns.

Radio PSAs are usually directed to the public service directors at local radio stations and are typically submitted in written script or pre-produced CDs. Written copies are often less expensive and more effective because they will be read by the radio announcer, who is a familiar voice to the audience. This is usually the radio station's preferred way of providing the service. If the organization decides to use a pre-produced version, the public service director can advise the organization about CD content and quality. Pre-produced PSAs are accompanied by a hard copy of the script and are labeled with the organization's name and telephone number and the title and length of the piece.

Television PSAs are usually sent to station program directors, traffic managers, or community relations/public service directors. Again, contacting the station before the production process begins is the best way to know what the station requires. PSAs that are for television can be distributed via videotape or satellite feed. You should ask the contact person about the preferred format. Also, enclose a hard copy of the script or storyboard, including the length of the spot, local statistics on the issue, and the organization's name, telephone number, and contact person. A storyboard is a depiction of the visuals and audio of the actual PSA.

Did They Work?

When executed correctly, PSAs can affect public opinion and behavior as well as inform and advocate. The success of a PSA can be evaluated in several ways. One measure is to consider the number of media outlets running the PSA. This is an indication of the organization's success in persuading stations and publications of the urgency and importance of the message. Media outlets can report to the organization how many times the PSA ran and, in the case of radio and television, at what times. You can then use this information, along with statistics on the average number of viewers, listeners, or readers, to estimate how many people the PSA reached.

PSAs themselves often become a source of media attention, bringing more media coverage to an organization than even the PSA itself might have achieved. Organizations can estimate the PSA's exposure by the amount of media attention and viewer feedback it receives. For example, if a PSA drives audiences to a Web site, an increase in visitors to the site may be an indication of the PSA's effectiveness or more memberships or increased donors.

Putting PR into Practice

Consider the client you chose for this course or an organization with which you are closely affiliated.

1. For what audience would you create a PSA? Is it a primary audience?

2. How do you know your client's issue has salience for this audience? What has research told you about this audience? How does this inform the appeal you will choose? Tone?

3. What is the primary message and what do you want this audience to do?

4. Do you need a spokesperson? Who? Explain your choice.

5. Write a 30-second elevator pitch that delivers your message concisely.

6. Using the format in the Example Gallery, create a 60-second PSA script for television, using your pitch as a guide.

7. Adapt the script to a 30-second radio PSA.

8. Create a print PSA.

An *Example Gallery* for Public Service
Advertisements and Announcements begins on the
following page.

Example Gallery
Public Service Advertisements and Announcements

CLIENT:	Emerald Heights Office of the Mayor	TIME:	30 seconds
TITLE:	Help Save Our Water	DATE:	August 22, 2012

SFX: WATER RUNNING IN BACKGROUND

FEMALE V/O:
Rainfall in the Emerald Heights watershed is at a 12-inch deficit for the year and the Emerald Heights reservoir is 10 inches below its normal level.

FEMALE V/O:
In order to ease the depletion of our area's water supply, please conserve water as much as possible. Limit watering of lawns and shrubs, or cleaning automobiles or boats, and eliminate ornamental uses of water in artificial waterfalls and reflecting pools. With your help we can avoid future mandatory restrictions.

MAYOR JUDITH GOLD:

Hi, I'm Judith Gold, Mayor of Emerald Heights, here to encourage all residents of Emerald Heights and the surrounding areas to scale back on water usage in response to our current drought conditions.

MAYOR JUDITH GOLD V/O:

Please help save our water. I thank you and your neighbors thank you!

Page 1 of 2

A city government public service announcement storyboard designed to persuade.

❶ HEADER: Includes the organization's name; the title, length, and date of the spot; and the name of the writer or producer.

❷ SOUND EFFECTS: Sound effects (SFX) directions in italics.

Example Gallery
Public Service Advertisements and Announcements

CLIENT:	Emerald Heights Office of the Mayor	TIME:	30 seconds
TITLE:	Help Save Our Water	DATE:	August 22, 2012

page 2 of 2

❸

**For More Information
Call the
Emerald Heights
Drought Hotline
555-2211**

MAYOR JUDITH GOLD

For more information about the current drought conditions, contact the Mayor's office Drought Hotline at 555-2211.

❸ CONTACT INFORMATION: The last shot includes information that viewers need to take action.

Example Gallery
Public Service Advertisements and Announcements

❶

CLIENT:	Formative Enterprises	TIME:	30 seconds
TITLE:	Get Fit, It's Fun!!!	DATE:	May 10, 2012

MALE V/O: Summer means kids are out of school and looking for things to do.

MALE V/O: Why not keep your kids fit? Encourage your kids to exercise.

❷

MALE V/O: Regular exercise is an important tool for children to improve their cardiovascular system, strengthen their growing bones and sustain good mental health.

MALE V/O: There are many ways for your children to exercise.

Television commercial storyboard for a corporate responsibility program.

❶ HEADER: Includes the organization's name; the title, length, and date of the spot; and the name of the writer or producer.

❷ FORMAT NOTES: Video elements in the left column depict the shot to appear on the video screen. Audio elements, or copy, on the right side coordinate with the visuals on the left.

Example Gallery
Public Service Advertisements and Announcements

CLIENT: Formative Enterprises   TIME: 30 seconds

TITLE: Get Fit, It's Fun!!!   DATE: May 10, 2012

page 2 of 3

MALE CHILD #1: Like bicycle riding and skate boarding!

FEMALE CHILD #1: Or playing soccer or swimming!

MALE CHILD #2:   What about tennis or running?

FEMALE CHILD #2:   Or even jumping on my trampoline?

MALE V/O: Yes, all of those activities are fun and great exercise.

Example Gallery
Public Service Advertisements and Announcements

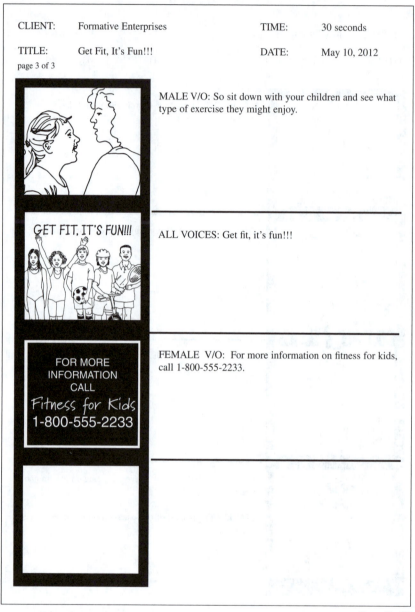

CLIENT:	Formative Enterprises	TIME:	30 seconds
TITLE:	Get Fit, It's Fun!!!	DATE:	May 10, 2012

page 3 of 3

MALE V/O: So sit down with your children and see what type of exercise they might enjoy.

GET FIT, IT'S FUN!!!

ALL VOICES: Get fit, it's fun!!!

❸

FOR MORE INFORMATION CALL
Fitness for Kids
1-800-555-2233

FEMALE V/O: For more information on fitness for kids, call 1-800-555-2233.

❸ CONTACT INFORMATION: The last shot includes information that viewers need to take action.

Example Gallery
Public Service Advertisements and Announcements

MAYOR JUDITH GOLD: HI, I'M JUDITH GOLD, MAYOR OF EMERALD HEIGHTS, HERE TO ENCOURAGE ALL RESIDENTS OF EMERALD HEIGHTS AND THE SURROUNDING AREAS TO SCALE BACK ON WATER USAGE IN RESPONSE TO OUR CURRENT DROUGHT CONDITIONS.

IN ORDER TO EASE THE DEPLETION OF OUR AREA'S WATER SUPPLY, PLEASE CONSERVE WATER AS MUCH AS POSSIBLE.

LIMIT WATERING OF LAWNS AND SHRUBS. DON'T CLEAN OFF AUTOMOBILES OR BOATS; AND ELIMINATE ORNAMENTAL USES OF WATER IN ARTIFICIAL WATERFALLS AND REFLECTING POOLS. WITH YOUR HELP, WE CAN AVOID FUTURE MANDATORY RESTRICTIONS.

PLEASE HELP SAVE OUR WATER. I THANK YOU AND YOUR NEIGHBORS THANK YOU.

FOR MORE INFORMATION ON THE CURRENT DROUGHT CONDITIONS, CONTACT THE MAYOR'S OFFICE DROUGHT HOTLINE AT 555-2211. THE HOTLINE'S NUMBER AGAIN IS 555-2211.

An audio PSA produced by a local government to encourage residents to assist in alleviating the water shortage.

❶ HEADER: Includes the organization's name; the title, length, and date of the spot; and the name of the writer or producer.

❷ BODY: Copy should be triple-spaced in all uppercase letters.

❸ FORMAT NOTES: All telephone numbers should be repeated at least two times.

Example Gallery
Public Service Advertisements and Announcements

❶

CLIENT:	Formative Enterprises		TIME:	30 seconds
TITLE:	Get Fit, It's Fun!!!		DATE:	May 10, 2012

❷

SFX:	*Distant sounds of kids playing in a park*
MALE V/O:	SUMMER MEANS KIDS ARE OUT OF SCHOOL AND LOOKING FOR THINGS TO DO.
MALE V/O:	WHY NOT KEEP YOUR KIDS FIT? ENCOURAGE YOUR KIDS TO EXERCISE.
MALE V/O:	REGULAR EXERCISE IS AN IMPORTANT TOOL FOR CHILDREN TO IMPROVE THEIR CARDIOVASCULAR SYSTEM, STRENGTHEN THEIR GROWING BONES AND SUSTAIN GOOD MENTAL HEALTH.
MALE V/O:	THERE ARE MANY WAYS FOR YOUR CHILDREN TO EXERCISE.
MALE CHILD #1:	LIKE BICYCLE RIDING AND SKATE BOARDING!
SFX:	*Sounds of a skateboard*
FEMALE CHILD #1:	OR PLAYING SOCCER OR SWIMMING!
SFX:	*Kids playing in a swimming pool*
MALE CHILD #2:	WHAT ABOUT TENNIS OR RUNNING?
SFX:	*A ball hitting a tennis racquet*
FEMALE CHILD #2:	OR EVEN JUMPING ON MY TRAMPOLINE?
MALE V/O:	YES, ALL OF THOSE ACTIVITIES ARE FUN AND GREAT EXERCISE.
MALE V/O:	SO SIT DOWN WITH YOUR CHILDREN AND SEE WHAT TYPE OF EXERCISE THEY MIGHT ENJOY. HELP THEM KEEP FIT, IT'S FUN!!!

An audio PSA developed by a for-profit organization to inform the public about the importance of kids' exercise.

❶ HEADER: Includes the organization's name; the title, length, and date of the spot; and the name of the writer or producer.

❷ SOUND EFFECTS: Sound effects (SFX) directions in italic.

Chapter 14 Speeches

What Are They?

Even with all of the technologically advanced tools available to communicators today, the ancient art of public speaking is still an extremely effective way to evoke emotion and to motivate and inspire an audience. Speeches can also be used as a platform for a communicator to voice concerns, promote causes, and influence public opinion.

A speech is a carefully prepared monologue designed to have an impact on an audience assembled to listen to a speaker. A speech's success depends on the speechwriter's ability to capture the speaker's persona and to anticipate the audience's reaction. Therefore, speechwriting is the most difficult assignment you will undertake as a public communication writer, requiring not only research on the target audience but also research on the speaker. It is no wonder that many career politicians keep the same speechwriter for years.

Whether a speech is directed at a large audience or a small group of individuals, its content can, if written and delivered appropriately and effectively, have an immense impact. And, unlike most public communication tools, a speech receives immediate audience feedback through nonverbal and verbal cues such as applause, facial expressions, body language, gestures, and a wide range of vocalizations.

Who Gets Them?

It is impossible to list here all of the possible audiences for speeches. The target audience for a given speech, depending on the purpose, could conceivably include every internal and external public. But a speechwriter *must* write directly to a specific target audience. Speechwriting and delivery require knowledge of the audience's beliefs, values, and attitudes. A good speechwriter conducts extensive, comprehensive research on the target audience *and* the speaker.

The target audiences for speeches are participating in a personal communication with the speaker. When a speaker delivers a speech, the audience immediately interprets the speaker's words, tone, rate of speech, and body language, all of which add meaning to the communication.

What Do They Do?

There are many reasons to speak in public, but speeches have three main functions. Speeches primarily aim to inform, to persuade, or to celebrate special occasions. The audience and occasion generally determine the purpose of the speech. While each type of speech has its own style and purpose, they all should convey a specific theme and/or message. If written well and delivered successfully, a speech can be an effective communication tactic.

Informative Speeches

The primary goal of the informative speech is to increase an audience's understanding and awareness of the speech's subject. It is critical to assess the knowledge base of the audience before you construct this type of speech. The relevance of the subject should be demonstrated early in the speech, and terms unfamiliar to the audience need to be clearly defined throughout the body of the speech. Supporting material should be chosen carefully in order to make the greatest impact in the most effective way possible. It is also important to define, describe, explain, and demonstrate the topic in the appropriate amount of detail. This type of speech can be a state-of-the-organization speech delivered by the executive director to an internal or external public, or it could be a talk from a public communication professional to explain a new community relations plan to a group of civic leaders.

Persuasive Speeches

The purpose of a persuasive speech is to get an audience to "buy" something—a person, a thing, or an action. This sometimes requires a change in the audience's attitudes, values, or beliefs about the something. The key messages should be personally relevant to the audience and demonstrate how a behavior change, product purchase, or vote will benefit them. If the speaker is promoting a change, it is critical to encourage only a small change. An emotional appeal that does not arouse fear or anxiety can help move the audience to act on the appeal of the speech.

Special-Occasion Speeches

Many different types of special occasions warrant a speech. In fact, most special occasions are an opportunity for the principal of an organization or company to deliver a desired message. As the speechwriter, you want to identify the purpose of the special occasion and acknowledge the tone of the event in the speech. Depending on the occasion, the objective of the special occasion speech can be to entertain, celebrate, commemorate, motivate, persuade, or inspire.

How Do They Help?

Speeches provide us with a unique opportunity to communicate ideas, views, values, or beliefs directly to a group of individuals or an audience without filters.

Speakers can attempt to inform, persuade, or celebrate with audiences with whom they have become familiar through the appropriate research. This public communication tool allows listeners to provide immediate feedback in the form of facial expressions, vocalizations, gestures, laughter, and/or applause. One of the unique features and benefits of a speech is direct connection with the audience and a chance to leave a lasting impression.

What Are the Pitfalls?

The success of a speech will be limited if the speaker does not deliver it effectively. As a speechwriter, you may write a perfect speech on a speaker's behalf, but the speaker may lack the training necessary to be effective. Training is key to the success of any speech.

Another limitation that can hamper a speech's success is the credibility of the speaker or of even the speech itself. If the speaker does not have intrinsic authority with an established reputation, then credibility must be earned. This can occur via a third-party introduction or even through the content and delivery of the speech. If credibility fails to be established, the purpose or goal of the speech can be lost.

How Should They Look?

Style Notes

Once the purpose of the speech has been determined, a number of factors must be considered in order to write an effective speech. After the subject matter has been decided on, the topic should be thoroughly researched.

Clearly, you will consider the audience when constructing the speech. Understanding the audience helps you as the speechwriter to determine the voice, tone, and vocabulary. Language should be adjusted to the audience's age and educational level and to their degree of familiarity with the subject. If you are writing a speech for an audience that is familiar with the subject, acknowledge and build on the existing intimacy. A speaker can better engage an audience by including personal references and details about audience members. If a speech is delivered to an audience that is unfamiliar with the subject, try to establish trust and credibility early in the speech.

Speakers cannot establish credibility without revealing a little of themselves. It is important to let the personality of the speaker permeate the speech. By doing so, a speaker is more apt to feel comfortable with the material of the speech. One of the most challenging aspects of speechwriting is writing on behalf of others; it is important to be as familiar as possible with the speaker so that some of the speaker's personal nuances can be included.

A speech must engage the audience in order to be effective, and writing "for the ear" is one way to capture the audience's attention. To draw listeners in and to make them comfortable with the information and the speaker, use words and examples to which they can relate.

One way to captivate an audience is to use repetition, consistently rein-forcing an idea; the listeners will ultimately absorb the underlying theme. Also, stating points in a concise way ensures appropriate emphasis. Rhetoric, persuasive language, and motivational words can help to draw in the audience and increase awareness of the speaker's subject.

A successful speech is as specific and to the point as possible, and it avoids using vague and confusing abstractions. Words that paint a picture reach the audience on a more emotional level than countless statistical references, although the minimal use of statistics is acceptable. A speech should aim for a reaction. It should appeal to the commonsense nature of listeners while perhaps striking a chord of passion with the audience.

Avoid mixing unrelated thoughts or ideas that distract the audience. A powerful yet concise 20-minute speech can say more than one that rambles for an hour.

You may consider including presentation aids such as graphs, charts, audio clips, video, slides, multimedia, models, or pictures. It is important to include only visuals that are appropriate to the subject, audience, and occasion. Such aids should be included only if they effectively illustrate a point, pique the inter-est of the audience, evoke some sort of emotion, offer levity, or provide context for an issue.

Format

At the center of an effective speech is adherence to a structural format. An organized and recognizable introduction, body, and conclusion will keep the speaker on track and give the audience a sense of where the speaker is in the speech. Without structure, a speech can digress in an infinite number of direc-tions without accomplishing its intended goal.

Introduction

The beginning of any speech must grab the attention of the audience within the first 30 seconds. It is during this pivotal part of a speech that the speaker and the speech either get noticed or disintegrate. An introduction should fit the objective of the speech while accommodating the personal style of the speaker. Select from tried-and-true options for introductions: an anecdote; a relevant well-known quote or brief story; a factual statement that will impact the audience; a surprise question or remark that will get the audience thinking; or the blunt announce-ment of the speech's topic. Here, you introduce the subject of the speech.

Body

After the speech has successfully grabbed the attention of the audience, it should move seamlessly to the body. This section is usually the lengthiest part. You want to build on points and arguments that support and defend the subject of the speech. Each point should be backed up with data relevant to the subject.

Don't include so many points that the audience becomes overwhelmed with an excess of information. Three to five points are usually sufficient. The body should be concise and consistent and present the speaker as a knowledgeable and credible source.

Conclusion

The closing of a speech should summarize the main points that were made earlier. It should provide "thinking material" for the audience to ponder or an action that the audience can take such as writing letters, volunteering, or making a donation. Many conclusions also extend acknowledgments to the audience and to those who made the speech possible.

Where Should They Go?

Today, the traditional method of speech delivery has undergone a transformation never imagined in ancient Rome. Until recently, speeches were usually thought to include speakers directing their comments to a group of individuals in the same location. But now, the distribution of a speech can extend way past the walls of an auditorium or even the borders of a country. Satellites and the Internet present the opportunity for global delivery.

A hard or electronic copy of a speech, called a transcript, can be distributed to sources outside the attending audience. Sometimes, distribution materials or other presentation aids may be included so that the impact of the speech can be experienced firsthand.

Videoconferencing and DVDs offer other ways to communicate and distribute a speech to an audience who may not have been able to attend it live. Not only is this audience able to read the speech and see the visual aids, they can actually watch the speaker deliver the speech.

Did They Work?

Speeches can be evaluated on many fronts. While the immediate feedback on a speech is important, it certainly means less than comments made hours or even days later. Measuring the success of a speech means determining whether the speech accomplished its intended goal. Did the audience gain a clear understanding of the information that was delivered during an informational speech? Did the persuasive speech change the views of the audience to align with those of the speaker? Was an emotional connection made between the speaker and the audience during the occasion being celebrated?

Another way to evaluate the success of a speech is to gauge the media attention given to it. It is important not only to note that the speech was covered, but also to ascertain what sound bites were used, what video clips were shown, or what quotes were printed.

Talented speechwriters and speakers are a valued commodity. If a speech is successful, the writer and the speaker are often approached with more requests for public speaking engagements.

Putting PR into Practice

Consider the client you chose for this course or an organization with which you are closely affiliated.

1. Select a speech topic and a primary audience to whom your organization's spokesperson might deliver a speech. Also consider an occasion on which the speech can be delivered. Ask yourself a few strategic questions.

   a. Why is the audience present for the speech? Why did they come?

   b. Does the occasion itself need to be recognized in the speech (e.g., an anniversary, an award or recognition, an announcement or endorsement)?

   c. Will the speech be used to inform or to persuade?

   d. As you know, the work of writing a good speech begins with understanding your audience. What research helps you to know this audience? What are the listener's attitudes, beliefs and values toward your topic?

   e. Is the audience well versed on the topic or have they come to learn? Determine whether any of the audience demographics are important to the speech.

   f. What is the purpose of the speech? What do you hope to gain?

   g. Is there a call to action? What do you want the audience to do?

2. Using the speech outline provided in this chapter, write at least three sentences that describe the main points for each of the main parts of a speech. Describe at least three examples of the main points. And describe at least three points of evidence for each argument.

3. Draft a speech for your organization's spokesperson.

An *Example Gallery* for Speeches begins on the following page.

Example Gallery
Speeches

Speech delivered by Willis Bennett, Executive Director of Each One Teach One, in Akron, Ohio on the occasion of the launching of the national campaign to reduce school and community violence

WE NEED YOU!

Let me first thank you for the opportunity to speak with you today at the launching of our national campaign on reducing school and community violence. The high attendance here today is an indication of your support for Each One Teach One and its mission.

Today I will not focus on the root causes of youth violence. I will not focus on the alarming statistics. I will not focus on yet another incident. I will, however, focus on the solutions. Now is the time for you and me to strengthen our commitment to helping point our youth in the right direction.

One of the objectives of Each One Teach One is to encourage family members, friends, adults, and teachers to do two things. First to take an active role in our children's lives, and two—to teach them the skills that will make them productive adults and citizens of this country. My charge to you is simply to get involved because we need you.

Each One Teach One needs you to help steer young people off the road of despair and onto a road of hope. We need you to invest in their lives. We need you to show them that violence is not the answer.

Even if the youth you know are not being pulled like a magnet to act out violent tendencies, we can all agree that our youth are vulnerable to the perils of their environments. Incident after incident shows that youth violence transcends race, gender and class. I challenge you to be a caring adult for some young person.

According to the National Commission on Children, 43% of female students in the 6th to 12th grade reported receiving support from three or more nonparent adults. For our males, the figure is only 39%. In addition, 65% of 7- to 14-year-olds say they would like to connect with an adult they can trust other than their parents. Sixty percent of 6th to 12th grade youth spend two hours or more per school day unsupervised. Each One Teach One needs you to be a part of the solution.

Page 1 of 2

Copy of a speech written for the head of a nonprofit organization to give at the launch of a national awareness campaign.

❶ HEADING: Event and purpose.

❷ TITLE.

❸ INTRODUCTION: The purpose of the speech.

❹ BODY: Between three and five main points.

Example Gallery
Speeches

Get involved by serving as an adopted family and become a safety net for a youth who would otherwise go astray. Get involved by encouraging our youth to serve their communities by joining one of the hundreds of service clubs that exist today. Get involved by offering to lead or sponsor a service club of a local school.

Get involved by serving as mentors, tutors, coaches, or even field-trip supervisors. Get involved by ensuring that your home is not a home where weapons are in the reach of our youth.

If you are a business owner, get involved by sponsoring after-school programs, apprenticeships, internships and scholarships. Business owners, you can also offer flexible or release time to parents so that they can attend parent-teacher meetings or other school functions.

All of you can help direct a young person onto the road of success. Vow today to join in the crusade to point our youth in the right direction. Become a caring adult in their lives and help them develop marketable skills. Encourage our youth to see that they too are part of the solution and not the problem.

I call on you to increase your investment in our youth. Our young people need structure, and they need to be physically and emotionally safe. Youth violence attacks the core of our communities and especially our families. It is like a cancer eating away at the fabric of our society. We need you!

As we launch this national campaign, I ask you to think of how you can make a difference. I remind you of the old African proverb, "It takes a village to raise a child." Guess what, you and I, we are all residents of that village. Each One Teach One needs you. Our youth need you. We need you!

⑤

Page 2 of 2

⑤ CONCLUSION: Review of main points and final thought or call to action.

Chapter 15

Video News Releases and Electronic Press Kits

What Are They?

Newsworthiness and relevance to the audience are the criteria by which to decide whether or not to use video news releases or electronic press kits. The information must be newsworthy to the media and relevant to the target audience in order to justify the cost of producing either of these public communication products.

Video news releases (VNRs) are the video version of printed news releases. An electronic press kit (EPK) is the video equivalent of a printed media kit. Both of these products convert printed words into visual images and sound bites. VNRs are carefully constructed 90-second to 3-minute news stories that allow an organization to maintain some control over its message. An EPK is usually a somewhat longer version of a VNR—closer to 15 minutes in length—and often supplies more extensive information related to an event. EPKs are generally targeted to entertainment-related shows or programs.

Both VNRs and EPKs are efficient ways for organizations to submit information about a newsworthy event or activity to television news stations across the nation. News outlets are encouraged to incorporate the supplied footage into their own news stories and programming. The goal of employing a VNR or an EPK is to acquire positive placement and/or mentions in a news program. Effective VNRs and EPKs result in news stories that ultimately give the sponsoring organization third-party credibility and high visibility and exposure to the specified target audience.

VNRs and EPKs should not be confused with printed broadcast news releases or media kits developed primarily for distribution to broadcast news outlets for their use as source materials to cover an event. Instead, VNRs and EPKs supply footage so that individual news stations can construct news stories that reflect their own styles and formatting.

VNRs and EPKs are produced by professional video production firms such as DS Simon Productions, Medialink, and Pathfire. But the public communication practitioner should be aware of the elements of a VNR and EPK and understand how to work with a production company. More importantly, VNRs and EPKs must have the best in media relations strategy and tactics behind them in order to have a chance of being used. Media relations experts must pitch the stories professionally and to the right person at news stations the first time. Because the competition is fierce, the first pitch is probably the only opportunity for success.

Video news releases and electronic press kits generally include background information **slates** (information slides, no sound), **b-roll** (a series of rough video images that incorporate a variety of different camera angles with natural sound), **sound bites** (7- to 15-second audio of quotes from an individual), and sometimes a pre-edited narrated news story. While including a finished news package is not recommended because it does not allow the targeted news outlets to develop their own news stories utilizing their individual style and format, many VNR and EPK producers choose to include them as guidelines for news directors and editors.

It is crucial for both VNRs and EPKs to be newsworthy and to have solid news angles. These two elements dictate whether or not a story will get coverage by news stations. Although a VNR or an EPK may be produced by an organization with a specific message in mind, too many mentions or references to the organization can make the material appear more like a paid advertising piece, a commercial, or an infomercial. Television news producers are not likely to include this type of material from the VNR or EPK. Most news departments consider themselves objective and neutral, and they do not want to provide free airtime to advertise a message, product, or organization in a biased manner. Therefore, the messages throughout any VNR or EPK should remain as objective as possible.

Because of the rising costs of covering the news and the decreasing news department budgets across the country, VNRs and EPKs are being used more and more frequently. These tools supply free and unrestricted footage to newsrooms for use as they see fit. The cost of producing a VNR or an EPK varies a great deal depending on the elements, time constraints, and complexity. Many cost factors must be considered when planning a budget for a VNR or an EPK. Elements such as preproduction planning, location shoot(s), postproduction editing, graphic composition, distribution, and monitoring of use affect the cost. Once these components have been determined and priced, an overall cost can be estimated. In general, an average-priced VNR runs between $10,000 and $50,000, while an EPK can run upward of $75,000.

Who Gets Them?

It is up to the communication practitioner to conduct the research that identifies and then locates a target audience for a VNR or an EPK. The ubiquity of television makes it an excellent choice for reaching a target audience with an important message. Television stations are well aware of who is watching their news segments. This information can be used to determine whether your target audience is watching. Clearly, if you want to reach soccer moms, you may find them watching the evening news, whereas it is unlikely you'll find their young players there.

What Do They Do?

The purpose of a VNR or an EPK is to promote an organization's event, news story, issue, product, or idea. These public communication products put an organization's message into visual terms while concentrating on subjects that are important to the sponsoring organization. VNRs and EPKs supply newsworthy information to the television news media in a format they can use. They allow an organization to create, frame, and shape a visual message and to disseminate it to specific news media outlets. VNRs are especially useful during times of crisis. They make it possible to distribute messages to the public or targeted audiences rapidly by uplinking the VNR signal to a satellite that can be simultaneously downlinked by most television outlets, which can disseminate the material to their audiences instantaneously.

VNRs are also sources of news for many television networks and affiliates. While news stations are affected by budget cuts and time constraints, VNRs provide story information (news), interview segments, and supplemental video and/or graphics free of charge and for unrestricted use to news producers who often construct their own stories using the raw materials provided. VNRs and EPKs are especially useful to small stations that have limited resources, allowing them to compete with stations that have larger staffs and budgets. Also, they provide professional and difficult-to-obtain footage to stations that would not ordinarily be able to afford coverage of the story.

VNRs and EPKs offer third-party credibility to organizations when they are used effectively by television stations. Instead of paying a significant amount of money for a contrived paid advertising spot, an organization can convey a message incorporated into a news story. The credibility of the information and the organization rises significantly when images and sound are presented in a television news story.

VNRs and EPKs also have an extended shelf life. Because they are offered free of charge and for unrestricted use, television producers can utilize the images found in VNRs and EPKs again and again. Typically, television producers pay for the rights to use some of the footage made available to them by video resource warehouses and catalogs, whereas VNRs and EPKs can supply the visuals they need without charging a fee.

How Do They Help?

VNRs and EPKs give organizations significant control over a message. If you develop an angle, incorporate crucial sound and footage, and send the finished product to specific television media outlets, you increase the possibility that the intended message will be communicated to the target audience. The information has the potential to reach millions of people at once, making VNRs and EPKs very cost-effective. Organizations can produce and distribute a quality VNR or EPK nationally and globally for approximately $10,000 to $100,000, depending on variables such as travel, number of shoots, satellite costs, and number of video copies. A mere 30-second spot commercial can cost hundreds of thousands of dollars to produce, excluding the additional expense of purchasing the time.

VNRs and EPKs are aired more and more frequently now than in years past. With budget constraints, increased media competition, and the 24-hour news cycle, VNRs and EPKs are more attractive to newsrooms than ever before. Stations receive video footage of events and activities that they can't physically cover themselves. Studies show that 100 percent of newsrooms use some portion of VNR or EPK footage at least once a year, although many maintain that they don't use unsolicited pieces at all.

VNRs and EPKs can add credibility to an organization and its campaign. They can position the organization as the authority on an issue or industry, and can also make the organization's message more memorable and meaningful to the public.

What Are the Pitfalls?

The news media are often critical of VNRs and EPKs because they are not produced by a network or station and are often referred to as "fake news."

Some news stations say that they refuse to air VNRs and EPKs because they cannot determine if the information provided is objective and, if it isn't, they don't want to place their credibility on the line. News stations may label the VNR or EPK untrustworthy and therefore refuse to use the footage at all.

Television news outlets also face the possible charge of deceiving the public when they air VNRs or EPKs. In most instances, viewers do not know they are watching a VNR or an EPK, and this can be seen as subjecting them to potential biases, especially when the sponsor is not clearly identified. Also, stations will not air VNRs that promote products or ideas that they would otherwise not choose to advertise.

It has become increasingly difficult to obtain a successful placement of a VNR or an EPK, even though their use by the television news media has increased significantly. An ever-growing number of VNRs and EPKs are pitched to television news outlets every day, making competition for that valued placement very difficult. As with many other public communication media tactics, the effective placement of the VNR or EPK can only be as successful as an organization's media list and media relations follow-up.

Ethics Note

Questions of ethical use of VNRs and EPKs are important to the public relations practitioner and newsgathering organizations. News editors have a code of ethics, as do practitioners (Chapter 4 discusses these codes). Many editors refuse to use the finished package VNR, as mentioned above, because the stories are clearly designed to place the producing organization in the most favorable light possible. A U.S. government cabinet agency, Health and Human Services (HHS), once distributed a VNR to promote a new Medicare law. The VNR included a very familiar manner of ending a news story: "This is Karen Ryan reporting."

The General Accountability Office (GAO) ruled that the VNR violated federal statutes because it was not identified as a production of the federal government. The ruling suggested the VNR was "covert propaganda." Viewers often do not know who is sponsoring the story they are seeing. It is important for news stations to include a reference to the source of the footage or information used in a news story.

How Should They Look?

Style Notes

Perhaps the most important element of any VNR or EPK is the visuals. Because they use a video format, VNRs or EPKs that rely too heavily on sound or background copy information will ultimately fail. The visuals should be able to tell a story using various shots and angles that complement the underlying message of the news story. The footage from the VNR or EPK that is most often used by news stations is hard-to-obtain video that the stations cannot shoot themselves. It is important, however, to avoid flashiness and heavy use of special effects and graphics unless it is absolutely necessary to do so. The footage should not look staged; instead, it should resemble the visual style of a news story.

Clearly, the information you provide must be factual and verifiable, adding to the credibility of not only the VNR or EPK but the organization as well. Offering an accurate account enhances the possibility that news stations will turn to the sponsoring organization as an authority in the future. Including sound bites from experts on the subject and third-party sources also adds credibility to the VNR. It is key to include more than one sound bite per newsmaker in order to offer the news producers various editing options. It is also often helpful to provide differing individual perspectives. This allows producers to create stories using the accepted formula in the news business referred to as *balance*—a presentation of facts as they are known, followed by reporting the two sides of the issue.

Process and Format

Producing a VNR or an EPK requires adequate planning. First, the subject must be newsworthy. Next, objectives and goals must be established and a target audience clearly defined. The purpose of the VNR or EPK must be evident in order to help create a concept and format. And finally, some form of evaluation should be in place prior to the actual distribution and dissemination of the piece, because once the VNR airs, it is more difficult and costly to track its use. While these determinants should always be considered no matter what the public communication tactic is, they are critical when considering VNRs and EPKs, which are so costly to produce.

Once a VNR or an EPK is ready for production, it should be produced digitally or on broadcast-quality tape with split-channel audio so that the television news video editor will have more control over the included sound elements.

Slates are used in several places throughout a VNR or an EPK. As mentioned earlier in this chapter, a slate is a video element that appears with no sound (unless a narration is used). They are generally stand-alone informational slides that appear right before the visuals they describe. Slates are used in order to avoid placing the titles or words over raw images, enabling individual news stations to use their own font (type) styles for titles or identification purposes.

The order of the elements may vary from project to project, but the format generally remains the same. VNRs and EPKs often include the following elements in this order:

- **Disclaimer**   A standard slate that gives the news station permission to use any footage supplied on the VNR or EPK. The disclaimer also gives news organizations the opportunity to use any portions of the VNR or EPK for future stories. The copy usually reads, "The following material is offered for your free and unrestricted use by [name of organization]."

- **Table of Contents**   This slate provides a detailed list of what will be seen within the body of the VNR or EPK and in what order. It often includes **time codes** (a tape-generated timing element) to indicate the time and length of shots.

- **Précis**   The précis provides background information on the news that is being seen in the VNR or EPK and how it relates to the sponsoring organization's key messages. This slate is often the main link a news station has to the themes and messages being conveyed by the organization. Of course, we would not call them key messages and themes. Our job is to weave them into the context and importance of the news story.

- **B-Roll**   This supplemental video footage provides news stations with vibrant visuals and natural sound (commonly referred to as "nat-sound"). The most frequently used b-roll is footage that news stations would have difficulty obtaining on their own. B-roll should include various scenes and camera angles and run for two to five minutes.

- **Sound Bites and Interviews**   Sound bites are the actual words spoken by individuals. They are also known as **SOT** (sound on tape). Most often, SOT consists of excerpts from an on-location interview, speech, opinion response, or question-and-answer session. Again, using sound bites from a third-party source helps to validate and add credibility to the VNR. A person's comments should reinforce the messages that are carried throughout the VNR and provide more information to help clarify the issue or topic. Sound bites should not exceed 15 seconds; the 7-second bite is ideal. It is important to include three seconds of pad time (dead space) on either side of the sound bite to allow for editing. In addition, sound bites should not be scripted, because it is hard to make scripted lines sound like real quotes from a real news interview. The individual being featured should not look directly into the camera, in keeping with standard news practice. An identification slate that includes the person's name and position or title should immediately precede any distinguishable sound bite.

- **Packaged Piece**   Packaged pieces (model stories) are rarely used, but many VNR producers choose to include a model news story because clients often want to see how a story may appear. This practice is discouraged for many reasons. For one, it often gives television news stations the impression that they are not in control and are being fed advertising and propaganda. As a consequence, they refuse to use any element of the story. Packaged stories are also a significant expense. Because a professional freelance television journalist will be needed, that cost must be added to the budget. These rates are generally quite high and often include union fees or add-ons. And finally, the time required to add a packaged piece can take away from the timeliness of the VNR.

- **Contact Slate**   This slate provides the name(s) and contact information of the source, including a telephone number and/or email address, in case there are questions or further inquiries from the news media.

- **Hard-Copy Request Information Slate**   This slate provides the name and contact information of the source for the news organization in case additional copies of the VNR or EPK are needed.

- **Script**   Although a script is optional, it is often considered helpful for editing purposes. The script resembles the format of a standard television news broadcast script. It is separated into two columns with a description of video images in the left column and audio in the right column. Slates are always located on the left side (because they are video elements), and identification slates always precede the person speaking on tape. The heading, which includes the sponsoring organization's name, **slug** (short title of the piece), length of the VNR, producer's name, and date, appears at the top of the script. Developing a script of desired images and sound bites prior to production helps organize a VNR or an EPK. Ordinarily, a script serves as a transcript to aid the news station in editing and writing its own stories.

Where Should They Go?

The newest development in the VNR and EPK business is distribution. Just as technology has revamped television in the past decades with videotape, satellite transmission, digital editing, and high definition television (HDTV), it has affected the way in which VNRs and EPKs are received. In the not-so-distant past, hard-copy videotapes were distributed through the mail to television stations. While hard copies of VNRs are still used by many stations, today they can be delivered in other ways that are convenient for news stations. But hard copies are still the standard of EPKs because they are often planned far enough in advance and generally are sent with additional printed material.

At this writing, the most common method of distribution for VNRs is via satellite transmission, but DVDs are becoming popular. Producers send media advisories and scripts to news directors and show producers by fax or email or make telephone calls to pitch the stories and advise the stations of the satellite window time for the feed. The media advisories contain a detailed summary, headline, keywords, satellite time and coordinates, and editorial and technical contacts for additional information. The stations then have a technician on hand to download the transmission at the appointed time.

Digital distribution is the newest way to distribute VNRs and EPKs. Internet applications and Web sites with video that can be downloaded provide immediate access to VNRs. If we consider benefits, these systems allow reporters to receive the information and tools they need for a story via email. An interesting digital development for distribution of VNRs is a system created by Pathfire in Atlanta. It is an interesting development for a few reasons. First, Pathfire stores and delivers footage on an ongoing basis. As a result, stations can have access for extended periods of time and are not limited to a window of time, as is the case with satellite transmission. This means the material can be captured at times that might be more convenient for the stations, and if the video is suitable for feature pieces, it can be captured at a later date. The other reason Pathfire is an interesting development is that it has CNN as a stakeholder in the company. Most CNN affiliates have the Pathfinder digital system and the company has distribution agreements with ABC, WB, and CBS affiliates, according to *PR Week*.

Did They Work?

The best way to evaluate the success of VNRs and EPKs is to evaluate their media placement. If a news station utilized the video in an effective way, the piece has conveyed the sponsoring organization's intended message to its target audience.

There are many reliable ways to track the placement of a VNR or an EPK. Although no tracking system can record 100% of the hits, tracking systems have become the standard in monitoring use of VNRs. SIGMA, from Nielsen Media Research, covers 212 markets. The producer injects an invisible code into the video signal using special equipment. Once the invisible code is injected, it can pick up broadcast signals. Information such as the time, date, broadcast duration, and location of airing is generated into a report, making it very simple to determine the reach of a VNR.

RTV Reports' VeriCheck, on the other hand, covers only 75 markets, but it can generate the same information as SIGMA. It is the most accurate form of tracking. This system relies on video-encoded invisible light (VEIL) technology, by which an invisible code is placed directly into the picture. Pulses of light create computer-readable bits of information, and data are sent to the distributor.

A cautionary note: Just because a VNR or an EPK was aired by a news station does not mean it was used effectively. Other factors must be taken into consideration, such as the way the media portrayed the story to the audience and the number of people in the target audience who were reached. Usage reports can help to sort out this information. A usage report contains detailed information organized by market, station, network affiliation, time and date of airing, and length of confirmed usage, and market maps and key demographics for each confirmed use. These reports are very helpful and alert the organization right away whether the VNR or EPK served its purpose.

Putting PR into Practice

Consider the client you chose for this class or an organization with which you are closely affiliated.

1. Ask yourself the following strategic questions:
   a. Why is a VNR appropriate for this client?
   b. What is the purpose of the VNR?
   c. What is the primary audience you are trying to reach through the VNR?
   d. Why is a news editor or producer likely to use the VNR?
2. A VNR is much more than a written news release, but you can begin with reviewing a news release you have already prepared for this client. Using the example in the Example Gallery, create a VNR script, keeping in mind the answers to the following questions:
   a. Who will narrate? Who is the primary spokesperson?
   b. What visuals will you use on camera? Remember: a series of talking heads is deadly boring.
   c. What b-roll will you include in the package?

An *Example Gallery* for Video News Releases
begins on the following page.

Example Gallery
Video News Releases

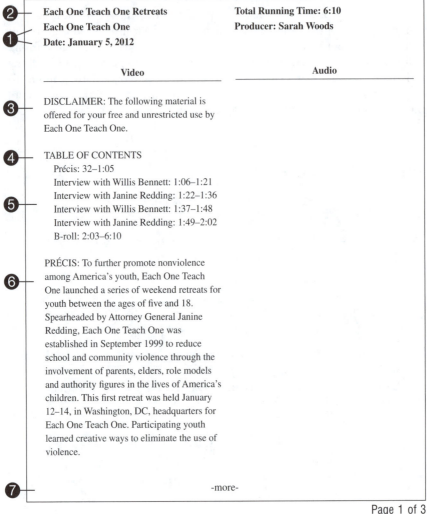

Each One Teach One Retreats
Each One Teach One
Date: January 5, 2012

Total Running Time: 6:10
Producer: Sarah Woods

Video	Audio

DISCLAIMER: The following material is offered for your free and unrestricted use by Each One Teach One.

TABLE OF CONTENTS
Précis: 32–1:05
Interview with Willis Bennett: 1:06–1:21
Interview with Janine Redding: 1:22–1:36
Interview with Willis Bennett: 1:37–1:48
Interview with Janine Redding: 1:49–2:02
B-roll: 2:03–6:10

PRÉCIS: To further promote nonviolence among America's youth, Each One Teach One launched a series of weekend retreats for youth between the ages of five and 18. Spearheaded by Attorney General Janine Redding, Each One Teach One was established in September 1999 to reduce school and community violence through the involvement of parents, elders, role models and authority figures in the lives of America's children. This first retreat was held January 12–14, in Washington, DC, headquarters for Each One Teach One. Participating youth learned creative ways to eliminate the use of violence.

-more-

Video elements in the left column, audio components in the right column. Image presented corresponds to the scripted words.

1 HEADING: Identifies organization, date, and length.

2 SLUG: Short title capturing the main news.

3 DISCLAIMER: Gives news outlet the right to broadcast the supplied footage.

4 TABLE OF CONTENTS: Lists the contents of a VNR in the order they appear, with time codes.

5 TIME CODES: Used to reference specific footage found in the VNR.

6 PRÉCIS: A 5- to 15-second slate with no audio element that provides background information about organization and news.

7 PAGE SLUGS: At the bottom of each page, -more- indicates script continues on the next page; at the end of the last page, -###- or -30- or -end- indicates the end.

Example Gallery
Video News Releases

Video	Audio
Slate #1: (MS) Willis Bennett, Executive Director of Each One Teach One	SOT #1 Bennett: "We can all agree that there's a youth violence problem in this country. It's time for adults to step in and become involved in the lives of our nation's children. SOT #2 Bennett: "The weekend retreats—like all Each One Teach One programs—provide youth with the essential tools to avoid violence. The youth teach each other so that they become involved and committed to the process."
Slate #2: (MS) Janine Redding, U.S. Attorney General	SOT #1 Redding: "The beauty of Each One Teach One is that it's not about lecturing our youth to avoid violence. It's about giving them the skills to choose an alternate path." SOT #2 Redding: "There's no question that we need to take active steps to curb youth violence. The Each One Teach One retreats are a sure step in the right direction."
Slate #3: Each One Teach One after-school program, Akron, OH B-roll Visuals of young students and their mentors on playground outside Akron Middle School working on constructive problem-solving methods. (WS) Playground at Akron, OH middle school (WS) Children on playground (MS) Three children talking and gesturing (CU) Two children smiling	NATSOUND

-more-

⑧ SLATE: Screen that identifies or introduces images that follow.

⑨ SOT: Sound on tape, a quote by someone related to the news story.

⑩ B-ROLL: Footage or compiled images shot at site of news story or event.

⑪ NATSOUND: Natural sound, audio present in the background of b-roll clips.

Example Gallery
Video News Releases

Video	Audio
Slate #4: Each One Teach One symposium, "Reaching Our Children," San Francisco, CA. Visuals of teachers, parents and students applauding keynote speaker, Oprah Winfrey, after her introductory presentation. (WS) Auditorium (MS) Audience clapping (CU) Oprah Winfrey	NATSOUND
Slate #5: Group counseling session at Each One Teach One workshop, Houston, TX Visuals of a circle of students and counselors debating effective conflict-solving techniques. Students discussing what strikes anger in them, counselors suggesting alternatives to violence. (MS) Students and counselors (CU) Three students	NATSOUND
Slate #6: Each One Teach One educational brochures and pamphlets Visuals of brochures and pamphlets.	NATSOUND

12 — Slate #7: For more information, contact: Christine Chow (202) 555-3777. For video information, contact: Sarah Woods (202) 555-3777.

Slate #8: Additional b-roll footage will be available Monday, January 15, 2012, from 3:00 p.m. to 3:30 p.m. EDT Galaxy 9 / Transporter 12 Audio 7.2+7.8.

-end-

Page 3 of 3

12 CONTACT INFORMATION: Two slates at the end. One offers more information, giving contact names and phone numbers. The second offers additional video via satellite or informs media outlets how to obtain a hard copy of the VNR.

Example Gallery
Video News Releases

Children's Exercise Ball Wins Youth Fitness Award

Total Running Time: 6:35

Formative Enterprises, Inc.

Date: March 6, 2012

Producer: Staci Kaufman
555-5597

Video	Audio

DISCLAIMER: The following information is offered for your free and unrestricted use by Formative Enterprises, Inc.

NATSOUND

TABLE OF CONTENTS:
　　Précis: 15–1:20
　　Rick Ripley, U.S. Secretary of Education 2:21–2:42
　　Jamie Molack, CEO of Formative Enterprises, Inc. 4:15–5:02
　　Sandy Meyer, Teacher 5:03–5:50
　　B-roll 1:21–4:14

PRÉCIS: The United States Secretary of Education, Rick Ripley, announced the winners of this year's National Youth Fitness Awards. In the category of "Outstanding Youth Fitness Product," the winner was Formative Enterprises' Youth Exercise Ball.

The award ceremony, held on Saturday, September 8th, in Washington, DC, honored individuals and organizations that have made significant strides in the area of improving children's fitness.

-more-

① HEADING: Identifies organization, date, and length.

② SLUG: Short title capturing the main news.

③ DISCLAIMER: Gives news outlet the right to broadcast the supplied footage.

④ TABLE OF CONTENTS: Lists the contents of a VNR in the order they appear, with time codes.

⑤ TIME CODES: Used to reference specific footage found in the VNR.

⑥ PRÉCIS: A 5- to 15-second slate with no audio element that provides background information about organization and news.

⑦ PAGE SLUGS: At the bottom of each page, -more- indicates script continues on the next page; at the end of the last page, -###- or -30- or -end- indicates the end.

Example Gallery
Video News Releases

Video	Audio
Slate: The National Youth Fitness Award Ceremony, Washington, DC B-roll (WS) Shots of the ceremony (MS) introduction of U.S. Secretary of Education Rick Ripley	NATSOUND
Slate: Rick Ripley United States Secretary of Education (MS) Rick Ripley	SOT Ripley: "Very rarely does an entire company dedicate itself to the physical fitness of this country's youth the way that Formative Enterprises seems to do on a regular basis. By incorporating fun, exercise, and fitness into one state-of-the-art product, Formative Enterprises has succeeded in creating a groundbreaking new product in the field of youth fitness."
(MS) Secretary of Education bestowing the Outstanding Youth Fitness Product Award to Formative Enterprises CEO, Jamie Molack (WS) Audience applauding	NATSOUND
Slate: Footage of the development of the Youth Exercise Ball (MS) Scientist and researchers reviewing sketches of the exercise ball (CU) Series of various clay and rubber models of the exercise ball (WS) Gymnasium filled with children testing prototype of the Youth Exercise Ball	NATSOUND
(MS) Manufacturing of the Youth Exercise Ball at Formative Enterprises	NATSOUND

-more-

8 SLATE: Screen that identifies or introduces images that follow.

9 SOT: Sound on tape, a quote by someone related to the news story.

10 B-ROLL: Footage or compiled images shot at site of news story or event.

11 NATSOUND: Natural sound, audio present in the background of b-roll clips.

Example Gallery
Video News Releases

Video	Audio
Slate: Formative Enterprises, Inc. Pointhaven, Illinois (WS) Various exterior angles of Formative Enterprises, Inc.	NATSOUND
Slate: Jamie Molack CEO, Formative Enterprises (MS) Molack	SOT #1 Molack: "It took nearly three years of research, development and testing before Formative Enterprises successfully perfected the Youth Exercise Ball. While we are thrilled about receiving such a prestigious award, our product team feels even more rewarded when we hear how children are using and enjoying our products every day." SOT #2 Molack: "Everyone at Formative Enterprises is dedicated to the happiness and well-being of children both in the U.S. and abroad."
Slate: Sandy Meyer Physical Education Teacher (MS) Meyer	SOT Meyer: "It used to be a chore to get some of my students to exercise, but now that I've incorporated the Youth Exercise Ball into my curriculum, they all enjoy becoming more physically fit."
Slate: For video or story information contact: ⑫ Staci Kaufman 555-5597	

-end-

⑫ CONTACT INFORMATION: Two slates at the end. One offers more information, giving contact names and phone numbers. The second offers additional video via satellite or informs media outlets how to obtain a hard copy of the VNR.

Example Gallery
Video News Releases

Video	Audio
Emerald Heights First Annual Community Day	**Total Running Time: 3:20**
Emerald Heights Office of the Mayor	**Producer: Steve Mangel**
Date: May 10, 2012	**555-2233**

DISCLAIMER: The following information is offered for your free and unrestricted use by the Emerald Heights City Government.

TABLE OF CONTENTS:
    Précis: 15–1:02
    B-Roll 1:03–2:01
    SOT Mayor Judith Gold 2:02–2:35
    SOT Artist Brady Lafay 2:36–2:55
    SOT 6-year-old Mandy Todd 2:56–3:05

PRÉCIS: To kick off a summer of fun and activities, Emerald Heights is holding a special weekend festival celebrating the 100th birthday of the city on May 24–26. Located conveniently in the City Hall Community Park, the First Annual Emerald Heights Community Day will have something for everyone to enjoy. In addition to rides, food, games and prizes there will be a local art exhibit highlighting some of the city's best artists.

In the evening there will be free concerts featuring a host of local bands showing off their talents at the Northwest Amphitheater.

    Slate: The First Annual Emerald
    Heights Community Day
    B-roll

-more-

1. HEADING: Identifies organization, date, and length.

2. SLUG: Short title capturing the main news.

3. DISCLAIMER: Gives news outlet the right to broadcast the supplied footage.

4. TABLE OF CONTENTS: Lists the contents of a VNR in the order they appear, with time codes.

5. TIME CODES: Used to reference specific footage found in the VNR.

6. PRÉCIS: A 5- to 15-second slate with no audio element that provides background information about organization and news.

7. PAGE SLUGS: At the bottom of each page, -more- indicates script continues on the next page; at the end of the last page, -###- or -30- or -end- indicates the end.

8. B-ROLL: Footage or compiled images shot at site of news story or event.

Example Gallery
Video News Releases

Video	Audio
	NATSOUND
*(WS) Pan of the festival (MS) Children playing games (CU) Children and clowns (MS) Various people on rides (MS) Mayor greeting people	
Slate: The art exhibit features some of the most promising artists in the area. (WS) People looking at art (CU) Child examining painting (MS) Artist talking with people	NATSOUND
Slate: The festival continued into the evening with a free concert. (MS) Band playing on stage (WS) Pan of the audience (CU) Dad dancing with boy on shoulders	NATSOUND
Slate: Judith Gold Mayor of Emerald Heights (MS) Gold	SOT Gold: "I can't think of a better way to celebrate our city's birthday than to throw a big summer party and invite all our citizens. Thanks to everyone for making the celebration so special."
* A standard abbreviation used in the video industry to describe the type of camera shot being used WS–Wide Shot MS–Medium Shot CU–Close-Up	SOT Gold: "We hope to make this first Community Day an annual event that will attract not just our city's residents, but anyone who wants to see what Emerald Heights has to offer."

-more-

⑨ SOT: Sound on tape, a quote by someone related to the news story.

⑩ SLATE: Screen that identifies or introduces images that follow.

⑪ NATSOUND: Natural sound, audio present in the background of b-roll clips.

Example Gallery
Video News Releases

Video	Audio
Slate: Brady Lafay 　　　Artist 　　　(MS) Lafay	SOT Lafay: "This art exhibition is a great opportunity for local artists to display their works as well as mingle with artists and other citizens. I've displayed my works at some of the most prestigious art shows in the country, but nothing beats a show in my own backyard."
Slate: Mandy Todd 　　　6 years old 　　　(CU) Todd	SOT Todd: "My mommy brought me here to celebrate my sixth birthday and Emerald Heights' birthday too. This is the biggest party I every had!!!"

12 — Slate: For video or story information contact:
Steve Mangel, Office of the Mayor
555-2233.

-end-

12 CONTACT INFORMATION: Two slates at the end. One offers more information, giving contact names and phone numbers. The second offers additional video via satellite or informs media outlets how to obtain a hard copy of the VNR.

Chapter 16 — Web Sites

What Are They?

The Web, of course, is yet another public communication medium for which we write. Even if we are not responsible for the day-to-day updating of an organization's site, we are asked to contribute stories, news releases, biographical sketches, condensed versions of remarks, and other written pieces.

Web sites have become an integral part of an organization's comprehensive public communication strategy. A visible presence on the Web is critical to remaining competitive. Strategic thinking and well-honed communication skills are crucial to creating and maintaining an organization's site.

A Web site helps to introduce an organization and its key messages to the public by providing a variety of financial, promotional, marketing, and educational information in one central location. This electronic connection allows people all over the world to learn, converse, persuade, trade information, and buy and sell products and services. Because Web sites have become valuable research tools that millions of people turn to each day, and because they are a source of even more message overload for audiences, an organization must create Web pages that are creative, informative, competitive, and professional.

One of the most important elements of any Web site is the home page. It is the first image audiences see when connecting to a site. A successful home page grasps and holds the target audience's attention, informs visitors about the organization, and persuades them to venture further into the site. In order to achieve all of this, aside from knowing the target audience, understanding how to write for the online world is most important.

Web pages cannot be narrowly defined because there are so many different varieties. There are certain elements most Web sites contain, but each site incorporates its own style and format.

Who Gets Them?

As with all public communication products, a Web site's target audience is determined by the goal of the organization and the research conducted to ascertain the interests of that audience. Remember, the goal is not to want *everyone* to be informed or persuaded. Depending on the type of organization and the purpose of the Web site, target audiences can include customers, clients, employees, stakeholders and stockholders, reporters, workshop participants, organization members, students, parents, community leaders, and government agencies.

What Do They Do?

Internet Web sites are designed to inform, entertain, sell, and/or persuade an audience. Each site contains a number of different pages designed to accomplish a variety of goals and objectives.

The aim of the home page is to provide the audience with an appropriate introduction and overview of the site as well as to pique its interest and to encourage further exploration through internal links and pages. Effective copy for a home page is clear and concise, communicating an organization's key messages in a comprehensive way. The subsequent pages are designed to amplify the organization's message.

Successful Web sites receive hundreds, thousands, and possibly millions of hits per day. Organizations that are not technologically capable should not try to utilize this tool without guidance from an experienced professional or consultant. While many organizations are looking toward the technological future, those that try to produce Web sites without the correct tools, resources, and experts may end up with disastrous results. An organization should take an honest and critical look at its technological limitations before embarking on the launch of a Web site.

Once a Web site is developed, hosting and updating the site must become the priority. It is crucial to update all pages consistently while monitoring visitor feedback. Hosting a site can take place either internally or externally, but should be taken very seriously. A meager product reflects poorly on the organization and may frustrate potential clients, partners, customers, or members.

Besides being utilized as an external communication tool, the Web can be used as part of an internal communication network. By implementing a comprehensive Intranet, organizations can effectively create organizational consistency and provide easier accessibility to information and multimedia data. Intranet networks are secure and cannot be viewed by external audiences. Instead, the information is usually limited to employees, members, or other constituencies. Information on these sites is usually sensitive and therefore not intended for public scrutiny.

How Do They Help?

Many public communication professionals, as well as their journalist counterparts, have turned to the Web as a timely, cost-effective, and unlimited way to communicate messages. Organizations have designed their Web pages to offer reporters links to print and broadcast news releases that can be immediately downloaded. This process saves time and effort for both the journalist and the public communication professional. Similarly, microsites (discussed in Chapter 9) are excellent tools for organizations facing crises, as they can be focused on a particular topic, issue, or event.

In comparison to many other communication tools, Web sites are an inexpensive and effective way to communicate an organization's various activities.

In times of crisis, Web sites provide the public and the news media with up-to-date information. During a milestone or celebration, Web sites are used to offer background material about events.

When writing stories, often reporters will check Web sites for up-to-date information. If your Web site is current and well organized, reporters will consult it regularly. Press releases, speeches, and other information posted for the purposes of working journalists should be written and presented in the usual accepted format and style and should be posted in a site newsroom. Remember that all the rules of writing for the news media should be observed when posting material to a Web site for reporters.

In a crisis situation, a Web site can serve two purposes. It can help keep reporters abreast of events and circumstances and it can serve as your organization's direct communication link to your key audiences.

Intranet Web sites provide an organization's users with critical information about health insurance, pay scales, stock information, biographies, and other organizational resources. These sites facilitate two-way communication of information throughout an organization. Intranet pages also provide an opportunity for management to communicate with employees between staff meetings.

What Are the Pitfalls?

Web sites can be limited by an organization's lack of technological resources. Without the right technology, an organization's Web site cannot remain competitive. Another major limitation is a lack of commitment on the part of an organization. It is important for the organization's executives to become familiar with the long-term costs involved in maintaining a site, such as hosting and updating. Not long ago, organizations that did not employ and utilize IT specialists and/or Webmasters could not produce and maintain an effective site. Today, there are enough available tools and resources to build and maintain a professional and effective site without the added cost of additional employees.

Sites can also be limited by their design and graphic animation. Incorporating too many digital graphics or high-resolution images may result in extended time for a user to log on to the site or download from the site. If the timing is delayed even by a few seconds, it can deter a potential user from visiting the site.

A common obstacle for Intranet systems lies with properly preparing internal users for the transition to the online network. Although organizations cannot ease every concern of their user base, workshops and seminars to familiarize and train users with the Intranet system can be very helpful. Without this type of guidance, many users will fail to embrace the technology, and all the energy and work that went into creating the system will have been wasted.

How Should They Look?

Style Notes

Web sites should always be clear, concise, and easy to navigate. A language known as Hypertext Markup Language (HTML) creates the home page and its subsequent pages. A variety of word-processing programs convert the HTML language into language that the audience can understand. Today, while HTML is still prevalent, there has been a proliferation of languages used to create Web sites.

The most effective Web sites include useful and direct information. Sites that use complex terminology are often ignored because they confuse and frustrate the audience.

Well-written copy plays a significant role in the success of a Web page. As in all writing, Web sites must carefully follow stylistic guidelines for grammar, punctuation, style, and spelling. Like all public communication copy, Web page content should be written in short, clear sentences. Avoid long paragraphs and use a bulleted list format when appropriate.

Web sites often incorporate headlines, subheads, and boldface fonts to grab the attention of the user. Organizing Web site content for quick and easy scanning means that users will not have to sift through a sea of unnecessary material. Internet users want their information fast. Most Web sites have less than a 15-second window to convince a visitor not to move on to another site. By creating large type and eye-catching headlines, the Web site designer and writer help ensure that the most important information will be seen and recognized instantly.

Effective Web pages contain a limited number of fonts—usually no more than two different typefaces. The design will look organized and more professional when one typeface is used for the text blocks and a different typeface is used for headlines and subheads. These font choices are sometimes altered by the use of boldface, underlining, or italics. Most designers limit their font sizes to 14-point type for all text, but 12-point is also acceptable. The length of each line should be short to allow for scanning and quick reading.

Web site visitors must scroll down a page when information, because of length of copy, cannot fit on one page and the page must be extended. Many Web pages lose their audience's attention when users are forced to scroll down to complete reading or to look for further information. For this reason, Web page content should not exceed the space provided by the monitor screen.

Color creates yet another opportunity to display great visuals. Unfortunately, not every computer has the same color options. Therefore, Web page designers should limit color to the Web-safe color palette standard for all color computer and printer systems.

Design elements and skilled writing make up only a portion of the formula for an effective Web site. Navigation tools also play a significant role in the effectiveness of a Web site. A Web page has both internal and external links. These links make up the navigation system. The internal links consist of individual elements or icons—such as words, pictures, or symbols—that appear on the Web page. When the mouse is clicked on one of these elements, the Web site visitor is transported to additional and supplemental information related to that icon. This information is usually found on other Web pages throughout the site. Navigation is important to us as writers because we want to be sure our audiences can reach our message.

External links are similar to internal links in that they generally appear as words, pictures, or symbols, but instead of transporting the visitor to different places within the organization's site, they take a visitor to a different, but related, site. Organizations that utilize information from other sources often include external links so that their visitors can also benefit from those sources. When a Web site uses an external link within its pages, the designer or Webmaster should obtain appropriate permission from the external link's host. Obviously, it is important not to include any external link that may compete with the sponsoring organization's site. Webmasters should continually monitor and update external links to ensure that the sites linked to the organization's Web site still exist. Audience members are often frustrated by links that lead to nowhere, so they stop visiting the original site.

Simple navigation that is easy to understand and consistent throughout the entire Web site is extremely important. The navigation elements should stay consistent on each page, and users should be able to access the home page easily no matter where they are in the site. It is most effective when a user can navigate throughout the entire site from any page.

An important navigation element included in every good Web page is a contact link. It is crucial that the audience be able to make contact with and offer feedback to the organization. Email addresses, street addresses, and especially telephone numbers are an important part of this link, especially for news media.

The last element in Web page design is graphics. As a writer, you want designers to choose graphics that fit the mood and theme of your words and the site. Animated graphics help draw attention to a Web site through the use of motion and sometimes sound. Judging appropriate use is important, as too much animation can detract from the message and become bothersome and confusing for the audience.

Format

Home Page

As the first page of the Web site, the home page is the organization's main identifier, incorporating a statement of purpose, a logo, key corporate information, and an introduction to the Web site's navigational system.

Internal Pages

These pages must be tailored to best benefit the organization's goals. Internal pages may be calendars of events, newsrooms and public information, backgrounders on the organization or issues, or archives. The list can go on. Internal pages also can target different audiences within the same Web site.

Headers

At the top of each internal page, there should be a short phrase that identifies and summarizes the purpose of the page.

Navigation Bar

A navigation bar should be easily visible on each page so that the visitor can move within the Web site without returning to the home page.

Logo

The organization's **logo**, or identifying symbol, should appear on each page in the site.

Where Should They Go?

Obviously, Web sites are available only through Internet/Intranet systems. Subscribing to search engines is an excellent way to ensure that an organization's Web site receives optimum attention. A search engine is a Web site that compiles information about different sites and categorizes them by subjects and keywords. Web site visitors enter information about the subject they want to research, and the search engine lists addresses and provides links to different sites that relate to their topic.

Another way to make sure that an organization's Web site is being visited is to include the Web site address, and an invitation to visit it, on all printed material distributed by the organization. News releases, stationery, brochures, business cards, advertisements, and paid advertising or public service media spots are all opportunities to plug an organization's Web site.

Organizations often trade links with one another. This means that Organization A will promote Organization B on its Web pages by including an external link to Organization B's site. In return, Organization B does the same. This creates both a partnership for the organizations involved and a service for the individual searching for information.

Did They Work?

Evaluating the success of Web sites on the Internet is one of the biggest obstacles to the technological revolution. It has become possible to determine exact demographic information on a Web site's audience through analytics that can tell you the age, gender, and geographic location of a visitor. But users can log on to a Web site under a different identity every time and of course do not have to answer survey questions honestly. It is hard to measure the true success of a Web site if an organization is not sure who is visiting its site. In addition, if a Web site gets 1,000 hits per day, that does not necessarily mean the site had 1,000 different users; in fact, the same person could be logging on each of those 1,000 times.

User appraisals may be problematic, but they are not the only way to determine the success of a Web page. Surveys on the Web site can help organizations garner information from visitors. Organizations can offer their email addresses to users for the purpose of getting email comments about the site.

Listening to the audience's feedback is one of the best ways to evaluate the success of a site.

The success of a Web site may also be evaluated based on consumer purchasing numbers or on how many visitors became members either while at the site or after visiting the site. An information-based site can be evaluated based on how many people contact it to find out more information about its cause.

The organizations with the most effective Web sites listen to their audience feedback and constantly monitor and update their sites based on the needs and/or wants of their audience.

Putting PR into Practice

The process for creating a Web site is much like the brochure and newsletter processes you read about earlier, and, as always, it begins with strategy. Most businesses and nonprofits today have Web sites. So it is no longer a question of whether or not a client will profit from having a site. Today, having a site is tantamount to existing. Instead, the question is how large the site will be and how to make it useful.

1. Consider your course client and answer a few strategic questions: Who are your client's primary audiences? Do they have access to the Internet? Who are your client's primary competitors? What is the extent of their Web presence? What is the primary objective for the client's Web site? What does your client want to communicate? What does your client want Web visitors to do while on the site?

2. To begin thinking about the Web site content and look and feel, list the topics of greatest interest to your client and its primary audiences. Arrange the list in order of importance. Group related topics. Use an organization chart design computer software application such as Microsoft Smart Art to create the architecture for your client's Web site.

3. Think about the navigation of the site as you proceed. Think of the uppermost box of the organization chart as the home page. All of the other boxes (pages) appearing on subsequent levels should be logical and navigational. For example, the first box (page) on the second level should likely be an "about us" page. Continue in this manner until you have exhausted the list. You will likely have six to ten pages.

An *Example Gallery* for Web Sites begins on the following page.

Example Gallery
Web Sites

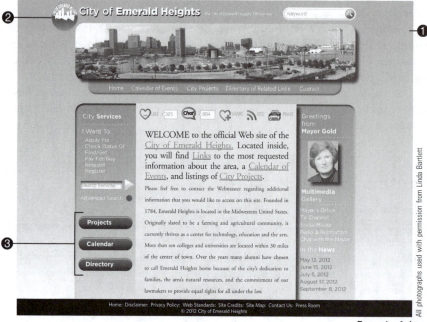

All photographs used with permission from Linda Bartlett

The home page of a city government Web site provides navigation to three Web pages.

❶ HOME PAGE: Contains basic, useful information, a clear introduction to the organization and its purpose, and clear links to the other pages of the site, including a contact link.

❷ LOGO: An identifiable logo appears on every page of the site. It should be colorful and eye-catching art that is simple enough to be recognizable to the reader.

❸ NAVIGATIONAL TOOLS: Clear and simple internal links that do not interfere with content and that facilitate navigation through the site and quick return to the home page.

Example Gallery
Web Sites

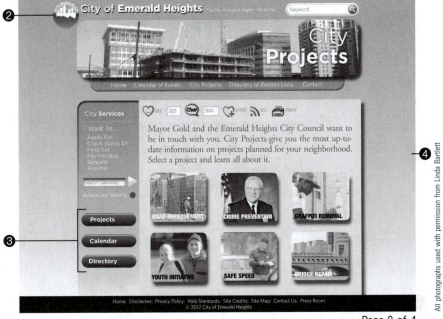

Page 2 of 4

❹ GRAPHICS: Eye-catching and colorful, but used to enhance, not overpower, the pages.

Example Gallery
Web Sites

Example Gallery
Web Sites

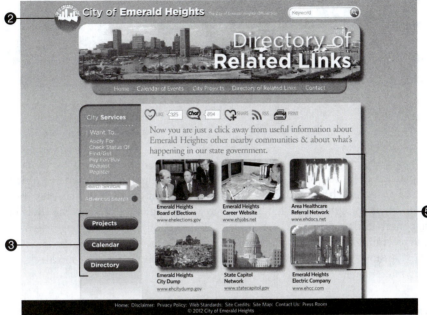

❺ EXTERNAL LINKS: Links to related sites on the Web are reference tools for additional information.

This appendix includes a few public relations *tools* commonly used by aspiring and practicing professionals. While each of these items is important, none required an entire chapter. A few, however, are mentioned in the chapters but are important enough to be highlighted here. This appendix presents the tools in alphabetical order for easy reference: billing, boilerplate language, email, employee publications, media advisories/media alerts, media clippings, memoranda, mission statements, news conferences, pitch letters, proposals, and videoconferencing.

Billing

Many organizations hire public relations firms, agencies, or freelance public communication professionals for their expertise in handling communication needs. One important business element that exists between the practitioner and the client is billing. The bill to the client covers account team or freelancer services fees, vendor services out-of-pocket expenses, and processing fees (i.e., administrative costs such as copying, telephone, and fax).

There are two ways of billing a client. An agency or a freelance practitioner can bill the client on an hourly fee basis or work for the client on a fixed monthly **retainer**: before the start of the project, the client and the agency or practitioner agree on a flat fee as a monthly payment. A retainer agreement helps the agency or freelancer control cash flow and the budget because payments are steady throughout the year. But the performance/compensation formula that exists under the hourly fee arrangement is practiced more often than the retainer arrangement in most agencies and by most freelancers because the chance of covering all costs is greater.

Under the hourly fee structure, the agency or freelancer is paid for the hours logged on the client's behalf. Agency staffs have different hourly rates based on experience, ability, and title as a team member. Junior and senior agency staff perform tasks suitable for their levels and are billed at different rates.

Agencies have minimum retainers that may vary slightly depending on the economy. Usually, the retainer is based on the estimated hourly fee. Overservicing or underservicing are the primary drawbacks to working on retainer. The agency executive or freelancer should explain the imbalance to the client each month and explain that the service time the client gets for the retainer fee will balance out over the life of the project.

Account teams and freelancers should always keep track of the time they spend on a client's behalf regardless of billing agreement—hourly or retainer. Many agencies use special software to keep track of billable hours, work performed for the client, and the expenses incurred.

Clients often raise questions about discrepancies in number of hours or when the bill exceeds what they expect. The key is to manage client expectations. If the account manager or freelancer senses that the bill is going to exceed the usual amount because of a big event or multiple projects on the client's behalf, she should prepare the client for extra charges *prior* to the time the bill is sent. It is also crucial for the account manager or freelancer to discuss the potential increased costs with the client beforehand and let the client decide whether the extra service is desired.

The billing method is usually included in the contract or the letter of agreement. The billable time begins after the client and the account manager or freelancer sign the contract. The previous time and effort are considered marketing costs and should not be charged to the client.

Boilerplate Language

Boilerplate language is the ubiquitous paragraph or two that can be added to news releases, brochures, newsletters, correspondence, Web sites, and other communication messages emanating from an organization. The boilerplate clearly and concisely describes the organization to its external audiences. Sometimes confused with an organization's mission statement, boilerplate language goes beyond the purpose or goals of the organization and provides information about what the organization does or makes, its primary audiences or customers, its nonprofit status, and its funding sources or other partnerships. Boilerplate language is highlighted in the examples in Chapter 10, News Releases.

Email

Email allows people to be in contact with one another quickly and easily through Internet/Intranet systems. It allows users to send a text message from one computer to another. Email can also be used to send spreadsheets, word-processing documents, programs, messages, faxes, photographs, video, audio, and PDF files. Many of the public communication collateral pieces discussed in the chapters of this book can be attached to an email message.

Email is a beneficial communication tool for several reasons. Most important is its speed. A written message is delivered within minutes or even seconds after being sent. Second, sending email is inexpensive. Whether the message is being sent to the next town or a neighboring country, to only one person or as many as hundreds of people, the cost is the same. Third, email is convenient. Expanding technology has made it possible to read or send email at any time and any place.

Unlike traditional letters, email messages can be saved and sent at a later time. Lastly, email can be sent to several recipients quickly and easily. Sending a message to either one or even a thousand users can be done simply by adding numerous email addresses. In addition, messages can be saved or printed for future reference, allowing members of the media to create e-folders for reference later. Convenience, cost effectiveness, and fast speed have made email one of the most often used tools of communication in today's world. Email addresses are expected on business cards, letterheads, and promotional pieces.

Although a very effective form of communication, email has disadvantages. Because email messages are sent or received through the Internet, email users are concerned about the safety and privacy of messages. It is possible that third parties can read, receive, or even block messages communicated through the Internet. Also, unlike telephone conversations in which responses are instantaneous, email receivers may not read or reply to a message within a desired period of time. In addition, the tone of an email message is difficult to interpret, often causing confusion and misinterpretation. Email users need to make a conscious effort to download and save their important messages because some Internet providers delete email messages after a specified time elapses. Moreover, although email allows immediacy of message exchange, it also has a negative effect in that it is too easy to send a quick message without enough thought or enough consideration of the consequences of the message. The question you should ask before sending an email message is whether this is the appropriate vehicle for the message and/or document.

There is a format and protocol for sending email messages. An email message consists of an envelope, a header, and a body. The envelope should specify the sender and receiver. The receiver's name will appear in the email address line. Additionally, the email sender should always remember to include his or her email address to allow for ease in response. The header provides a glimpse of what the sender is expressing in the message. This may be a simple greeting or a catchy or funny phrase. The body contains the message or information from the sender. There are several structural components to the body of the message. The first part of the body is the greeting, which should be friendly and similar to a one-on-one conversation. Right from the beginning, the sender should make the reader aware of the subject of the message and the reader's role in the communication. Like all public communication writing, the email message should be clear and concise. It should not include jargon or anything that could be misconstrued by the reader. You should always keep in mind the purpose of writing the message and keep it clearly stated to avoid confusion or frustration. Just as the sentences in the email should be kept short, so should the message itself. The sender's goal in this particular process should be to engage with a short, specific, and accurate message.

Employee Publications

Distributed as an internal publication within an organization, printed or electronic employee publications are a means of keeping all employees informed and connected—whether they are located in headquarter offices or regional and production sites and whether they are full-time or part-time employees. In essence, print publications provide employees with a tangible link to one another and to the organization. An employee publication resembles a newspaper, a newsletter, or a magazine in format.

An employee publication can help an organization promote and meet its objectives and strategic goals. It outlines the organization's goals and encourages employees to have a vested interest in its success. These publications can help boost employee morale and generate enthusiasm and should be among the most reliable, accurate, and credible sources of information for an organization's workforce.

The success of employee publications is determined by several factors. They must be seen as honest by employees and cover some of the tough topics such as loss of revenues, layoffs, or unfavorable media attention. The publication should be timely and should keep employees up-to-date on the organization's goals, mission, and objectives. Finally, a successful employee publication should be proactive and respond to readers' feedback.

The obvious limitations for employee publications are the time, energy, and money dedicated to their creation, distribution, and reading. Another limitation is that it is difficult to keep them timely. If important news needs to be circulated as fast as possible, the employee publication definitely is not the best communication tool to use.

Media Advisories/Media Alerts

The media advisory—sometimes called a media alert—is one of the core components of a news media kit and an essential tool for media relations professionals. Designed to provide important facts about an event in a comprehensive fashion so that editors and reporters can make decisions about news coverage, it can be delivered to the news media as a separate "stand-alone sheet," updating reporters on one-on-one interview opportunities and providing details for video and photo opportunities. When written well, the media advisory will attract media coverage.

Don't confuse a media advisory with a fact sheet (see Chapter 6, Media Kits), a media relations tool often found in news media kits that succinctly summarizes the main details about an organization, product, service, or program. A handy reference to help reporters get on top of a story or a quick grasp or overview of the subject, a fact sheet explains the subject in straightforward, factual terms. It does *not* supply the details found in the media advisory.

Assignment desk editors and reporters are the usual audience for media advisories. It is the kind of document that field producers can use in planning interviews, but it has to be passed on to them, as practitioners rarely contact field producers directly.

The advisory outlines the elements of the event that are most important to the news media. Like all public communication tools that go directly to the media, the media advisory must anticipate the needs of the news media in providing coverage. It outlines the event and its significance in a short paragraph and then delineates important information such as the names and titles of specific newsmakers attending and/or participating in the event, the exact times and locations of opportunities for the news media to take photographs of the event, media credential information, video opportunities with the newsmakers, scheduled times and locations for one-on-one interviews, and other logistical information.

Media Clippings

Clipping bureaus provide media clipping and monitoring services to help their clients keep track of what the online and offline media are saying about the client's organization. Media clippings can be newspaper clippings and audio and video clippings. With the development of technology and the popularity of Internet use, many clipping services have not only changed their way of delivering service, they have also expanded their services to include monitoring chat rooms, news groups, and online forums.

Clipping-bureau staff read, monitor, and search local, national, and international media daily and select stories according to the subjects or keywords specified by the client.

Media clippings can be delivered through mail, fax, or email, and the client can log on to the clipping bureau's Web site as a subscriber to view the clippings online. Service charges vary according to the number of media outlets covered as well as the breadth of the topic.

Memoranda

A memorandum, also called a memo, is a written message directed to a person or people in an organization. While a memorandum can be used externally, it is usually thought of as an internal business letter. Memoranda are used for a variety of purposes, including short reports, brief proposals, meeting outlines, delineation of points of agreement, notes, and reminders. When used externally, they usually outline a formal agreement between parties.

Memos are intended to increase communication within an organization. They are usually meant to inform readers of a particular issue. They can help to open up the lines of communication, allowing a number of people to be aware of several issues.

Like all business correspondence, memos should be written as clearly and concisely as possible. For that reason, the best memo is one that follows clear guidelines. A page slug identifies the document as a "memorandum." Every memo should state clearly the date, the recipient (a "to" section), the sender (a "from" section), and the subject.

The "to" section specifies to whom the memo is directed. It should include a name and title. If it is an external document, it should include the name of the recipient's organization. The memo can be sent to several receivers, or copies can be sent to others in the form of a "C."

The "from" section includes the sender's name, title, office location, and department name. It may include a telephone number and email address. Every part of the "from" section is crucial because this information allows the receiver(s) to respond.

The heading of a memo contains a brief description of the memo's subject. This will prepare the receiver(s) for what they are going to read in the memo.

The body of a memo should be single-spaced within paragraphs and double-spaced between paragraphs. Paragraphs should not be indented. If the memo is written to an external audience, it is usually hand-carried and presented in a meeting, but it may be faxed or emailed.

An effective memo is short, concise, highly organized, and never late. It should anticipate and answer all questions that a reader might have. It never provides unnecessary or confusing information.

Mission Statements

Mission statements are written definitions of purpose that distinguish organizations from each other. Usually a broad concept, a mission statement explains an organization's ethics and goals and attempts to delineate a specific rationale or principle for the organization's existence. The statement helps enhance the organization's credibility and provides high standards to which the organization can aspire.

A mission statement reflects the ideals and goals of the organization. It not only helps create the organization's identity, but it also helps reinforce established values and keeps the organization and its employees and partners focused on a common goal. Overall, the mission statement is an important message for all of the organization's publics.

Despite its benefits, mission statements are not always taken seriously because an organization's top executives usually create the statement and other employees do not always feel like real stakeholders. Also, mission statements lose relevance over time and must be updated regularly.

An organization's mission statement must be clear and concise—free of jargon and complex language. The tone and length should be dictated by how the organization wants to be perceived by all of its publics and should articulate the future direction of the organization's development. Lastly, top management should seek the support and involvement of all employees when developing the statement.

An organization's mission statement should be prominent in most of its public communication products, including annual reports and brochures and on the Web site.

News Conferences

A news conference is a forum to which members of the media are invited to cover an important announcement and to engage in a question-and-answer exchange with the company's or organization's principal(s). Organizations hold news conferences when they have important news, ranging from a new product launch to a celebrity's visit to clarifying a misunderstanding or offering solutions to problems that have plagued the public.

A news conference enables a company or an organization to deal with a large number of reporters at one time. It also allows reporters to better understand a complex issue and may lead to in-depth interviews.

Although a news conference is an effective way to disseminate information, it also has limitations. Reporters are inundated with invitations to news conferences, and most are not "newsworthy" events. As a public communication practitioner, you must make sure the reason for a news conference is a major development that is relevant and newsworthy.

Many reporters are hesitant to attend news conferences because the stories they get from news conferences lack exclusivity. You should be aware and explain to the organization's principals that uncontrollable factors, such as breaking news events, can prevent reporters from attending a planned news conference. Finally, a news conference consumes both time and resources. Planning and coordinating a news conference can be expensive. It requires reserving a room, inviting the reporters, creating a media kit, renting equipment, and distributing materials.

The following guidelines can help to ensure the success of a news conference:

- Target and invite all relevant news outlets. Because news media outlets work under tight time constraints, it is important to know and accommodate reporters' deadlines. The invitation should describe the general nature of the news conference so that a news editor can make the best assignment.

- Choose a convenient location and the right day and time if your announcement is not breaking news or a crisis. Select a room for the news conference that is comfortable and efficient for working reporters. Interruptions by cellular phones, pagers, or telephone calls should be avoided.

- The spokesperson should express three major points during a news conference. Focusing on three main points will help communicate a simple and clear message to reporters. Written facts, statistics, and visual aids should be used to support these points and to avoid inaccuracies and misunderstanding.

- While the spokesperson should always be aware of time constraints, she or he should always answer each question completely, truthfully, and succinctly. Answering a question with "yes" or "no" is not acceptable. Instead, the spokesperson should take a minute to compose his or her thoughts before answering the question.

- The spokesperson should focus on nonverbal communication as well as verbal communication. This includes maintaining eye contact with reporters at all times.

- Have all experts available to answer questions.

- A reporter's job is to look for new or controversial angles of a story. Our job as public communication practitioners is to help the spokesperson anticipate all possible questions. The spokesperson should remain composed when answering questions and avoid answering emotionally.

- Neither the public communication practitioner nor the spokesperson should answer a reporter's question with "no comment" or ask to be "off the record." A "no comment" remark can be construed as withholding information. "Off the record" does not exist; it is naive to assume a reporter will not use information provided. A decision to hold a news conference is a decision to be on the record. A spokesperson can always "take a question" and follow up with an answer to the reporter before his or her deadline.

Pitch Letters

The pitch letter is another important media relations tool. It is directed to print and broadcast news editors and broadcast news producers, inviting them to cover an event or offering them a news interview with a spokesperson. Pitch letters are sometimes used as cover letters for news media kits. This often is determined by whether the kit was requested or is mailed from a media list. For example, if a reporter or editor received a news release and expressed interest in covering an event but was unable to do so, send a media kit from the event but do not include a pitch letter with the kit. A personal handwritten note will do. If the kit is sent as part of distribution to a media list, a pitch letter can be sent as a cover. If it can be avoided, do not send a media kit with a pitch letter that offers a client or spokesperson for an interview not associated with an event.

Considering our target audience, we must write pitch letters that are personal, short (no longer than one page) and attention-grabbing. Editors and producers receive hundreds of letters a week; they have no time to try to discern the point of the letter. So when writing a pitch letter, you must get to the point right away and try to be interesting in your pitch. Remember, there is a lot of competition for this audience's attention, so you must offer a benefit. Here are a few tips for writing a good pitch letter.

- Be sure you know the name of the current editor or producer and address your salutation and envelope to that person.
- Let the editor or producer know you've done your homework and have some knowledge of who their viewers, listeners, or readers are. For example, "I know that your listeners depend on you to bring them the most up-to-date information on government waste."
- Be as creative or novel as possible: "Government Watch has a 'waste-ometer,' and we want to discuss money squandered in building Route 1."
- Provide the benefit to the editor or producer. Why should they provide news coverage or conduct an interview? See this event or interview opportunity through the editor's or producer's eyes. Be specific about why it will be a benefit—an interesting and exciting interview.

- Remember, visuals are important to television, and sound is important to radio. In our example, a money-guzzling "waste-ometer" might be a good visual and provide sound.
- Provide specific details about the event and logistics for covering the event.
- Be sure to indicate that you will call to follow up on the letter. If the pitch is for an interview, let the producer or editor know you will call in a few days, by the end of the week, or next week.

There are only two reasons for sending a pitch letter by fax or email. If you are involved in a breaking news story, time is of essence and you can offer a spokesperson for an interview in the quickest way possible. Again, stating the benefit is very important because you are taking license by offering an interview in this manner. Second, if you work regularly with a producer, editor, or even reporter who covers your beat, you have an existing working relationship. It is appropriate to send information by email or fax, but always ask or indicate your intentions. In these cases, it is most likely you will have called the pitch before sending correspondence.

If your pitch letter and follow-up call are successful and result in an interview, you will want to send a letter confirming the details right away. Be sure to indicate you will send a confirmation letter and ask if there is a preference for fax or email. Your confirmation letter is an important media relations tool. It is both tactical and strategic. As you confirm the logistics and details of the scheduled interview, you have the opportunity to review the subject and areas of interest to the news outlet. You can gently remind the producer, editor, or reporter of the primary message by providing a brief summary of your original pitch letter. Caution: don't try to provide a road map for how the interview should proceed, because news people do not want to be told how to approach a story or interview. Instead, gently lead with information that is helpful to the editor, producer, or reporter and that reinforces the primary message you want your spokesperson to deliver.

Your confirmation letter should begin by confirming the specific day, date, time, and location of the interview. Include every detail of the scheduling, including who will meet you and your spokesperson, best entrances to use, and details for contact should changes occur. Close your letter with a thank you and remind the editor or producer why this interview is such a good idea and how it will engage the audience. Your confirmation letter should be kept in your files, and copies should be sent to anyone who is responsible for your spokesperson's schedule and public appearances, such as executive or administrative assistants, schedulers, political advance staffers, and press secretaries.

Proposals

A proposal is a written document that attempts to describe, suggest, or pitch an idea to a potential client. Its purpose is to influence or persuade a potential client to take a specific action. The proposal should provide the potential client sufficient information to understand the steps he or she would take to reach a satisfactory conclusion. It also allows the potential client to see different problem-solving tactics that might be employed in the process.

The standard format of a proposal consists of six sections. First, the introduction explains the public communication professional's understanding of the situation, opportunity, or problem. Then it outlines the foreseeable complications that could occur if the opportunity isn't taken or the problem isn't solved.

The second section is the discussion, which outlines the requirements for the project and explains the objectives. This section usually has three subsections. The requirements subsection explains the opportunity, or the problem and solutions, and lays out the research to be conducted to determine target audiences. Next, a detailed analysis subsection delineates the steps required for completing the project. Here, the practitioner presents alternative approaches. The analysis subsection distinguishes this plan from competitors' plans, demonstrating a comprehensive understanding of the situation and explaining the advantages of this approach. In the approach subsection, logic should be the focus. The reader should be able to see how and what measures will be taken to solve the problem.

The third section outlines the proposed project. This section is the most detailed and most important. You make specific commitments and predictions for the future in this section, outlining what will happen and how. This should include strategies and a timeline of when different components and elements of projects are due.

The fourth section reviews the qualifications and experience of the project staff. Résumés of principal participants or consultants should be included in this section as well. It also tells where, when, and how you have been successful in completing similar projects for other companies or organizations. This section establishes your credibility and the credibility of your team so that the client will feel confident of your capabilities.

The evaluation is delineated in the fifth section. It states the how, when, where, and why of the evaluation to be conducted to determine the success of the project and to provide information for the research phase of the next project.

The sixth section outlines the budget and includes line items for the major components of the project. The client wants to know the cost of the project, so be as detailed and comprehensive as possible.

A complete and thorough proposal requires and consumes a great amount of time, money, and energy. Safeguards should be taken to avoid wasting them.

First, it is critical that we, as advisors, understand the problem or opportunity correctly and completely. Otherwise, the proposal and its analysis will be incorrect or lack depth.

Second, thorough and accurate research is critical to developing an effective proposal. Strategies, tactics, themes, and messages created without thorough research of the problem and the audiences are worthless. Inadequate research is a sure indication that you may not be competent in the field.

Third, an effective proposal should attempt to answer the problems facing the client. Last, the proposal should be well organized and well written. Sentences should be concise and project elements should follow sequentially so that the client understands each of the elements. Great ideas can be lost in poorly executed proposals. The ultimate goal of a proposal is to get us to the next step—giving a presentation to the client.

Videoconferencing

Videoconferencing is an interactive tool that uses video, computing, and communication technologies to allow people in different locations to communicate face-to-face. It lets people conduct meetings, give presentations, talk to vendors, and meet new business prospects or colleagues in different cities, all without the expense of time and the inconvenience of traveling. Conference participants can be at two or more locations either domestic or international.

In addition to helping save time and costs, videoconferencing encourages participation that would be impossible if travel were involved. The time savings and cost effectiveness also make it possible for people to participate in activities they might otherwise have declined. Another benefit of videoconferencing is that it allows meetings to take place with little advance notice and allows people to have briefer, more frequent interaction. And the visual capabilities of videoconferencing make it possible for participants to share graphics or videotapes interactively.

Many vendors provide full videoconferencing services. This can include providing conference rooms, setting up equipment at sites, and videotaping the conference for future reference. Service is usually charged by the hour and the number of sites. Price varies according to how many sites are involved and whether the service is point-to-point or point-to-point with conversion. Point-to-point refers to a direct link between two sites in a network or communication link. Point-to-point with conversion is required if the mode and speed of the videoconferencing equipment differ from site to site.

An *Example Gallery* for Public Communication Toolbox
begins on the following page.

Example Gallery
Public Communication Toolbox

Emerald Heights
Office of the Mayor
1 City Hall
Emerald Heights, USA 62220
555-2233

CONTACT:
Steve Mangel, Director of Media Relations
Office: 555-2233
Cellular: 555-1133
Email: smangel@emeraldheights.gov

MEDIA ADVISORY

The selection process is underway for a new school superintendent for the Emerald Heights School District. Mayor Judith Gold is conducting a national search and promises to involve local community residents, as well. Two public forums will be held to provide residents with the opportunity to share their thoughts and recommendations for a new school superintendent with Emerald Heights officials. The Emerald Heights School District continues to rank number one in the state and among the top ten in the country.

WHO: Mayor Judith Gold
             Members of the Emerald Heights School Board

WHAT: Two public forums to give citizens and other interested parties the opportunity to share with city officials the qualities they would like to see in a new school superintendent.

WHEN: Wednesday, January 20 at 6:30 p.m.
             Thursday, January 21 at 6:30 p.m.

WHERE: Stone View High School
             222 Main Street
             Emerald Heights, USA 62220

WHY: Select a new school superintendent.

A media advisory from a city government informs news media of a public forum.

❶ CONTACT: Located below letterhead; contact's name, title, phone number(s), and email address.

❷ INTRODUCTORY PARAGRAPH: Basic information about event.

❸ PRIMARY INFORMATION: Who, What, Where, When, and Why.

Example Gallery
Public Communication Toolbox

2623 North Ave.
Western, CA 90200
Phone: (800) 555-5597
Fax: (800) 555-5599
www.formativeenterprises.com

Formative Enterprises, Inc.

CONTACT:

Staci Kaufman, Public Affairs Director

(800) 555-5597

Email: skaufman@formativefindings.com

MEDIA ADVISORY

As part of the National Fitness Initiative recently passed by Congress, Formative Enterprises, the nation's premier manufacturer of youth fitness products, is launching a new youth exercise program called *Get Fit, It's Fun!* This series will be available free of charge in low-income neighborhoods. Key executives from Formative Enterprises, along with members of Congress, youth athletic directors and participants, will be on hand at a demonstration and informational talk discussing the advantages of the new program.

WHO: Jamie Molack, CEO, Formative Enterprises
Congressman Chad Lathem
Senator Rona Jackson
Catherine Morris, Community Relations, Formative Enterprises
John Peters, Athletic Director, Western Youth Center
Maggie McBride, Director of Youth Services, Chicago, Illinois
Program Participants

WHAT: Informational talk and demonstration of a *Get Fit, It's Fun!* new youth exercise program being offered free of charge to children of low-income families. Interview opportunities will be available with all speakers.

WHEN: April 26 at 1:30 p.m.

WHERE: Western Youth Center
555 Plainview Avenue
Western, California 90200

WHY: The demonstration is designed to heighten awareness of a new and innovative exercise program offered free of charge to children of low-income families.

Parking and media passes are available. Contact Staci Kaufman at (800) 555-5597.

A media advisory from a corporation informs news media of an event and availability of participants.

1. CONTACT: Located below letterhead; contact's name, title, phone number(s), and email address.
2. INTRODUCTORY PARAGRAPH: Basic information describing the goal or mission of the client.
3. PRIMARY INFORMATION: Who, What, Where, When, and Why.
4. SPECIAL INFORMATION OR INSTRUCTIONS: Additional notes at the bottom of the page for special instructions, including media credentials and alternative entrances to the event.

Example Gallery
Public Communication Toolbox

2623 North Ave.
Western, CA 90200
Phone: (800) 555-5597
Fax: (800) 555-5599
www.formativeenterprises.com

Formative Enterprises, Inc.

M E M O R A N D U M

TO: Lori Roberts, Director of Human Resources

FROM: Jamie Molack, President

DATE: April 2, 2012

RE: Formation of Search Committee for V.P. of Product Development

C: Devon Mayhue, Chief Financial Officer

I would like to arrange a meeting to discuss the formation of a search committee that will be responsible for seeking out a superior candidate to fill the newly created position of Vice President of Product Development. Please submit to me a list of current staff who you believe should serve on the panel by the close of business today. At that time, we will coordinate a time and location convenient for all participants.

Thank you for your attention to this matter.

A internal memorandum.

❶ PAGE SLUG: Identifies the document as a "memorandum."

❷ TO: To whom the memo is being sent.

❸ FROM: From whom the memo was sent.

❹ DATE: The calendar date the memo was written.

❺ RE: What the memo is about.

❻ C: Individual(s) who receives a copy of the memo.

❼ BODY: Written message.

EachOneTeachOne

1836 Jefferson Square, NW/Washington, DC 20036

MISSION STATEMENT FOR EACH ONE TEACH ONE

- Reduce school and community violence around the nation

- Identify children who demonstrate patterns of violent behavioral problems at an early age

- Promote children's skills in showing self-control and rebuffing the use of violence or aggression

- Provide creative outlets, workshops, seminars, retreats and positive influences for children between the ages of 5 and 18 that will help deter them from violent behaviors

- Encourage "*Each One Teach One*," meaning family members, friends, adults, children, and teachers should take an active role in children's lives and teach them the skills that will make them productive adults and citizens of this country

Mission statement of a nonprofit voluntary organization.

The following profiles provide background information on the organizations highlighted in the examples presented in this book.

"EACH ONE TEACH ONE"

A Nonprofit Organization

Overview of the Problem

In a day and age when elementary and high school students are gunned down in the classroom, something must be done to curb youth violence in America. America's youth are exposed to violence from a variety of channels: from television, video games, movies, and explicit song lyrics, young adults are desensitized to violent behavior. It's almost as if the lines between reality and fiction are blurred for our youth. It is the responsibility of the parents, elders, role models, and authority figures of this country to steer America's youth back in the right direction. The old African proverb is true: "It takes a village to raise a child."

Background Information

Each One Teach One was established in response to the Inglewood tragedy that occurred in Akron, OH, on January 18, 1999, in which a 14-year-old boy shot and killed three of his classmates and his teacher. Spearheaded by U.S. Attorney General Janine Redding, this organization was officially launched in September 1999 in Washington, D.C. It is funded by the Presidential Safe Schools/Healthy Students Initiative and will receive an annual budget of $1,500,000 for the next three years.

The nation's capital was chosen as the original site due to staggering youth statistics. One-third of Washington, D.C., children live below the poverty level and nearly 39 percent in high-risk families. Sixty-six percent of D.C. students are eligible for free and reduced school lunch. During 2007–2008, the dropout rate was reported at 30 percent, more than twice the national urban figure; only 60 percent of D.C. youth graduate from high school. Healthy lifestyles for thousands of D.C. children are hindered by environmental and societal realities such as poverty, drugs, gangs, and child abuse. Each One Teach One wants to change these statistics by providing positive services to combat these issues.

Mission/Objectives

- Reduce school and community violence around the nation among American youth
- Identify children who demonstrate patterns of violent behavior at an early age
- Promote children's skills in showing self-control and rebuffing the use of violence or aggression
- Provide creative outlets, workshops, seminars, retreats, and positive influences for children between the ages of 5 and 18 that will help deter them from violent behaviors
- Encourage family members, friends, adults, and teachers to take an active role in children's lives and teach them the skills that will make them productive adults

Board of Directors

Ken Durham, Office of Juvenile Justice & Delinquency

Janine Redding, U.S. Attorney General

Rick Ripley, U.S. Secretary of Education

George Salazar, Ohio Attorney General

Damon Smith, MD, U.S. Surgeon General

Vivian Holmes, Department of Education

Executive Staff

Willis Bennett, J.D, Executive Director

Sarah Woods, Communications Director

Christine Chow, Comptroller

Donald H. Holmes, Ed.D, General Counsel

Patrick Smathers, Director of Volunteers

Rose Ward, Vice President of Operations

Nathaniel Mitchell, Program Coordinator

Membership

Currently, Each One Teach One has a staff of 35 full-time employees and 50 volunteers who work with the 1,000 students identified as aggressive and enrolled in the program to participate in various activities.

Functions

- Prepare *Hand To Hand*, the official quarterly newsletter of the organization
- Research corporations for potential partnership opportunities
- Brainstorm topic ideas for workshops, seminars, retreats, and symposiums and implement them
- Develop and distribute techniques for handling aggressive children/students
- Provide counseling services for aggressive children
- Meet with school administrators and assist them with recognizing problem students
- Host events for children in the program
- Develop and maintain organization's Web site
- Prepare and organize for Each One Teach One Holiday Gala fundraiser

CITY OF EMERALD HEIGHTS

Municipal Government

Overview and Background

This fictitious town is located somewhere in the Midwestern part of the United States. Founded in 1784, it was originally slated to be a farming and agricultural community. Now the area thrives as a center for technology, education, and the arts. More than 10 colleges and universities are located within 30 miles of the town center. Emerald Heights is considered a politically moderate community that focuses a great deal of its attention on protecting the area's natural resources. Rich in its cultural diversity, Emerald Heights currently has a population of 51,250. Its land mass is approximately 40.120 kilometers and it has no natural surface water.

Mission/Objectives

- Provide equality for all under the laws of Emerald Heights
- Protect and defend the area's natural resources
- Promote the Emerald Heights area as a leader of technology, education, and the arts in the Midwest while offering a safe and happy place for all of its residents

Community Officials

Judith Gold, Mayor

Norman Harrison, Deputy Mayor

Harmon Louis, Director of Housing Services

Pamela Stephens, Director of Health Services

Margie Allen, Education Supervisor

Steve Mangel, Communication Director

Kevin Taraman, Comptroller

Vin Arnold, Chief of Police

FORMATIVE ENTERPRISES, INC.

A Private For-Profit Company

Overview and Background

Founded in 1994, Formative Enterprises, Inc., is the nation's premier manufacturer of youth fitness products. Located in Western, California, Formative Enterprises grosses over $20 million in annual sales while putting nearly 25 percent of profits back into the community. This private for-profit company employs approximately 250 men and women nationwide. Offering a wide variety of exercise and fitness equipment through retail and online sales, Formative Enterprises tailors all exercise equipment to fit the sizes and abilities of its young users. Identifying the needs of today's youth has become a major concern for Formative. The company works very closely with youth centers across the country while developing healthy and safe exercise regimens that kids will find fun and invigorating.

Mission/Objectives

- Promote health and fitness to the youth of America so that they can become healthy and fit adults
- Organize and sponsor state and federal youth exercise programs that will be offered free of charge to children of low-income households
- Identify youth exercise patterns and tailor programs to meet the needs of children of all ages

Executive Staff

Jamie Molack, President and Chief Operating Officer

Devon Mayhue, Chief Financial Officer

Robert Josephson, Senior Vice President

Karen Stone, Vice President of Manufacturing

Leon Staples, Vice President of Product Development

Lisa Tanner, Vice President of Marketing

Lori Roberts, Director of Human Resources

Staci Kaufman, Public Affairs Director

Writing and Editing Exercises

Exercise A

Underline or circle the correct bolded words in the sentences below.

1. He was **accused of/accused with** the crime.

2. He asked her **to whom/to who** she sent the flowers.

3. She said the weather will not **affect/effect** her plans.

4. He **lay/he lie** down on the bed.

5. He walked **in/into** the room.

6. The highway closed **due to/because of** the snowstorm.

7. Susan lives **further/farther** away.

8. Everyone in the class understood the assignment **accept/except** the professor.

9. **Whose/who's** in charge of today's lesson?

10. Susan said she is **all right/alright**.

11. Alyssa is one of the skaters who **skate/skates** with the new students.

12. No other explanations **have/has** been presented to the team.

13. Neither Celeste nor Denise **is/are** included on the program.

14. It's a school where nationally **renown/nationally-renown/nationally renowned/nationally-renowned** students dominate.

15. I am exhausted. I feel I have been through the **ringer/wringer**.

16. At this writing, her intern is the **front runner/front-runner/ frontrunner**.

17. Acme is a **wholly owned subsidiary/wholly-owned subsidiary.**

18. She knew her **God father/godfather** would take care of the speeding ticket.

19. The wedding, **which/that** was planned quickly, will now be in November.

20. Walk two blocks down to the house **which/that** has black shutters.

21. See **their/there/they're**, no matter how many times I ask for **their/there/ they're** attention, **their/there/they're** still distracted.

Exercise B

Look at the words (or partial words) below and add "able" or "ible" where appropriate.

1. Account

2. Break

3. Comfort

4. Credit

5. Destruct

6. Fashion

7. Fathom

8. Flex

9. Illeg

10. Incred

11. Indestruct

12. Invis

13. Irrespons

14. Irrit

15. Laugh

16. Permiss

17. Remark

18. Suit

19. Tax

20. Valu

Exercise C

Rewrite the numbers in the sentences below where needed. Not all require rewriting.

1. 1,000 people attended her wedding.

2. Susan said there were one hundred and forty-five entries.

3. The service began at eight a.m.

4. The New York Stock Exchange bell rings promptly at 9 a.m.

5. The vote was 221 in favor and fifteen opposed.

6. With 700 pages left, he will never get the book read in time. He is on page 10.

7. A gain of fifteen and a half percent is unheard of in this market.

8. He left for the airport at exactly 12:00 today.

9. A tweet cannot exceed one hundred forty characters.

10. Chapter sixteen was the most exciting of all twenty-three.

Exercise D

Correct the sentences below so that they are written in AP Style.

1. Figures from the Chamber of Commerce indicate that eight in ten future job openings in the US will require education beyond a High School diploma.

2. The United States currently ranks 17th in science and 25th in math on international assessments.

3. Currently, 31% of high school students do not graduate on time with a regular diploma.

4. 30 percent of college students currently require non-credit remedial education before they can begin work on their Bachelor's Degree.

5. By 2018, the existing postsecondary education system will produce three million less college graduates than required by the labor market.

6. 53% of business leaders reported that their companies faced difficulties in recruiting employees with the needed skills, technical training, and education.

7. Employers spend $400 billion dollars per year in providing formal and informal training to employees.

8. Business leaders from across the country including GE, The Boeing Company, and IBM, met for 2 days in a special session to discuss how companies can assist States and Districts with the management capacity they will need to successfully implement and sustain the changes.

9. U.S. officials said in an interview that the sudden collapse of the government of Syrian president Bashar al-Assad might mean a break down in controls.

10. The WW-I era weapon amounted to canisters filled mostly with mustard gas.

11. Tex. governor Rick Perry's Presidential campaign announcement came at the very last minute, weeks after other GOP hopefuls.

12. Americans, no longer, believe they will make money next year than this year according to Michigan Universitys survey.

13. American expectations following a recession used to rebound this time they didn't.

14. Over 9 hundred thousand students will begin school in northern Va. this fall.

15. The meeting is being held in the west wing of the White House not the Oval Office.

16. The dean's speech to the new freshman class included repeated references to September 11.

17. Almost everyone had forgotten that former President, Jimmy Carter, was from Plains, Georgia.

18. What time do they expect the processional to pass through Md.?

19. She was stationed for three years in Denver, Col.

20. He said the further away he gets from Texas the better.

Start-of-Course Writing and Editing Test

When you apply for an entry-level position at a PR agency or communication department, you will be asked to complete a writing test. It is likely you will have to edit copy for a news release, brochure, speech or article. Edit the following draft newsletter article, providing AP style and correcting spelling, punctuation, and usage errors. Use editing marks and insert page slugs.

NEWS RELEASE

August 15, 2012

FOR IMMEDIATE RELEASE

**EMERALD HEIGHTS DECLARES BID FOR 2020 SUMMER
OLYMPIC GAMES**

Great Hope As U.S. Olympic Committee Completes Revenue-Sharing Talks

EMERALD HEIGHTS, Midwest, USA—Emerald Heights will bid for the year 2020 Summer Olympics, hoping to show the world that the United States (U.S.) can mount a competative bid in spite of the late date. Bids are due on September the first.

U.S. Olympic Committee President Scott Blackmun and Emerald Heights Mayor Judith Gold confirmed the citys' candidacy on Friday in New York, NY at a ceremony immediately after the International Olympic Committee (IOC) and the USOC announced a revenue sharing agreement acceptible to all parties.

"America is pleased to have Emerald Heights as our choice for a bid," said President Obama in a White House statement. The President made a personal appeal for Chicago to host the 2016 games.

The U.S. which lost out in its race to host the 2016 Olympics in Chicago and its 2012 New York bid was not expected to pull off a bid on such a short notice. A visibly relieved Blackmun said, "We didn't want to submit a bid unless it was world-class. Now we can."

The revenue-sharing disputes were resolved following weeks of bickering and negotiating. Since 2006, the USOC has been under pressure to take a smaller share of the IOC's global sponsorship revenues and U.S. broadcast rights. Under the current agreements, that were open-ended, the USOC gets 12.750% of the U.S. TV rights and 20% of the global sponsorship.

The issue has became such a flashpoint that it helped undermine the New York bid for the 2012 Olympics and the Chicago bid for 2016.

IOC president Jacques Rogge, who attended Friday's ceremony, said on Thursday the IOC hoped the United States (U.S.) would submit a bid.

Rome, Madrid, and Tokyo have officially declared bids for 2020 and Istanbul is expected to do so as well. South Africa is still a possibility according to its olympic committee, but France has withdrawn its intentions. Right now looks like a 5 city competition.

The IOC will select the 2020 host city in 2013.

Emerald Heights has never hosted the hosted the Summer Olympics but the U. S. hosted in St. Louis in 1904, Los Angeles in 1932 and 1984 and Atlanta, in 1996. The Winter Games in Lake Placid, New York in 1932 and 1980, Squaw Valley, CA in 1960 and Salt Lake, UT in 2002.

Rogge said he was confidant Emerald Heights would make a strong bid.

"Emerald Heights will be the smallest city to organize a Olympic games" said Rogge. 50,000-plus residents of the city are going to be very excited."

The IOC and USOC said Emerald cities' bid will be an inspiration to other small towns across the world.

Emerald Heights Mayor Judith Gold who was the driving force behind the bid said her government would provide full support.

"There is no point in bidding if you don't win," said Gold. "The city government will give blood, sweat, and tears to provide money and facilities to make sure Emerald Heights is the sight of our country's 9th Olympic games. This is an incredable opportunity." -###-

-###-

Page 2 of 2

End-of-Course Writing and Editing Progress Test

When you apply for an entry-level position at a PR agency or communication department, you will be asked to complete a writing test. It is likely you will have to edit copy for a news release, brochure, speech or article. Edit the following draft newsletter article, providing AP style and correcting spelling, punctuation, and usage errors. Use editing marks and insert page slugs.

Emerald Heights Public Schools Newsletter Article

Last Fall, the Emerald Heights Public School District (EHPS) received a 5 year, 15,000,000 dollar grant from an anonimous donor. Emerald Heights is one of six school districts in the Midwest who received the grants. The donor acknowledged that all of the districts' demonstrated the potential to benefit from exploring and implementing new ways to educate students in math and science but lacked the resources to do so. The donor also stressed that EHPS was known for its accountibility systems.

School superintendent George Mills said, "this grant is an incredable gift and just what the district needs to really help our students. 75% of our students have expressed interest in going in to math and science carrieers. And our home town has jobs for them."

The ultimate goal of the grant is to improve students' achievement in math and science—fostering the leaders of tomorrow. The school district will use it's gift to develop rigorous, systemwide math and science curricula and to help teachers increase there skills through professional development. In addition, the school district will strive to improve the way that it works with its partners in the community to improve students' educational experiences. 12 thousand students attend EHPS schools .It is a diverse student body with 22 percent African American and 34 percent Latino students. Emerald Heights school administrators identified another challenge that needed to be addressed. The District was not benefiting from technological advances. One of the major goals identified by the District was to enhance the information technology (IT) system.

"This is an incrediable opportunity for our students. We have curriculum, professional development, and management projects that will profit from this gift" said EHPS Superintendent George Mills. Mills has pushed for tougher standards in math and science in the District.

Better Technology

Through the grant, the District plans to invest 4,000,000 dollars towards the implementation of a new IT system, with the help of businesses in the community who dedicated IT staff and identified cost saving measures that will ultimately reduce the cost of the project by 1,000,000 million dollars. The new system will put student data in the hands of teachers and administrators so that they can track student progress and make better decisions. In addition, it is a time saver. All teachers K–12 will be able to take attendance using the new system. While it now takes teachers ninety minutes per week to perform their attendance duties they will be capible of finishing in fifteen minutes, which means more time for teaching.

Wireless Internet access will be available in all District schools, which makes e-mailing and accessing online resources easier. The District will launch a new web site that is designed to be a creative, user-friendly way to communicate with students, parents, employees, and the community. This web site provides students with instructional resources, exccess to local and national educational sites, and valuable information to help them in their daily academic lives. Parents will have access to important information which includes dates, times, and locations of District events, daily school lunch menus, messages from the superintendent and other essential news about what is happening in the District. Teachers will have easy access to instructional resources. As a "one-stop shop" for District information, the new web site (www.ehps.org) delivers easy-to-access phone numbers, e-mail, instructional resources, and media presentations. Design work has been underway accept for the Parent Portal which will allow parents and students to check assignments, progress, and grades online. Thanks to the new grant, that work will begin soon.

Editing Marks

The editing marks provided below are used widely in the fields of public relations and journalism. They are presented with their meanings and demonstrated in accompanying copy. Editing marks will become more familiar to you through the course for which you are using this book and during your practice in the field. Use them to edit your own work and to understand the edits of others.

EDITING MARKS

EACH ONE TEACH ONE KICKS OFF 2012 ANTI-VIOLENCE CAMPAIGN

Awareness Against Youth Violence

NEWS RELEASE

WASHINGTON, DC —

Each One Teach One, a nonprofit organization dedicated to reducing youth violence, will begin its 2006 anti-violence campaign, "Breaking Anger Down" with a seminar on the prevention of youth violence on Saturday, February 18, 2012. The seminar, to be held at the *Each One Teach One* headquarters, 1836 Jefferson Square, NW, will include 15 presentations on youth violence and 8 recent developments in the effort by Willis Bennett, the Executive Director of *Each One Teach One*, Janine Redding, the United States attorney general, and Rick Ripley, the U.S. Secy. of Education.

"These activities are vital to helping our children grow and learn about productive ways to resolve problems. There is too, too much violence in our youth to day to let this continue, said Ripley.

The seminar will also include interactive activities for children and parents on controlling and curbing the use of violence and group discussions on how to effectively practice self control and conflict resolution techniques. Students and their mentors can discuss what provokes anger and together they can create possible alternatives the use of

-more-

Violence. Counselors will assist in fostering creative, productive solutions to the types of conflicts that happen everyday.

Bennett Willis, the executive director of *Each One Teach One*, spends much of his time talking to students and teachers in the Washington DC area, planning and promoting *Each One Teach One* activities and events. "We want to provide our youth with the tools necessary to avoid violence. If the youth then begin to teach each other, they become involved and committed to the process. If they are committed, then we are successful," says Bennett.

For more information, please contact Sarah Woods at (202) 555-3377 or email at swoods@eachoneteachone.org.

Each One Teach One was launched in September of 1999 in response to the growing number of tragedies from youth violence. The organizations program includes seminars, workshops and retreats as well as counseling services and fund-raisers. Volunteers have also created a monthly newsletter and a Web site for the nonprofit organization.

-###-

Symbol	Meaning
⌐	flush right
⌒	no paragraph
⌐	paragraph
⋏	insert comma
/	lowercase
=	uppercase
◯	spell it out
N	insert space
◡	remove space
✄	delete
⌐⊏	center
⊏	flush left
∿	transpose
ⱽ ⱽ	insert quotation marks
⊗ ⊙	insert period
⩦	insert hyphen
⋀	insert word

Glossary

Actuality See sound bite.

Audit diary A record and description of the activities that transpire during a communication audit.

B-roll Raw video footage with natural sound only.

Backgrounder One-page description of the organization and its mission, history, goals, and principles.

Banner The name of a newsletter; also called a nameplate.

Biography Background information about principals of an organization or event.

Bleed Artwork or text that runs off the edge of a page.

Blog Short for Web log, is an online posting. Blogs are often closely associated with the author.

Blueline stage Last stage of a proof made directly from a printer's plate.

Boilerplate Background information on an organization—who they are, their mission, and other information. Usually found at end of news release.

Caption Phrase or sentence that describes a photo, illustration, or graphic.

Contact information The name and telephone and fax numbers or email address to request additional information.

Cross headline Headline copy that stretches across more than one panel in a brochure.

Curling The buckling of paper as a result of excess moisture.

Date of distribution The date the intended public relations media will be sent to the target audience.

Dateline Location of the event or story.

Deck head An introductory line that offers supplemental information not included in the headline; also known as a subhead.

Digital printing Computerized printing process that outputs directly from computer files, eliminating negatives and plates.

Disclaimer Gives the media permission to use information supplied in an electronic press kit (EPK), video news release (VNR), or audio news release (ANR).

Embargo A future date and time the media can release information.

Executive summary Two- to three-page summary of the contents in a communication audit.

Fact sheet Numbered or bulleted information relevant to the organization or event.

Feature story A human-interest story about a particular person or event. Often included in a media kit.

Font Typeface.

Four-color process (CMYK) The printing process in which the four process colors—blue (Cyan), red (Magenta), yellow, and black (K)—are placed on the paper in a series of dots to create the illusion of millions of colors.

Gravure A type of printing that incorporates recessed images.

Headline A sentence that titles an article summarizing the main ideas of the story.

Ink affinity Speed at which ink will dry on one side.

Inverted pyramid style The arrangement of facts within a story proceeding from the most important to the least important information.

Johnson box opener An indented, boxed, and/or introductory block of copy that introduces a product or third-party endorser in a direct mail piece.

Lead The first one- or two-sentence paragraph that summarizes the news with the five W's—who, what, when, where, and why.

Lead amplifiers Information such as quotes, statistics, or other pertinent story details that expands the information first presented in the lead paragraph.

Letterhead The stationery heading that reflects the image and tone of the campaign and includes the logo and title of the organization.

Letterpress A printing method that uses images from raised surfaces.

Logo The identifying symbol of an organization and/or event.

Masthead Contains all the publication information for the newsletter, including the publisher, editor, address, and editorial statement.

Microsites Also known as landing pages, minisites, or weblets, they are a single page or cluster of pages that supplements the primary Web site. They usually focus on a single event, cause, product, or service.

Mini-bios A collection of abbreviated biographies of key individuals that highlight only the information relevant to the subject of the media kit in which they are included. Each bio is usually two paragraphs in length.

Navigation bar A group of icons that allows the user of a Web site to move easily between pages.

Offer The proposal to accept.

Offset A type of printing that uses lithography to create a soft, smooth color transition.

Page slugs Symbols located at the bottom and/or top of each page that indicate whether the copy continues by using "-more-" or conclude by using "-end-," "-###-," or "-30-."

Panels Faces of a brochure designed to present information.

PDF Also known as Adobe PDF® (portable document file). Cross-platfom file format that allows all computers to read documents if they have free Adobe Acrobat Reader® installed (www.adobe.com).

Pitch To offer or suggest a story idea or news angle to news media representatives.

Position paper A document outlining a cause or an issue and explaining an organization's position on the issue and why.

Précis Background information on the news that is being provided in a video news release (VNR) or an electronic press kit (EPK).

Premiums Collectibles, coupons, and upcoming offer information often included in a direct mail package.

Publicity photos Pictures and/or graphics that amplify a story.

Pull quotes A section of copy drawn from an article, usually used to highlight, emphasize, or draw attention to certain important points. It is set in type that is much larger than the body type.

Quadrants The four equal rectangles formed by dividing a page in half vertically and horizontally.

Response card A postcard that urges the target audience to take action.

Retainer A flat fee that client and agency/practitioner agree on as a monthly payment before the start of the project.

Rules Solid lines that separate editorial material.

SAR Summary annual report, a shorter and less complicated annual report that is divided into brief summation sections.

SFX Sound effects. Directions that are found in italics on the right side of a script for a public service announcement, along with the audio elements.

Shell Folder with graphics, logo, organization, event, date, and theme. Contains the items of a media kit.

Sidebars Blocks of copy, often boxed for effect, that offer a unique perspective on the article they accompany.

Slate A screen that identifies or introduces images that follow.

Slug Short title capturing the main news.

SMT Satellite media tour.

Social network sites (SNS) Online forums for people with shared interests—be they personal (family and friends), professional (industry- or networking-focused), or reflective of a specific interest, such as a hobby or the work of a particular artist.

SOT Sound on Tape, a quote by someone related to a broadcast news story.

Sound bite Quote on tape that is approximately 8–15 seconds in length.

Spot color Highlighted color on borders, boxes, and/or titles.

Standing feature A recurring piece found in a newsletter.

Tag line Copy added to the end of a public service announcement (PSA)

that gives local information related to the PSA.

Teaser A promotional phrase that entices audience to open the direct mail package.

Time codes Generated from videotapes and used to reference specific places in the footage.

Twitter A social networking and micro-blogging service that allows twitterers to "tweet" to one another. Tweets are 140 character messages that allow twitterers to send a short update on any topic to their audience at any time.

White space The empty or unused portion of the total space used in brochures, newsletters, magazines, and other printed material.

Widget A small program that can be easily added to a Web site, blog, or profile page to add an element of interactive content. For example, the content-related ad that runs across of the top of a Web site is a widget.

Wiki A type of Web site built through collaboration. Users contribute the content via their own browsers, which is edited, updated, or even changed completely by successive users. Some wikis are open to all Internet users, whereas others require membership or specific qualifications to participate.

Index

Note: page numbers in *italic* indicate illustrations.